PRACTICAL STATISTICS FOR EDUCATORS

Ruth Ravid

UNIVERSITY
PRESS OF
AMERICA

Lanham • New York • London

Copyright © 1994 by
University Press of America® Inc.
4720 Boston Way
Lanham, Maryland 20706

3 Henrietta Street
London WC2E 8LU England

Library of Congress Cataloging-in-Publication Data

Ravid, Ruth.
Practical statistics for educators / by Ruth Ravid.
p.   cm.
Includes index.
1. Educational statistics—Study and teaching.   2. Educational tests
and measurements.   I. Title.
LB2846.R33   1994   370'.21—dc20   94–4720 CIP

ISBN 0–8191–9498–0 (cloth : alk. paper)

 The paper used in this publication meets the minimum requirements of
American National Standard for Information Sciences—Permanence
of Paper for Printed Library Materials, ANSI Z39.48–1984.

To My Students -- The source of my
inspiration and reward

CONTENTS

Preface
Acknowledgments

Part One: Introduction

Chapter 1: Getting Started   3
Qualitative and Quantitative Measures   3
Variables and Scales of Measurement   4
     Nominal Scale, 5   Ordinal Scale, 6
     Interval Scale, 7   Ratio Scale, 7
     Comparing the Four Scales, 8
Parametric and Nonparametric Statistics   9
The Process of Statistical Hypothesis Testing   10
     Errors in Decision Making, 12
Degrees of Freedom   12
"And Finally . . ."   13
SUMMARY   13

Chapter 2: Sampling Procedures   17
Populations and Samples   17
Descriptive and Inferential Statistics   18
Parameters and Statistics   19
Methods of Sampling   20
     Simple Random Sample, 20   Systematic
     Sample, 21   Stratified Sample, 22
     Cluster Sample, 22   Incidental
     (Convenience) Sample, 23
Sample Bias   23
Size of Sample   24
SUMMARY   25

Part Two: Descriptive Statistics

Chapter 3: Organizing and Graphing Data   **31**
Organizing Data   31
   Grouped Distributions, 33
   Cumulative Frequency Distributions, 36
Graphing Data   37
   Histogram and Frequency Polygon, 37
   Graphing Cumulative Distributions, 43
   Pie Graph, 44   Bar Diagram (Bar Graph), 45
   Line Graph, 49   Pictogram, 50
   Stem-and-Leaf Diagram, 51   Box Plot, 55
SUMMARY   56

Chapter 4: Measures of Central Tendency   **59**
Mode   59
Median   60
Mean   62
Comparing the Mode, Median and Mean   64
   The Mean of Combined Groups, 66
Calculating the Mode, Median and Mean:
   A Summary of the Steps   68
SUMMARY   70

Chapter 5: Measures of Variability   **73**
The Range   74
Variance and Standard Deviation   75
   Deviation Score Method, 76
   Using the Variance and SD, 83
   Factors Affecting the Variance and
   SD, 85   Comparing the Variance and
   SD for Populations and Samples, 86
Additional Notes: Computations of
   Variance and Standard Deviation   87
   Computations of the Raw Score
   Method, 87

Computations of Variance and Standard
    Deviation for a Population: A Summary
    of the Steps   92
      The Deviation Score Method, 92
      The Raw Score Method, 93
SUMMARY   94

Part Three: The Normal Curve and Standard Scores

Chapter 6: The Normal Curve and Standard Scores   **99**
The Normal Curve   99
Standard Scores   104
    Z Scores, 104   T Scores, 107   Other
    Converted Scores, 108   The Normal
    Curve and Percentile Ranks, 109
SUMMARY   112

Chapter 7: Interpreting Test Scores   **115**
Norm-Referenced Tests   116
    Percentile Ranks, 117   Stanines, 119
    Grade Equivalents, 119
Criterion-Referenced Tests   121
SUMMARY   122

Part Four: Measuring Relationships

Chapter 8: Correlation   **127**
Graphing Correlation   127
Pearson Product Moment   131
    Evaluating the Correlation Coefficient, 133
    Hypotheses for Correlation, 134
    Computing Pearson Correlation, 135
Factors Affecting Correlation   139
Further Interpretation of the
    Correlation Coefficient   142
Intercorrelation Tables   143

Correlation Tables   146
Spearman Rank-Order Correlation   147
SUMMARY   150

Chapter 9: Prediction and Regression   **153**
Simple Regression   155
The Standard Error of Estimate, S_E, 158
An Example of Simple Regression, 161
Graphing the Regression Equation, 165
The Coefficient of Determination, r^2, 166
Multiple Regression   167
SUMMARY   169

Part Five: Inferential Statistics

Chapter 10: _T_-Test   **175**
Hypotheses for _T_-Test   176
Using the _T_-Test   178
_T_-Test for Independent Samples, 179
_T_-Test for Paired (Dependent) Samples, 184
_T_-Test for a Single Sample, 186
SUMMARY   189

Chapter 11: Analysis of Variance   **191**
One-Way ANOVA   193
Hypotheses for One-Way ANOVA, 193
Conceptualizing One-Way ANOVA, 194
Steps in the Computation of ANOVA, 196
Further Interpretation of the _F_-Ratio, 200
An Example of One-Way ANOVA, 202
The One-Way ANOVA Summary Table, 206
Post Hoc Comparisons, 207
Two-Way ANOVA   209
Conceptualizing Two-Way ANOVA, 209
Hypotheses for Two-Way ANOVA, 211
Graphing the Interaction, 211   The Two-

Way ANOVA Summary Table, 214
An Example of a Two-Way ANOVA, 215
SUMMARY   218

Chapter 12: Chi Square   **221**
Assumptions Required for Chi Square   222
Using Chi Square   223
One Variable Chi Square: Goodness
  of Fit Test   223
  Equal Expected Frequencies, 223
  Unequal Expected Frequencies, 228
Chi Square for Two Variables: Test
  of Independence   229
Using Percentages in Chi Square   233
Sample Size   234
Computation of Expected Frequencies
  for Chi Square with Two Variables   235
SUMMARY   237

Part Six: Reliability and Validity

Chapter 13: Reliability   **241**
Understanding the Theory of Reliability   242
Methods of Assessing Reliability   243
  Test-Restest, 243   Alternate Forms, 244
  Measures of Internal Consistency, 245
  Inter-Scorer Reliability, 247
The Standard Error of Measurement   248
Factors Affecting Reliability   250
  Heterogeneity, 250   Test Length, 250
  Difficulty of Items, 251   Quality of Items, 251
How High Should Reliability Be?   251
SUMMARY   252

Chapter 14: Validity   **255**
Content Validity   256

Criterion-Related Validity   257
   Concurrent Validity, 257
   Predictive Validity, 257
Construct Validity   258
Face Validity   259
Assessing Validity   260
Test Bias   261
SUMMARY   262

Part Seven: Putting It All Together

Chapter 15: Simulations and Examples   **267**
Introduction   267
Sample Passages and a Step-by-Step
   Explanation of the Answers   271
    Sample Passage 1   271
    Sample Passage 2   272
Simulation Passages   274
Answers   284

Appendixes

Appendix Table A: Areas and Ordinates of the
   Normal Curve in Terms of x/σ 311
Appendix Table B: Values of the Correlation
   Coefficient (Pearson's r) for Different Levels
   of Significance   317
Appendix Table C: Distribution of t 318
Appendix Table D: The 5 Percent and 1 Percent
   Points for the Distribution of F 319
Appendix Table E: Distribution of Studentized
   Range Statistic   327
Appendix Table F: Distribution of Chi Square   331
Glossary of Symbols   332
Glossary of Formulas   334
Index   341

Preface

"I would rather have a root canal than take the statistics course," joked one of my students several years ago. However exaggerated, this statement probably represents the attitude of many of the students we encounter in our statistics courses. I also have noticed that several of my students take the required statistics course just before graduation. The message? Put off this course until it is the only thing separating you from your degree. Only at that point do you grudgingly take it.

At the same time, there are those students who look forward to the statistics courses. They enjoy the logical, sequential nature of statistics and can immediately see how their newly-acquired knowledge can be applied to their work environment.

Instructors of statistics courses need to accommodate students with various levels of interest and knowledge. These instructors strive to challenge the interested students and maintain their motivation, while at the same time help the others overcome their fear of research and statistics.

Students who take statistics courses as part of their degree program may end up using statistics as consumers of and/or as producers of research. Most probably fall into the first category, that of consumers. Professionals who want to keep current in their field need to be able to read literature, and to understand research studies reports. A course in statistics, coupled with a course in research methodology, can help people become educated consumers of research.

Elementary and high schools have consistently increased the amount of statistical concepts being introduced into their curricula, and children in today's classrooms are asked to predict, hypothesize, test, observe, and record. Mastery of basic statistics helps teachers feel comfortable and knowledgeable when teaching these skills to their students. In addition, educators need to have a fair level of understanding of standardized test scores and norms, which are commonly used in most, if not all, schools. Thus, there is even a greater need for universities to include research and statistics courses in their programs.

There are educators who are likely to continuously initiate and conduct research studies in their classrooms and schools. However, even those who do not conduct formal research should always study, question, and monitor the teaching-learning process. All educators, whether school teachers, early childhood educators, or school principals, should acquire knowledge of basic statistics. Having this knowledge helps one in the quest to become that questioning, critical, and intellectually-curious professional.

Practical Statistics for Educators, as the title indicates, was written specifically for educators. The book tries to show the application of research and statistics to education; a special effort was made to present examples relevant to this field. The book grew out of frustration with the textbooks which are currently used in statistics courses offered in colleges of education. My students indicated to me time and again that my explanations "were better" than those in the texts we were using, and suggested that I write my own statistics text. I started by writing a few chapters and trying them out in class. My students liked these chapters and encouraged me to continue to write.

The book is divided into eight parts. Part One, *Introduction*, includes Chapter 1, Getting Started; and Chapter 2, Sampling Procedures. Part Two covers *Descriptive Statistics*, and includes three chapters: Chapter 3, Organizing and Graphing Data; Chapter 4, Measures of Central Tendency; and Chapter 5, Measures of Variability. Part Three, *The Normal Curve and Standard Scores*, could have been included in Part Two, but we decided that the topics covered in Part Three merit their own part. Part Three, then, includes Chapter 6, The Normal Curve and Standard Scores, and Chapter 7, Interpreting Test Scores. Part Four, *Measuring*

Relationships, discusses Correlation (Chapter 8); and Prediction and Regression (Chapter 9). Both chapters in this part could also have been included in Part Two (Descriptive Statistics), or in Part Five (Inferential Statistics). However, we felt that the topic of correlation and prediction should be discussed in a separate part. Part Five, *Inferential Statistics*, includes three chapters: Chapter 10, T-Test; Chapter 11, Analysis of Variance; and Chapter 12, Chi Square. Part Six, *Reliability and Validity*, contains two chapters, Reliability (Chapter 13); and Validity (Chapter 14). Part Seven, *Putting It All Together*, contains Chapter 15, Simulation and Examples. Finally, the appendixes include statistical tables of critical values, a glossary of symbols, a glossary of formulas, and an index.

Acknowledgments

I would like to acknowledge the help and support of the following people who have contributed to the creation of this book:

Professor Rebecca Barr, who encouraged and guided me, especially at the initial stages of writing the manuscript.

Professor Jan Perney, who has always been gracious and generous with his time, for reviewing many portions of the manuscript, and for providing helpful suggestions and ideas.

Professor Paula Jorde Bloom, for her advice, support and encouragement, and for providing continual feedback while pilot-testing the book in her classes.

Dr. Kenneth Rasinski, who reviewed the entire manuscript and provided excellent comments and suggestions regarding the book's content, accuracy, and style.

Barbara Leys, my graduate assistant in 1991-92, who helped refine and improve the manuscript. Her insight and ideas were extremely useful and contributed greatly to the book.

Cynthia Ahlman, my graduate assistant in 1992-93, who diligently worked on the manuscript, paid attention to detail, and assured the book's uniformity of style and appearance. I learned to trust Cindy's judgment and advice as she took charge of various aspects of the writing process, including the creation of the index.

Greta Michael who has always been willing to help and has encouraged me for the past two years. I highly respect Greta's opinions and value her support and friendship.

Finally, I would like to thank my family for their love, support, and patience. To my husband, **Dan**, and to my children, **Cory** and **Ossie**, who offered helpful editorial comments and suggestions and encouraged me to complete this book.

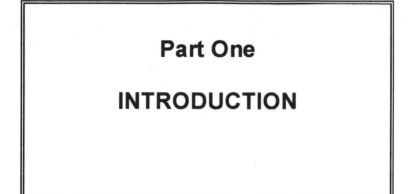

Part One

INTRODUCTION

Chapter 1
GETTING STARTED

Like all other disciplines, the field of statistics has its own jargon and language. This chapter will introduce you to several basic concepts and terms used in statistics. Additional concepts and terms are introduced throughout the book.

Qualitative and Quantitative Measures

One way to classify research methodologies is to characterize them as being typical of the **qualitative** or the **quantitative** paradigm. One of the most obvious differences between the two paradigms is the type of data which is collected. In qualitative data analysis, data typically are presented in a *narrative* form; whereas in quantitative data analysis, the findings are typically presented in a *numerical* form. Qualitative researchers usually make extensive use of observations and interviews, while quantitative researchers try to maintain objectivity and may not even be present when data are collected. Qualitative research is context-based, recognizing the uniqueness of each individual and each setting. Quantitative researchers believe that findings can be generalized from one setting to other similar settings, and are looking for laws, patterns, and similarities.

In the past, researchers identified themselves as either "qualitative researchers" or "quantitative researchers," and the two paradigms were seen as completely different from each other.

Today, while recognizing the differences between the two paradigms, more and more researchers see the two as complementary and support using both of them together in research studies.

In a typical quantitative study, data are collected to describe phenomena or to test hypotheses. Statistical techniques are then used to analyze the data. *This statistics book, like most other statistics books, is geared toward the analysis of quantitative, numerical data.*

Variables and Scales of Measurement

Measurement is defined as assigning numbers to observations according to certain rules. Measurement may refer, for example, to counting the number of times a certain phenomenon occurs or the number of people who responded "yes" to a question on a survey. It also refers to using tests to assess intelligence, or to measuring height, weight, and distance. Each system of measuring uses its own units to quantify what is being measured (e.g., meters, miles, dollars, percentiles, frequencies, and text readability level).

A **variable** is a measured characteristic that can assume different values or levels. Some examples of variables are age, grade level, height, gender, and political affiliation. By contrast, a measure that has only one value is called a **constant**. For example, the length of each side of a square with a perimeter of 24 inches is a constant; that is, all sides are equal (as opposed to other geometric shapes where the sides may have different lengths). Or, when all the participants in the study are third graders, then grade level is a constant.[1]

---

[1] **A HINT**: The decision whether grade level or any other characteristic (e.g., socioeconomic status) should be a constant or a variable depends on the design of the study. For example, in studies attempting to measure a particular type of growth over time (e.g., cognitive abilities or social skills), grade level may be a variable, and several grade levels will be included in the study. On the other

A variable may be continuous or discrete. **Continuous variables** can take on a wide range of values and contain an infinite number of small increments. Height, for example, is a continuous variable. Although we may use increments of 1 inch, people can differ from each other by a fraction of an inch. **Discrete variables**, on the other hand, contain a finite number of distinct values between any two given points. Some test scores are a discrete variable. For example, on a certain test, a student may get a score of 20 or 21, but not a score of 20.5.

It is important to remember that in the case of intelligence tests, for instance, while the test is only capable of recording specific scores (discrete variable), intelligence itself is a continuous variable. On the other hand, research reports may describe discrete variables in the manner usually prescribed for continuous variables. For example, in reporting the number of children per classroom in a given school, a study may indicate that there are, on the average, 26.4 children per room. In actuality, the number of children in any given classroom would, of necessity, be indicated by a whole number (e.g., 26 or 27). Reporting the discrete variable in this manner lets the researcher make finer distinctions, allowing for more sensitivity to the data than would be possible if adhering to the format generally used for the reporting of discrete variables.

There are four commonly used types of measurement scales: **nominal, ordinal, interval**, and **ratio**. For all four scales we use numbers, but the numbers in each scale have different properties and should be manipulated differently. It is the duty of the researcher to ascertain the scale of the numbers used to quantify the observations in order to determine the appropriate statistical test which should be applied to analyze the data.

Nominal Scale   *Label, Categorize*

In nominal scales, numbers are used to label, classify, or categorize data. For example, the numbers assigned to the

---

hand, in a study where three instructional methods are used with first graders, grade level is a constant.

members of a football team comprise a nominal scale, where each number represents a player. Numbers may also be used to describe a group in which all members have some characteristic in common. For example, in coding data from a survey to facilitate computer analysis, boys may be coded as "1" and girls as "2". In this instance, it clearly does not make sense to add or divide the numbers. We cannot say that two boys, each coded as "1", equal one girl, coded as "2", although in other contexts, 1+1=2. Similarly, it will not make sense to report that the average gender value is, for example, 1.5! For nominal scales, the numbers are assigned arbitrarily, and are interchangeable. Consequently, instead of assigning 1 to boys and 2 to girls, we can just as easily reverse this assignment, and code boys as 2 and girls as 1.

Ordinal Scale *- ordered based on size*

For ordinal scales, the observations can be ordered based on their magnitude or size. This scale has the concept of *less than* or *more than*. For example, students may be rank-ordered in comparison to their classmates using achievement as a criterion. We know that a student who is ranked 10th in the class has a higher grade point average (GPA) than a student ranked 50th. However, we do not know how many points separate these two students. The same can be said about the three medal winners in the long jump at the Olympic games. It is clear that the gold medalist performed better than the silver medalist, who, in turn, did better than the bronze medalist. But we should not assume that the same number of inches separate the gold medalist from the silver medalist, as separate the silver medalist from the bronze medalist. Another example is the typical grading system in which a grade of A is higher than a B or a C, but it cannot be assumed that the difference between an A and a B is the same as the difference between a B and a C, or a D and an F. Thus, in an ordinal scale, observations can be rank-ordered based on some criterion, but the intervals between the various observations are not assumed to be equal.

Interval Scale *ordered based on size but all have equal intervals*

Interval scales have the same properties as ordinal scales, but they also have equal intervals between the points of the scale. Most of the data we will use in this book are measured using an interval scale. Temperatures, calendar years, IQ, and achievement test scores, all are considered interval scales. The difference between a temperature of 20°F and 25°F is 5°F, and is the same as, let's say, the difference between 65°F and 70°F. However, we cannot say that a temperature of 90°F is three times as hot as a temperature of 30°F; or that a child with an IQ of 150 is twice as smart as a child with an IQ of 75, because an interval scale does not have an absolute, or true, zero. An absolute zero is a point lacking completely the characteristic being measured. In Fahrenheit temperature, the temperature of 0° does not imply lack of heat (the absolute zero is -273°C, where the molecules do not move at all). The zero point in an IQ scale is not a true zero, because we cannot say that a person who received a score of zero on our IQ test has no intelligence at all. We probably can find other questions which this person can answer, but these questions were not asked.

Ratio Scale *– same characteristics but have absolute 0 true 0 point*

Ratio scales have the same characteristics as interval scales, but in addition they have an absolute zero. Thus, we can compare two points on the scale and make statements such as: this point is twice as high as that point, or this person is working half time (as opposed to full time). Height, for example, is a ratio scale. We can say that a person whose height is 3'2" is half as tall as a person whose height is 6'4". Height has a true zero point, usually the floor on which the person stands while being measured. Or, for example, in a race, the absolute zero point is when the gun sounds and the stopwatch is pressed to start the counting. Ratio scales exist most often in the physical sciences but rarely in behavioral sciences such as education, psychology, or sociology.

Comparing the Four Scales

Most data and measures used in educational and psychological research are assumed to be interval. Many of the most common and powerful statistical tests (e.g., *t*-test, analysis of variance, and regression) use interval or ratio scales. At times, assuming that certain measures comprise an interval scale involves, possibly, stretching somewhat the rules for such a scale. For example, a **Likert scale**, which uses responses from "strongly agree" to "strongly disagree", is often scored on a scale of 5 to 1. That is, a response of "strongly agree" is assigned 5 points, and a response of "strongly disagree" is assigned 1 point. However, one may question whether the interval, or distance, between "strongly agree" and "agree" is the same as the interval between "neutral" and "disagree". Researchers tend to treat the Likert scale as an interval scale and by doing so, they can use more powerful and more convenient statistical tests to analyze the data. Some fictitious examples from Lincoln Elementary School may help to illustrate some of the differences between the scales:

Example 1: The six buses which carry the children to and from school are numbered 1 through 6. All the children on each bus live in proximity to each other, so, in essence, each bus represents a neighborhood. In this case, the numbers assigned to each bus serve as labels and comprise a *nominal* scale.

Example 2: A photographer wants to take a picture of Mrs. Smart's seventh-grade students. The photographer asks the children to line up, according to their height, from the shortest to the tallest child. Each child is then assigned a number from 1 to 35, to help the photographer set up the class picture. These numbers comprise an *ordinal* scale. The child assigned #5, for example, is taller than the child assigned #4, but the difference in height between these two children is not necessarily the same as the difference between any other two students who are assigned two consecutive numbers.

Example 3: Mr. Bright, the fifth grade teacher, looks at the list of scores obtained by his students on the latest mathematics test. These test scores comprise an *interval* scale. Mr. Bright can see that several students in the class have some difficulties with addition and division. He wants to motivate his students to practice these two skills, and suggests that they calculate the average height of the students in the class. The list of the heights of all students comprises a *ratio* scale.

Parametric and Nonparametric Statistics

There are different research situations which call for the use of two types of statistics: parametric and nonparametric.[2] **Parametric statistics** are applied to data from populations which meet the following assumptions: the variables being studied are measured on an interval or a ratio scale; subjects are randomly assigned to groups; the scores are normally distributed; and the variances of the groups compared are similar. When these assumptions are being met, the parametric tests are more efficient and powerful than their nonparametric counterparts. However, in many research situations in behavioral sciences, it is hard to meet all the required assumptions. As a result, findings should be interpreted cautiously. It is probably safe to say that many researchers always use interval or ratio scales when applying parametric tests, while it is more common for researchers to violate the other assumptions.

Nonparametric statistics are used with ordinal and nominal data, or with interval and ratio scale data that fail to meet the assumptions needed for parametric statistics. Nonparametric statistics are easier to compute and understand, compared with parametric statistics. Chi square, for example, (see Chapter 12) is a nonparametric statistic. *T*-test (see Chapter 10) and analysis of variance (see Chapter 11) are examples of parametric statistics.

---

[2] **A HINT:** Nonparametric statistics are also called assumption-free, or distribution-free statistics.

The majority of the statistical tests you are likely to read about in the literature are classified as parametric.

The Process of Statistical Hypothesis Testing

A research study often begins with a hypothesis (an "educated guess") which guides the investigation. After the hypothesis is proposed, a study is designed to test that hypothesis. The data collected in the study enable the researchers to decide whether the hypothesis is supported.

We actually use two hypotheses to explain phenomena and to make predictions about relationships or differences between variables in the research study. These two hypotheses are the null hypothesis and the alternative hypothesis. The **null hypothesis** (represented by H_0) predicts no relationship or no difference between variables. For example, the null hypothesis may predict no difference (beyond that which may be attributed to chance alone) between the experimental group and the control group as a result of an intervention. Or, the null hypothesis may state that two variables, such as IQ and reading comprehension, are not related. In most cases, the null hypothesis (which may also be called the **statistical hypothesis**) is not formally stated, but it is always implied. The **alternative hypothesis** (represented by H_A or H_1) gives direction to the design of the study and guides the investigation. It predicts that some relationship or difference exists between variables. For example, the alternative hypothesis may predict that students in a group using a new experimental reading method will score significantly higher on the end-of-year reading test, compared with students in the group using the traditional reading method. Or, the alternative hypothesis may state that there is a positive correlation between IQ and reading comprehension.

Studies yield statistical results which are used to decide whether to retain (i.e., accept) or reject the null hypothesis. Once this first decision is made, the researcher can then determine whether the alternative hypothesis has been confirmed. It should be mentioned, however, that this statistical decision is made in terms of *probability*, not *certainty*. We cannot *prove* anything; we can only describe the probability of obtaining these results due to sampling error. For example, we may want to compare the means from experimental and control groups using a statistical procedure called the *t*-test (see Chapter 10). The null hypothesis states that the difference between the two means is zero. The statistical results may lead us to two different conclusions: (a) it is unlikely that the two means came from the same population, and the difference between them is too great to have happened by chance alone; or (b) the difference between the two means is not really greater than zero, and the two means probably did come from the same population. In such cases, even if we observe differences between the two means, we attribute them to sampling error, and not to some systematic differences resulting from the experimental treatment.

Regardless of the research hypothesis presented at the onset of the study, the statistical testing and the evaluation of the findings start with a decision regarding the null hypothesis. Once we calculate the sample statistic, we compare the obtained value to the appropriate critical value, which is often determined from statistical tables. If the obtained value exceeds the critical value, the null hypothesis is rejected. *Rejecting* the null hypothesis means that the probability of obtaining these results by chance alone is very small (e.g., 5% or 1%). We conclude that the relationship, as predicted by the alternative hypothesis (H_A), is probably true. *Retaining* the null hypothesis means that these results (e.g., difference between two means) may be due to sampling error, and could have happened by chance alone more than 5% of the time.

In most statistical tests, the probability level of 5% (p of .05) serves as the cutoff point between results considered **statistically significant** and those considered **not statistically significant**.[3] The p level (i.e., level of significance) indicates the probability that we

---

[3] **A HINT:** The term *significant* does not necessarily mean the same as "useful in practice" or "important".

are rejecting a true null hypothesis. If the probability level (p value) is 5% or less ($p \leq .05$), the findings are reported as statistically significant.[4] If the probability level (p value) is higher than 5% ($p > .05$) we usually report the findings as not significant, instead of reporting the actual p level.[5]

The probability level, when set at the onset of the study, is represented by the Greek letter ∝ (alpha). The convention is to use an alpha of .05. However, in exploratory studies, researchers may set alpha at .10. In other studies, the researchers may want to set the alpha level at .01, so as to have a higher level of confidence in their decision to reject null.

Errors in Decision Making

If we reject the null hypothesis (H_O) when in fact it is true and should not be rejected, we are making a Type I error. If we retain the null hypothesis, when in fact it should be rejected, we are making Type II error. The proper decision is made if we reject a false null hypothesis, or when we retain a true null hypothesis.

Degrees of Freedom

In order to consult tables of critical values (found usually in the appendix), the researcher needs to know the degrees of freedom (df). Essentially, df is **n-1** (the number of people in the study, minus 1), although there are some modifications to this rule in some statistical tests. The exact way to calculate df will be presented in the discussion of the statistical tests included in this book.

---

[4] **A HINT:** When the results are statistically significant, report the highest (the best) level of significance. For example, if results are significant at the $p < .01$ level, report that level, rather than $p < .05$. Of course, you can always report the exact p value (e.g., $p = .035$).

[5] **A HINT:** However, researchers may choose to report the exact p value when $p > .05$, especially when the p level is close to .05 (e.g., $p = .056$).

And Finally...

Statistical analysis is based on observations, which are collected using certain instruments and procedures. If the instruments lack in reliability or validity, any conclusions or generalizations based on the results obtained through using these instruments are going to be questionable. Similarly, when a study is not well designed, one may question the results obtained from such a study. Problems resulting from a poorly designed study and bad data cannot be overcome with fancy statistical analysis. Just because the computer processes the numbers and comes up with "an answer" does not mean that these numbers have any real meaning. Remember what is often said regarding the use of computers: "garbage in - garbage out." This adage applies to the use of statistics, as well.

Summary

1. Research methodologies can be classified into **qualitative** and **quantitative**. Qualitative research is context-based and findings are usually presented in words. Quantitative research assumes that the findings, presented typically as numbers, can be generalized to other settings. The focus of this book is on quantitative statistics.

2. **Measurement** is defined as assigning numbers to observations according to certain rules.

3. A **variable** is a measured characteristic that can vary and assume different values or levels.

4. A **constant** is a measured characteristic that has only one value.

5. Variables may be continuous or discrete. **Continuous variables** can take on a wide range of values and contain an infinite number of small increments. **Discrete variables** contain a finite number of distinct values between two given points.

6. Measurements are divided into four scales: **nominal, ordinal, interval**, and **ratio**.

    Nominal: Numbers are used to label, classify or categorize observations to indicate similarities or differences. This is the least precise form of measurement.

    Ordinal: Observations are ordered to indicate *more than* or *less than* based on magnitude or size. The intervals between the observations, however, cannot be assumed to be equal.

    Interval: Observations are ordered with equal intervals between points on the scale. Since there is no absolute zero point, inferences cannot be made which involve ratio comparisons.

    Ratio: Observations are ordered with equal intervals between points. This scale has an absolute zero; therefore, comparisons can be made involving ratios. This is the most precise form of measurement. Ratio scales are generally used in physical sciences rather than in the behavioral sciences.

7. **Parametric statistics** are applied to populations which meet certain requirements. **Nonparametric statistics** can be applied

to all populations, even those that do not meet the basic assumptions.

8. Parametric statistics are used more often by researchers and are considered more powerful and more efficient that nonparametric statistics.

9. Nonparametric statistics can be used with nominal, ordinal, interval, and ratio scales. Parametric statistics can be used with interval and ratio scales only.

10. Many research studies start with a hypothesis that guides the investigation. A study is then designed to test that hypothesis, called the **alternative hypothesis**. It is represented by the symbol H_A or H_1.

11. After collecting the data, the process of statistical hypothesis testing starts with a decision regarding the **null hypothesis**, represented by the symbol H_0. This hypothesis predicts no difference or no correlation between the variables under consideration.

12. The study's statistical results are used to decide whether the null hypothesis should be retained or rejected. Rejecting the null hypothesis can lead to the confirmation of the alternative hypothesis; retaining the null hypothesis may lead to a decision not to confirm the alternative hypothesis.

13. Results may be reported as **statistically significant** or **not statistically significant**. When the results are statistically significant, the exact level of significance may be reported.

14. Statistical results are reported in terms of probability, not certainty. Results that are significant are likely to be reported in terms of probabilities (p value), using terms such as $p < .05$ or $p < .01$.

15. In order to consult the statistical tables of critical values, the appropriate **degrees of freedom** (*df*) need to be calculated for each of the tests.

Chapter 2
SAMPLING PROCEDURES

Sample s/B representative of the population; it is used to generalize a population

at least 1 characteristic in common

Populations and Samples

A **population** is an entire group of persons or elements that have at least one characteristic in common. Examples would include all the residents of a particular suburb, all high school mathematics teachers in a district, or all the states in the U.S. A population may have more than one characteristic, or trait, in common. For example, we may talk about a population of female students in the state university freshman class who come from one-parent families.

In real life, rarely do we study and measure entire populations. The most notable example of a study of an entire population is that of the census, which is conducted once every 10 years. Clearly, including *all* members of a population in a study is expensive, time consuming, and simply impractical. Yet, most research studies are concerned with generalization; that is, with obtaining rules and findings that describe large groups. Thus, quite often, the researchers draw a sample and use it to gain information about the population. A **sample**, then, is a small group of observations selected from the total population. A sample should be *representative* of the population, because information gained from the sample is used to estimate and predict the population characteristics which are of interest.

As an example, suppose we want to know what the parents of the students in the elementary school district think about sex education. In a large district, we may have as many as 10,000 parents and it might be too expensive to survey every household. Instead, a sample of 500 parents may be selected and surveyed. The results of this survey can be said to represent all the parents in the district. (Of course, as with every survey, the response rate has to be adequate to assure that the results truly reflect the total population.)

Descriptive and Inferential Statistics

The field of statistics is often divided into two broad categories: descriptive statistics and inferential statistics. **Descriptive statistics** classify, organize, and summarize numerical data about a particular group of observations. The number of students in the district, the mean grade point average of the students in the biology honors class, and the ethnic make-up of a given university, are all examples of descriptive statistics. These statistics, which describe only one group, cannot be generalized to other populations.

Inferential statistics (which may also be called **sampling statistics**), involve selecting a sample from a defined population and studying this sample. Then, conclusions are drawn and inferences are made about the population based on the observations of the sample. In political polls, for example, a pollster may survey 1500 voters and use their responses to predict the national elections results the next day. In another example, an educational researcher who is conducting a study in which cooperative learning is used in five junior high school science classes may use the results of the study to predict the efficacy of implementing this method in similar junior high school science classes. The rationale behind inferential statistics is that since the sample represents the population, what holds true for the sample probably also holds true for the population.

Descriptive and inferential statistics are not mutually exclusive. In a sense, inferential statistics include descriptive statistics. When a sample is observed and measured, we obtain descriptive statistics for that sample. However, inferential statistics can take the process one step further and use the information obtained from the sample to estimate and describe the population to which the sample belongs. Whether or not a given statistic is descriptive or inferential depends not on the type of statistic, but on its purpose. For example, the mean score on a spelling test is a descriptive statistic if the teacher wants to compare the scores of the students on the test which was given on Friday, to the scores of the same students on the same test given at the beginning of the week. However, the same spelling test can be given in another study done in the district in which a group of second graders, selected at random, were using a new method to learn spelling; and another group of randomly selected second graders were using the traditional spelling method. The results from the two methods can be compared to each other to determine if, indeed, the new method was more effective (i.e., if second graders using the new method scored significantly higher on the spelling test). If this were the case, the language arts coordinator in the district may recommend that other second grade teachers in the district use the new method.

Parameters and Statistics

A **parameter** is a measure of a characteristic of an entire population. For example, the mean ACT score of a district's high school students is a parameter. A **statistic** is a measure of a characteristic of a sample. In most research studies, we are interested in obtaining information about the population parameters, but instead of measuring the parameters directly by measuring every member of the population, we draw a sample, measure the sample to obtain the statistics, and then use the statistics to estimate the corresponding population parameters. For example, a market research firm may want to find the reaction of consumers to a new cereal packaging. The firm may select a sample, interview the people, and record their reactions. The firm will then generalize the findings from the sample to the total population of the potential cereal consumers. In another example, we may want to find out if the mean IQ in the state of Illinois is indeed 100. We may choose a sample of 1,000 people and measure their IQ scores. This sample mean IQ is a statistic and it can be used to estimate the mean population IQ, the parameter, which is the focus of the study.

It becomes clear, then, that the sample selected should be representative of the population, because the sample statistics are used to estimate and predict the population parameters. There are a number of procedures which may be used to draw a sample. The next section describes several of the sampling techniques that are widely used by researchers.

Methods of Sampling

The majority of research studies in behavioral science are interested in studying populations by using samples representative of these populations. In many physical sciences studies it is quite simple to obtain a representative sample. For example, if the scientist wants to study the quality of the water of a pool, all that is needed is to scoop out a small jar with pool water and analyze this sample. We would all agree that the sample is representative of the pool water. In behavioral sciences, such as education, psychology, and sociology, the task of obtaining a representative sample is much more complicated.

There are several sampling methods which may be used in research. In choosing the method to use, the researcher has to decide which one is appropriate and feasible in a given situation. All sampling methods share the same steps, or sequence: first, the population is identified, then the sample size required is determined, and lastly, the sample is selected.

Simple Random Sample

In selecting a **simple random sample**, every member of the population has an equal and independent chance of being selected for inclusion in the sample. That is, the selection of one member in no way increases or decreases the chances of another member to also be selected. Sampling procedures whereby the first 100 people who stand in line are chosen, or every other person from a list is selected, do not fit the definition of a random sample. When the first 100 people are selected, those who stand behind them do not have a chance of being included in the sample. Likewise, choosing every other person means that persons next to those being selected do not have a chance of being included.

In theory, if the random sample is large enough, it will truly represent the population in every respect, and be a true reflection of the population. On the other hand, selecting 10 people from a population of 1,000, even if done by using random sampling procedure, may result in a sample that is not truly representative of the population.

The typical idea that comes to mind when we think of a random sample is drawing names out of a hat. While a random sample can be drawn this way, such a process is not efficient. There are more practical means of achieving the same results, using what we call a table of random numbers. Found in several statistics textbooks, this table may be used by hand or by computer, and offers a faster way of drawing a random sample.

Systematic Sample

In a **systematic sample**, every Kth member (e.g., every 5th or 10th person) is selected from a list of all population members. The procedure starts by ascertaining the size of the population and the desired sample size. The population size is then divided by the sample size to obtain the value of K. For example, if we have a population of 500 and need a sample of 25, we divide 500 by 25, to obtain a K of 20. In other words, we select every 20th member to achieve the desired sample size of 25.

A systematic sample can be a good representation of the population when the names on the list from which the sample members are selected are listed randomly. Since this is rarely the case, the sample may be biased. For example, certain nationalities tend to have many last names that start with the same letter. Thus, a whole group of people of the same nationality may be excluded from the sample if the names of those selected are listed just before and just after that group of names.

Stratified Sample

To obtain a **stratified sample**, the population is first divided into strata, or subgroups, and then a random sample is taken from each stratum. Stratified sampling is used extensively in market research, in political polls, and in norming standardized tests. The final sample represents, proportionally, the various subgroups in the population. A stratified sample may be used when there is a reason to believe that various subgroups in the population may have different opinions or behave differently because of some characteristics that the group members have in common. An example may help to illustrate this sampling procedure.

Suppose a large urban elementary school district with 5,000 teachers wants to survey its teachers about their attitudes toward merit pay. Instead of surveying all 5000 teachers, a stratified sample of 250 may be selected. The teachers may first be divided into strata based on variables such as grade level taught (primary, intermediate, or upper), subjects taught, and annual salary (in increments of $5,000). For example, we may have a stratum of intermediate grades, social studies teachers, whose annual salary is $40,000-$45,000. From each subgroup, a random sample may be drawn. The resulting sample of 250 teachers will include, proportionally, all subgroups from the total district population of 5,000 teachers. Thus, the sample which will participate in the survey will be a miniature of the population where each stratum is represented in proportion to its percent in the population.

Cluster Sample

In **cluster sampling**, groups or clusters, rather than individuals, are selected. By comparison, in simple random, systematic, and stratified sampling procedures, individuals are selected, one at a time, for inclusion in the sample. A cluster is any group whose members share common characteristics. These clusters may be classrooms, schools, families, or city blocks. Cluster sampling procedure is useful when the clusters are naturally occurring groups, and it may be impractical or impossible to select individuals from these clusters.

For example, suppose a publisher wants to try out a new textbook for eighth-grade science classes. Out of the 50 states in the U. S., three may be chosen at random. From each state, three counties may be randomly selected, and from each county, three school districts may be chosen at random. From each district, one school may be randomly selected, and from each school, one eighth-grade classroom may be randomly selected. All eighth-grade classes selected from all three states may be asked to field-test the new textbook.

Incidental (Convenience) Sample

Occasionally, the researcher conducts a study using an accessible sample, such as the researcher's own classroom or school. For example, college psychology professors may choose, for convenience and cost cutting purposes, to use their own students to conduct an experimental study. Or graduate students working on their dissertations may use their schools to collect data. In fact, a fair number of research studies in education and psychology are done using an available, convenience sample.

The main problem in using an incidental sampling is that it is not always clear what population the sample belongs to, since the study did not start by choosing a sample from a defined population. Great care should be exercised in generalizing the results of the study to a larger population.

Sample Bias

A biased sample contains a systematic error, or differs systematically from the population. Sample bias does not refer to *random* differences between the sample and the population, but rather to *systematic* differences. If, for example, a political poll is conducted by randomly selecting respondents from the telephone book, the resulting sample is likely to be biased because it excludes voters with unlisted telephone numbers, or voters who do not have telephones.

A well-publicized example of such sample bias occurred during the 1936 presidential elections when Republican Alf Landon ran against Democrat Franklin D. Roosevelt. The *Literary Digest* predicted a victory by Landon after receiving a 25% response rate from 10 million written ballots which were mailed out. The mailing list for the ballots was based on telephone books and state registries of motor vehicles. Of course, the list left out a big segment of the population that did vote in the presidential election, but was not included in the survey because they did not own a telephone or a car.

Another possible sample bias stems from using volunteers in a study. Even though the volunteers may come from a clearly defined population, they may not be "typical" of the other members of that population. Conducting a study with volunteers and then generalizing the results to the population at large can lead to incorrect conclusions.

A biased sample may also occur when it is based solely on the responses of people who had mailed back their completed surveys. Those responding are similar to people who volunteer to participate in a study. Therefore, their responses may, or may not, represent the rest of the population. In many cases, those who respond to surveys feel strongly one way or another about the topic of the survey, whereas the majority of people do not bother to respond. Yet, quite often, the responses of those who did return their surveys are generalized to the total population.

Size of Sample

As sample size increases, it is more likely to be representative of the population, especially when the sample is randomly selected. In determining whether a sample truly represents the population, it is important to consider the sampling procedure, as well as the size of the sample used. For example, simple random sampling is highly regarded; however, if the randomly selected sample consists of five students, it is probably not an adequate representation of the population. By the same token, size alone does not guarantee an accurate sample, and a large sample may also be biased. In general, the researcher should try to obtain as large a sample as is feasible. A minimum of 30 subjects per group is recommended in most studies. In well-designed experimental studies, a smaller sample size is acceptable. As the population gets larger, a smaller portion sample may be sufficient to provide accurate representation. When the population is greater than 10,000, a sample of 1,000 to 1,500 may give adequate precision.

Summary

1. **Descriptive statistics** classify, organize, and summarize numerical data about a particular group of observations.

2. **Inferential statistics** involve selecting a sample from a defined population, studying the sample, and using the information gained to make inferences and generalizations about that population.

3. Descriptive and inferential statistics are not mutually exclusive and the same measures can be used in both types. The purpose or the use of the statistics determines whether they are descriptive or inferential.

4. A **population** is the entire group of persons or things that have some characteristic in common.

5. A **sample** is a group of observations selected from the total population.

6. A **parameter** is a measure of a characteristic of the entire population.

7. A **statistic** is a measure of a characteristic of the sample.

8. A sample should be **representative** of the population, because the statistics gained from the sample are used to estimate the population parameters.

9. The majority of research studies in behavioral sciences are interested in studying populations by using samples representative of the populations.

10. In selecting a **random sample**, every member of the population has an equal and independent chance of being selected. The table of random numbers is often used to draw a random sample.

11. In **systematic sampling**, every Kth person is selected from the population. K is determined by dividing the total number of population members by the desired sample size.

12. A **stratified sample** is obtained by first dividing the population into strata (subgroups) and then selecting, at random, members from each stratum. The final sample represents, proportionately, the various subgroups in the population.

13. In **cluster sampling**, clusters (rather than individuals) are selected. A cluster is any naturally occurring group whose members share common characteristics.

14. An **incidental sample** is a convenient, or available, sample used by the researcher. Researchers have to exercise great caution in determining the population to which they can generalize results from a convenience sample.

15. A **biased sample** contains a systematic, rather than just random, error.

16. As sample size increases, it is more likely to be an accurate representation of the population, although size alone does not guarantee that the sample is representative. A large biased sample is still biased.

17. In many research studies, a sample size of at least 30 is desirable. When the population is greater than 10,000, a sample size of 1,000 - 1,500 may accurately represent this population.

Part Two

DESCRIPTIVE STATISTICS

Chapter 3
ORGANIZING AND GRAPHING DATA

Organizing Data

Occasionally, an educator may have a list of scores recorded next to each other in no particular order. An example might be the scores each student received on a social studies test, which are recorded in the teacher's grade book, next to each student's name. In order to see how the students performed on the test, or to assign letter grades, the teacher may want to organize the scores in some manner. The first logical step is to **order** the scores. The convention is to order them from the highest to the lowest. If there is a limited number of items on the test and the range of the scores is also limited, there are likely to be several students who have obtained the same score. Instead of listing those duplicate scores several times, the next step for the teacher is to **tally** the scores, thereby creating a **frequency distribution**. Frequency distributions lend themselves well to graphic presentation, usually in the form of frequency polygons and histograms.

Consider these scores on a 30-item test given to a class of 25 students (Table 3.1):

Table 3.1   Scores of 25 Students on a 30-Item Test

27	16	23	22	21
25	28	26	20	22
30	24	29	17	28
24	17	23	24	26
19	21	18	23	25

Now, let's order and tally the scores, creating a frequency distribution (Table 3.2):[1]

Table 3.2   A Frequency Distribution of a 30-Item Test

Score	Frequency
30	1
29	1
28	2
27	1
26	2
25	2
24	3
23	3
22	2
21	2
20	1
19	1
18	1
17	2
16	1
	$N=25$

---

[1] **A HINT:** Always add up the scores in the "Frequency" column to make sure it equals the total number of scores in the distribution (i.e., N).

Frequency distributions can be graphed using frequency polygons or histograms (discussed in this chapter). Frequency distributions can also be converted to cumulative frequencies. (See Table 3.6.)

[handwritten margin note: range of scores is 20 pts or less - list each; more than 20 pts range - group intervals]

Grouped Distributions — *[handwritten: range]*

If the range of the scores (i.e., the distance between the highest and the lowest score) is 20 points or less, we list each individual score and indicate its frequency. However, if the range of scores is more than 20 points, we may want to combine every few scores together to avoid having a very long list of scores. Thus, we create **class intervals**, in which every few scores are grouped together. The biggest disadvantage in using class intervals is that we lose details and precision. That is, because scores are grouped, we cannot tell what was the *exact* score that was obtained by each person.

There are two rules to remember concerning class intervals: (a) all class intervals should have the same width; and (b) all intervals should be mutually exclusive (i.e., a score may not appear in more than one interval). In creating class intervals, two decisions need to be made: one regarding the **number** of intervals, and the other regarding the **width** of the intervals. There is no clear consensus as to the desired number of intervals. Several textbooks recommend 8 to 15 intervals, while others recommend 10 to 20 intervals. We recommend a total of 8 to 20 intervals (with close to 8 intervals for narrower ranges, and closer to 20 for wider ranges). As to the width of the intervals, an odd number is recommended (e.g., 3, 5, or 7) in order to have an interval midpoint that is a whole number. For example, the interval of 48-50 has a width of 3 points (50, 49, and 48) and its midpoint is 49. By comparison, the interval of 47-50 has a width of 4 points (50, 49, 48, and 47) and its midpoint is 48.5, which is not a whole number.[2]

---

[2] **A HINT:** The convenience of having a whole number as a midpoint will become more apparent when we discuss graphs later in the chapter.

As with ungrouped scores, the highest class intervals should be listed on top, and the lowest interval should be listed at the bottom of the column. Within each interval, the lowest score should be listed on the left side and the highest score on the right side (e.g., 38 - 40).

To practice creating class intervals for a frequency distribution, Table 3.3 contains scores for 25 students. The scores are already ordered for your convenience.

Table 3.3 Test Scores for 25 Students

80	68	58	52	45
78	65	57	51	43
75	64	56	50	42
72	63	55	48	41
71	60	54	47	40

We can choose an interval width of 3 points, resulting in 14 different intervals (Table 3.4); or an interval width of 5 points, resulting in 9 intervals (Table 3.5). Both options are acceptable and are within the guidelines of 8 to 20 intervals. However, be aware that the decision as to whether to use interval width of 3 or 5 points will result in a different-looking graph.

Note the following points: (a) there are fewer intervals when a width of 5 points is used and each interval is wider, thus likely to include more people; (b) although the lowest score obtained was 40, the lower border of the lowest interval includes scores below 40 (e.g., 36) in order to follow the rule of equal width in all intervals. Similarly, if the highest score obtained would have been 79, instead of 80, we could have extended the highest interval up to 80, to assure equal intervals throughout the list.

[handwritten notes at top:]
• highest on top   lowest @ bottom
• Choose odd # for interval 3 or 5
○ no more than 8 to 20 # created by using intervals

Table 3.4 A Frequency Distribution of 25 Scores
With Class Intervals of 3 Points

Class Interval (3 points)	Frequency	Midpoint
78-80 *[high]*	2	79
75-77	1	76
72-74	1	73
69-71	1	70
66-68	1	67
63-65	3	64
60-62	1	61
57-59	2	58
54-56	3	55
51-53	2	52
48-50	2	49
45-47	2	46
42-44	2	43
39-41	2	40
	N=25	

[handwritten: Low, 3 pts in between; 8 to 20 min to max]

Table 3.5 A Frequency Distribution of
25 Scores With Class Intervals of 5 Points

Class Interval (5 points)	Frequency	Midpoint
76-80	2	78
71-75	3	73
66-70	1	68
61-65	3	63
56-60	4	58
51-55	4	53
46-50	3	48
41-45	4	43
36-40	1	38
	N=25	

Cumulative Frequency Distributions

Another way to organize data is to create a **cumulative frequency distribution**. Cumulative frequencies show the number and percentage of scores at or below a given score (Table 3.6).

accumulated scores

Table 3.6 Cumulative Frequencies

(Col. 1) Score	(Col. 2) Frequency	(Col. 3) Cumulative Frequency	(Col. 4) Percent Frequency	(Col. 5) Cumulative Percentage
20	1	20	5	100
19	1	19	5	95
17	2	18	10	90
16	4	16	20	80
14	4	12	20	60
10	3	8	15	40
8	2	5	10	25
6	2	3	10	15
5	1	1	5	5
	N=20			

3 people scored a 6 or less

Table 3.6 starts with a frequency distribution (columns 1 and 2), and then the third column is added. The "Cumulative Frequency" column (column 3) is created from the bottom up. To create this column, ask yourself: how many people had a score of 5 (i.e., the lowest score obtained) or less? Answer: 1; so 1 is recorded at the bottom of the third column. How many had a score of 6 or less? Answer: 3, which is recorded next. How many had a score of 8 or less? Answer: 5. And so on, until the column is completed.

The fourth column, "Percent Frequency," expresses in percentages the proportion of people who have obtained the same score. For example, we can see that 5% ($n=1$) of the examinees had a score of 20; and that 20% ($n=4$) of the examinees had a score of 16.

The cumulative frequencies in column 3 are converted to cumulative percentage, recorded in column 5. The conversion can be done by starting either at the top or at the bottom of column 5. First, you have to know the total number of scores in the distribution, which is 20 in our example ($N=20$). If you work your way from the bottom up, ask yourself what percentage is 1 out of 20? (1 is the first entry at the bottom of column 3 which is now converted to cumulative percentages.) The answer is: 5%. Or, you may ask, what percentage is 3 out of 20, and 5 out of 20? The answer is: 15% and 25%, respectively. And so on, until the column is completed.

A cumulative frequency can be depicted visually using a graph called an **ogive** or an **"s" curve**. (This graph is illustrated in Figure 3.8, along with an explanation of the graph.)

Graphing Data

Graphs are used to convey information. They transform numerical data into a visual form. The graphs enable the reader to see relationships not easily available by looking at the numerical data. There are various forms of graphs, each one appropriate for a different type of data.

Histogram and Frequency Polygon
A frequency distribution, such as the one in Table 3.7, may be represented by a **histogram** (Figure 3.1, part a) or by a **frequency polygon** (Figure 3.1, part b).

Table 3.7 A Frequency Distribution

Score	Frequency
6	1
5	2
4	4
3	3
2	2
1	1

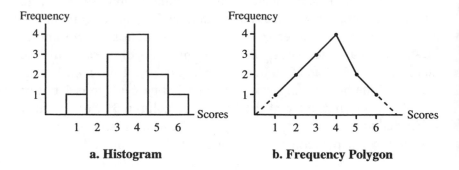

Frequency

4
3
2
1

Scores

1 2 3 4 5 6

a. Histogram

Frequency

4
3
2
1

Scores

1 2 3 4 5 6

b. Frequency Polygon

Figure 3.1 Histogram and frequency polygon of the data in Table 3.7

There are several guidelines to follow when drawing these graphs:

1. The vertical axis always represents frequencies, and the horizontal axis always represents scores (or class intervals).
2. The lower values of both axes are at their intersection, and they increase as they move away (up, or to the right) (Figure 3.2).

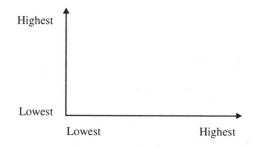

Highest

Lowest

Lowest   Highest

Figure 3.2 Graphing the lowest and highest values on each axis

3. The frequency axis (the vertical) always starts from a frequency of 0 (zero). The scores axis (the horizontal) may start with a score of 0, or with a higher score. If the first score to be recorded is higher than 1, we indicate skipping scores by a break

in the horizontal axis. For example, if the lowest score to be graphed is 15, we indicate skipping the first 14 scores as shown in Figure 3.3.

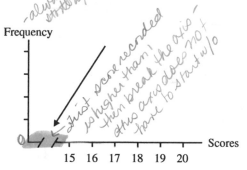

- always start w/o
- first score recorded is higher than 1 then break the axis / this axis does not have to start w/o

Figure 3.3 Graphing frequency distributions when the lowest score on the horizontal axis is higher than 1

4. Whenever possible, the vertical axis should be shorter than the horizontal axis (about 3/4). Doing so gives the graphs a more natural appearance and reduces distortions.

5. The bars of the histogram should touch each other to indicate that the scores are on a continuum.

6. When a score or an interval has a frequency of 0 (zero) (see Table 3.8), the histogram or frequency polygon should be drawn as demonstrated in Figure 3.4.

Table 3.8 A Frequency Distribution

Score	Frequency
6	1
5	2
4	3
3	2
2	0
1	1

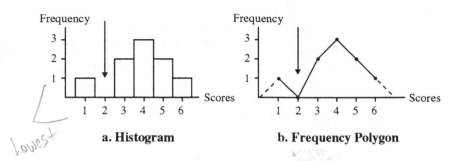

a. Histogram   **b. Frequency Polygon**

Figure 3.4 Histogram and frequency polygon of the data in Table 3.8

7. When drawing a frequency polygon, bring the two sides (tails) down to the horizontal line. This can be done in two ways:

    a. A broken line going all the way to the horizontal axis (Figure 3.5, part a).

    b. A solid line coming close, but not touching the horizontal axis (Figure 3.5, part b).

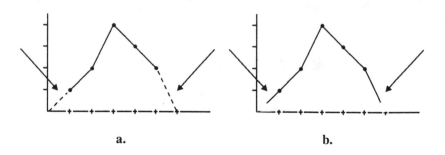

a.   b.

Figure 3.5 Two ways of graphing the tails of a frequency polygon

Both the histogram and the frequency polygon can be used to graph individual scores, as well as scores grouped into class intervals[3]. When graphing class intervals, midpoints are used to indicate the intervals. Table 3.9 shows English test scores of 25 students, and Figure 3.6 presents the same data using a frequency polygon.

Table 3.9 A Frequency Distribution With Class Intervals and Midpoints

Class interval	Frequency	Midpoint
38 - 42	1	40
33 - 37	3	35
28 - 32	4	30
23 - 27	6	25
18 - 22	5	20
13 - 17	3	15
8 - 12	2	10
3 - 7	1	5

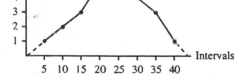

Figure 3.6 Graphing a frequency distribution with class intervals using interval midpoints (data in Table 3.9)

---

[3] **A HINT:** Where there are many scores, graphing them using a frequency polygon is likely to show a normal curve. For more information, see Chapter 6.

Differences between histogram and frequency polygon. To some extent, the decision whether to use a histogram or a frequency polygon is a question of personal choice. Frequency polygons may be easier to draw, whereas histograms are somewhat easier to read and interpret. One advantage of the polygon over the histogram is that two groups can be graphed and compared on the same graph using a polygon. For example, Figure 3.7 shows test scores of a group of 15 boys and 15 girls on a biology test. As can be easily seen, the girls performed better than the boys, although the range of scores is the same for both groups.

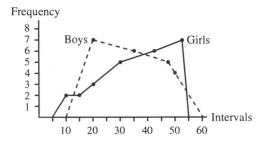

Figure 3.7 A frequency polygon comparing scores of boys and girls

Several textbooks list another difference between a histogram and a frequency polygon. These books suggest using the histogram for data that naturally occur in discrete units. For example, IQ scores may be 101, 102, or 103, but not 101.5 or 102.5.[4] A frequency polygon is recommended for observations that can take on in-between values, even when we record and graph only discrete units. For example, we may record the height of the students in our class, rounded off to the nearest inch. On the frequency polygon graph we would show only data points such as 5'1," 5'2," or 5'3," but in reality we have students whose height is somewhere between 5'1" and 5'2," or between 5'2" and 5'3."

---

[4] **A HINT:** Although IQ scores for an *individual* may only be whole numbers, *group* mean score may have decimal places, such as 103.4 or 104.8.

Graphing Cumulative Distributions

To graph a cumulative frequency distribution, we draw an **ogive**, which can be described also as a special case of a frequency polygon. The horizontal axis is used for recording the scores and the vertical axis is used for recording the cumulative frequencies or the cumulative percentages. (See Table 3.6, columns 3 and 5.) A typical ogive tends to be flat at the lowest and the highest points, and is steep at the middle.[5] This is why the ogive is also called the "s" curve.

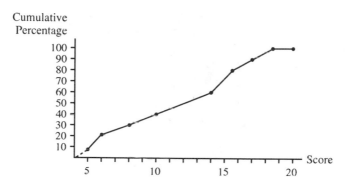

Figure 3.8 An ogive of a cumulative distribution showing the data in Table 3.6

Looking at Figure 3.8, we can read the same information as that presented in Table 3.6. For example, we can determine that a person with a score of 17 scored as well as, or better than, 90% of those who took the test.

---

[5] **A HINT:** This is especially true when the distribution includes many scores.

Pie Graph

The **pie graph** (or **pie chart**) is used when the subparts add up to 100%. When drawing a pie graph, the different sections of the pie should be identified and numerical information should be added in the form of percentages and/or the actual numbers. To illustrate a pie graph, Figure 3.9 depicts the proportion of four feeder schools in the total population of a high school.

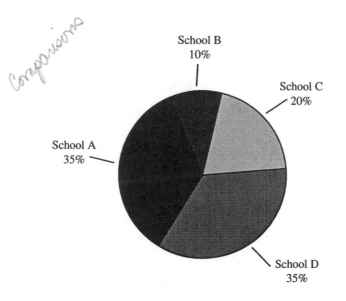

Figure 3.9 A pie graph showing the percentages
of students from four feeder schools

Pie graphs lend themselves well to comparison. For example, a small private college, in its alumni quarterly report, may present two pie graphs: one showing a breakdown of donations made to the college in 1992-1993 year (Figure 3.10, part a), and the other showing a breakdown of donations made to the college in the following year, 1993-1994 (Figure 3.10, part b). In order to compare the donation patterns from year to year, the percentage of money contributed by each group is indicated on each of the graphs.

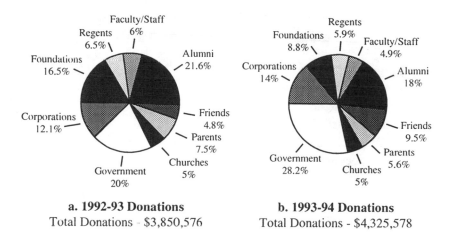

a. **1992-93 Donations**
Total Donations - $3,850,576

b. **1993-94 Donations**
Total Donations - $4,325,578

Figure 3.10 Two pie graphs showing donations
made to a college in two consecutive years

Drawing pie graphs by hand may prove a somewhat complicated task. It is difficult for most of us to convert percentages into sections of a pie. Computer graphic programs are clearly a great help here!

Bar Diagram (Bar Graph)

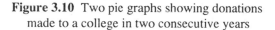

The **bar diagram** shows a series of bars next to each other. The bars do *not* touch, and they are usually ordered in some way (from lowest to highest, or vice versa). This type of graph is used for categorical (nominal) data. For example, we may want to compare degree plans of undergraduate students from several majors who plan to go to graduate school within the next five years (Table 3.10 and Figure 3.11). The college majors are categorical data which do not imply a continuum, even though in the graph they are listed next to each other.

**Table 3.10 College Majors and Percentages of Students
Who Plan to Go to Graduate School**

College Major	% Who Plan to Go to Graduate School
A. Education	25
B. English	40
C. Psychology	85
D. Accounting	15

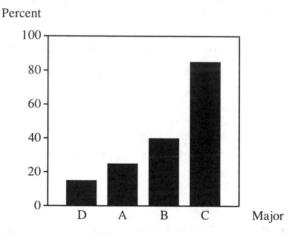

Figure 3.11 A bar diagram showing the data in Table 3.10

The bars may also be drawn horizontally, to allow for easier identification and labeling of each bar (Figure 3.12).

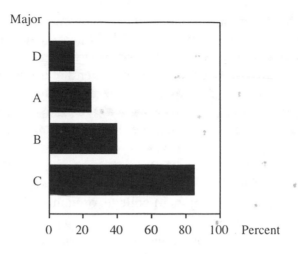

Figure 3.12 A horizontal bar diagram showing
the same data as in Figure 3.11

Occasionally, two bars may be drawn next to each other. For
example, we may want to ask the same question as before concerning degree plans, but in addition to comparing several majors,
we also want to compare male and female students (Figure 3.13).

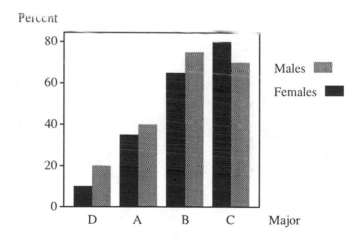

Figure 3.13 A bar diagram comparing male and female students
from different college majors and their graduate degree plans

One of the most common mistakes of students is to get this graph mixed up with a histogram. Although a bar diagram looks somewhat like a histogram, the two should not be confused, as they are used for different purposes. Remember that a histogram is used *only* for frequency distributions and the two axes are always reserved for frequencies (the vertical), and for scores or class intervals (the horizontal). Unlike a bar diagram, the scores in a histogram comprise an interval or a ratio scale, and they are on a continuum; therefore, the bars *do* touch each other to show continuity. The bars in a bar diagram represent nominal, categorical data (e.g., majors in college, or names of states), and do not imply a continuum.

How to draw the bar diagram. The scale one chooses can affect the message conveyed by the graph. Let's look at the data presented in Figure 3.14, showing the graduation rate (in percentage) of four high school districts. In part a, the differences between the four districts seem much less pronounced than in part b. Figure 3.14, part b magnifies the differences and shows more details, but may also present an exaggerated picture of the differences.

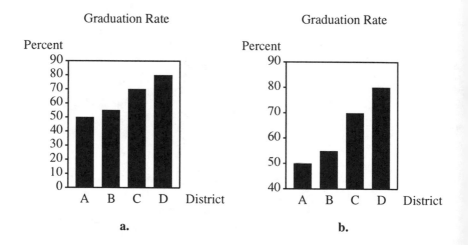

Figure 3.14 Graduation rate in four high school districts:
A comparison of two graphs showing the same data

Line Graph

This is the most commonly used graph. When we say "graph," we probably mean this form of a graph. A **line graph** is used to show relationships between two variables which are depicted on the two axes. The horizontal axis indicates values that are on a continuum (e.g., calendar years or months). The vertical axis can be used for various types of data (e.g., test scores, temperatures, and income). Table 3.11 shows mean test scores of second grade students in one school over the last four years, and Figure 3.15 shows the same information graphically.

Table 3.11 Mean Test Scores of Second Graders, 1991-1994

Year	Mean Test Score
1991	50
1992	70
1993	60
1994	90

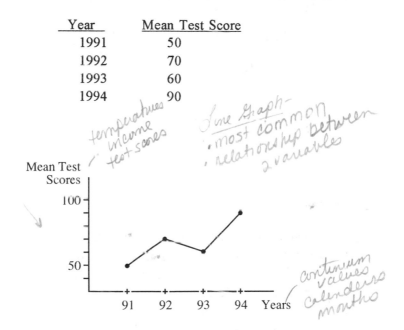

Figure 3.15 A line graph showing the data in Table 3.11

A big advantage of the line graph is that more than one group can be shown on the same graph simultaneously. If colors are not available, each group can be presented by a different kind of line (e.g., broken or solid) (Figure 3.16). Notice that the line graph is different from a frequency polygon. The line graph is used for a different purpose and does not have frequencies in the vertical axis.

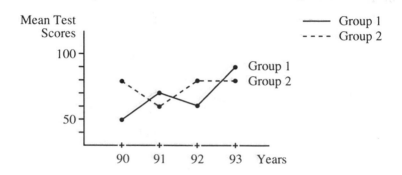

Figure 3.16 A line graph showing mean test scores of two groups over a four year period

Pictogram

Newspapers (such as *USA Today*) and magazines are likely to use **pictograms** to present data graphically. A pictogram is actually a modified form of the bar diagram, where a different number of figures are used to indicate the height of the bars. For example, a school district may wish to show the changes in the number of students enrolled in the district schools over the last six years (Figure 3.17). In this pictogram, each human figure represents 100 students.

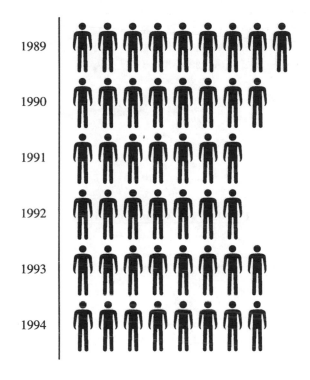

Figure 3.17 A pictogram showing the number of students in the district over a six year period (each human figure represents 100 students)

Stem-and-Leaf Diagram

The **stem-and-leaf** diagram is a modification of the histogram, allowing the display of more information in the same amount of space. When class intervals are depicted using a histogram, the midpoints are usually indicated; however, there is no information about the *exact* score of each person in each interval. The stem-and-leaf diagram brings back precision and details which are lost when scores are grouped into class intervals. Consider the following scores (Table 3.12):

Table 3.12 Test Scores of 26 Students

15, 19, 20, 23, 28, 33, 35, 37, 39,
40, 46, 46, 48, 48, 49, 51, 54, 55,
57, 62, 65, 68, 70, 77, 79, 85.

The first step is to create a frequency distribution with class intervals (Table 3.13).

Table 3.13 A Frequency Distribution With Class Intervals

Class Interval	Frequency
10-19	2
20-29	3
30-39	4
40-49	6
50-59	4
60-69	3
70-79	3
80-89	1

Next, we need to choose a **leading digit** for each interval. For the data in Table 3.13, the leading digits are 1, 2, 3......8 and they comprise the **stem**. The **leaves** are the second digit of each score (Figure 3.18). For example, according to Tables 3.12 and 3.13, the class interval of 10 - 19 includes two scores: 15 and 19. Thus, the stem is the digit 1 (the first digit on the left), and the leaves are 5 and 9. Adding the leaves to the stem provides information about the exact scores (15 and 19, in this example).

Stem	Leaves
1	5, 9
2	0, 3, 8
3	3, 5, 7, 9
4	0, 6, 6, 8, 8, 9
5	1, 4, 5, 7
6	2, 5, 8
7	0, 7, 9
8	5

Figure 3.18 Stem-and-Leaf graph showing the data in Table 3.13

By inspecting the stem-and-leaf graph we can get an idea about the shape of the distribution (e.g., symmetric or skewed), and about any possible extreme scores (also called outliers). Adding bars around each line of scores shows the similarity between a horizontal histogram and a stem-and-leaf diagram (Figure 3.19).

Stem	Leaves
1	5, 9
2	0, 3, 8
3	3, 5, 7, 9
4	0, 6, 6, 8, 8, 9
5	1, 4, 5, 7
6	2, 5, 8
7	0, 7, 9
8	5

Figure 3.19 Stem-and-Leaf graph showing the same data as in Figure 3.18, with bars added around the leaves

Box Plot

The **box plot** (also called **box-and-whiskers**) is another way to describe data. This graph can show the location of the median of a set of scores, as well as the spread of these scores.[6] To create the box plot, the scores are first ordered and divided into four quartiles, identified as Q_1, Q_2, Q_3, and Q_4. The two middle quartiles (Q_2 and Q_3) are included in the box, and the two extreme quartiles (Q_1 and Q_4) are the "whiskers". The median is shown by a line in the middle of the box (Figure 3.20).

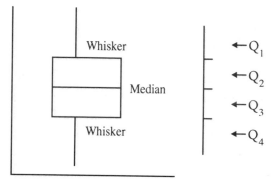

Figure 3.20 A box plot (box-and whiskers)

Let's look at an example of a box plot. An eighth-grade mathematics teacher practices estimation with her students. Each student is asked to estimate, to the nearest inch, the length of a 30-inch stick. The students' estimates are recorded as "prepractice." Then the teacher practices with the students various ways of estimating length, and each student is asked to estimate again the length of the stick. These estimates are recorded as "postpractice." Following are the prepractice and postpractice scores for 20 students (Table 3.14).

---

[6]**A HINT:** See Chapter 4 for a discussion of the median.

Table 3.14 Prepractice and Postpractice Scores for 20 Students

Student Number	Prepractice	Postpractice
1	13	24
2	18	25
3	22	25
4	24	26
5	27	27
6	28	28
7	28	28
8	29	29
9	29	29
10	30	30
11	32	31
12	32	31
13	33	32
14	35	32
15	38	32
16	39	33
17	39	34
18	42	34
19	45	35
20	49	36

Figure 3.21 shows two box plots, one for the prepractice scores and one for the postpractice scores. Notice that the postpractice scores are clustered closer to each other, when compared with the prepractice scores. The two middle quartiles which include the middle 50% of the scores are spread between the scores of 28 and 38 for the prepractice scores, and from 28 to 32 for the postpractice scores.

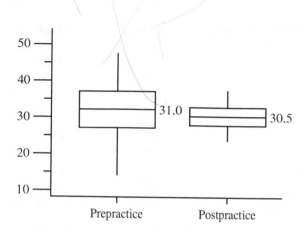

Figure 3.21 A box plot of the data in Table 3.14

The mathematics teacher concludes that as a result of the practice session, the most extreme scores were eliminated on the postpractice test, the range of scores decreased, and the whiskers became shorter. Figure 3.21 shows that, as a result of the practice, the students have improved their estimates of the length of the stick.

Summary

1. The first step in organizing data is to **order** the scores in some manner. The most common method is to order them from the highest to the lowest score.

2. After the scores have been ordered, the researcher then **tallies** the scores, thereby eliminating the need to list duplicate scores several times.

3. A **frequency distribution** is the list of scores which have been ordered and tallied.

4. Scores should be listed individually if the range of scores is 20 points or less.

5. If a frequency distribution has a range of more than 20 points, **class intervals** can be created in which scores are put into small groups. When class intervals are used, however, detail and precision are lost.

6. When using class interval, all intervals should have the same width and no score should appear in more than one interval. It is recommended that a total of 8 to 20 intervals be used. An odd number is recommended for the width of the intervals so that the interval midpoints are whole numbers.

7. Data may be organized using a **cumulative frequency distribution**, which shows the number and percentage of scores at or below a given score.

8. **Graphs** convey numerical information in a visual form.

9. **Histograms** and **frequency polygons** are used to represent frequency distributions.

10. There are guidelines to follow when drawing either the histogram or frequency polygon:

    a. The vertical axis represents frequencies and the horizontal axis represents scores or class intervals.

    b. The lower values of both axes are at the point of their intersection.

    c.   The vertical axis should be somewhat shorter than the horizontal axis.

11.   When drawing histograms or frequency polygons, the midpoints are used to mark class intervals.

12.   The bars of the histogram should touch each other.

13.   A cumulative distribution may be graphed using an **ogive** (also called an **"s" curve**).

14.   The **pie graph** is used when the subparts add up to 100%.

15.   The **bar diagram** (or bar graph) is used to represent nominal, categorical data. It has a series of bars that do *not* touch each other, usually arranged by height.

16.   The **line graph** is used to show changes in value over time. The horizontal axis has data on a continuum (e.g., years or months).

17.   The line graph may be used to show several groups in comparison to each other.

18.   The **stem-and-leaf diagram** is a modification of the histogram for class interval data, allowing for the presentation of more detailed information.

19.   The **box plot** (also called **box-and-whiskers**) can show the location of the median of a set of scores, as well as their spread. To create a box plot, the scores are first ordered and divided into four quartiles. The median is then shown by a line in the middle of the box, which represents the middle 50% of the scores.

Chapter 4
MEASURES OF CENTRAL TENDENCY

[handwritten: a single # that represents a set of scores]

[handwritten: center]

A measure of central tendency is a summary score. It is a single score that represents a set of scores, allowing us to describe and compare distributions of scores. In other words, this summary score is a single number typical of a frequency distribution. A measure of central tendency is often called an "average," although the word *average* is also used to describe "typical" or "normal." There are three commonly used measures of central tendency: mode, median, and mean. The decision as to which of these three measures should be used in a given situation depends on which measure is the most appropriate and the most representative of the scores.

Mode *[handwritten: # which occurs most frequently]*

The **mode** is the score that occurs with the greatest frequency. For example, in the distribution of 5, 8, 6, 8, 5, 9, 8, and 6, the mode is 8 (Table 4.1). To find the mode, tally the scores and check which score occurs the most. Since 8 repeats the most (3 times), it is the mode.

[handwritten: tally scores / ✓ which score occurs most]

To be a mode score should be at least repeated 2 times

Table 4.1   Test Scores of 8 Students

Score	Frequency
9	1
8	3
6	2
5	2

To be considered a mode, a score should repeat at least twice. If two scores have the same frequency, the distribution is called **bimodal**. A distribution may also be classified as **amodal** (has no mode) if no score repeats more than once. If three or more scores repeat the same number of times, we have a **multimodal distribution**. The following is an example of a bimodal distribution (Table 4.2):

Table 4.2   A Bimodal Distribution

	Score	Frequency
Both 4 & 5 are	6	1
the mode	5	2
	4	2
	3	1
	2	1

In a frequency polygon, the mode is the peak of the graph (Figure 4.1, part a). In a bimodal distribution, there are two peaks, both the same height (Figure 4.1, part b).

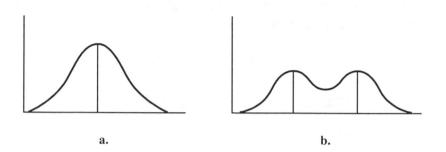

a.   b.

Figure 4.1 Frequency polygons with one mode (part a) and two modes (part b)

Median 50%↑ ─── median
50%↓

The **median** is the point in the distribution where 50% of the scores are above it, and 50% are below it. For example (Table 4.3):

Table 4.3 Test Scores of Seven Students

Score
10 ⎫
8 ⎬ 3 scores
7 ⎭
6 ─── median
4 ⎫
2 ⎬ 3 scores
1 ⎭

The score of 6 is the median, because 3 scores are above it and 3 are below it. The median is a point, and does not have to be an actual score obtained on the test. In the following test scores of

7.5 — *→ not actual score on test but OK*

10, 8, 7, 6, the median is 7.5, although the teacher may assign only full points on the test.

Sometimes, the median is estimated rather than calculated exactly.[1] For example, in the distribution of scores presented in Table 4.4, we will use 7 as the median, although there are 3 scores above it and only 2 scores below it.

Table 4.4   Test Scores With a Median of 7

Score
11
10   *median = 7*
9
7
7
6
5

$\overline{X}$ = sample mean

M = population mean

Σ = sum of

N = number of scores

Mean

The **mean**, also called the **arithmetic mean**, is sometimes referred to as the average. The mean is used more than the mode or the median. It is used in both descriptive and inferential statistics. The statistical symbol of the mean is $\overline{X}$ (pronounced "ex bar") for the sample mean; and μ, the Greek letter mu (pronounced "mu"), for the population mean. In research, many times the mean of the sample $(\overline{X})$ is used to estimate the population mean (μ). Quite often, we are interested in finding the mean of the population; however, it may not be practical or possible to find that

---

[1] **A HINT:** The exact median can always be calculated, using a somewhat lengthy procedure, not included in this book.

mean. Therefore, we select a sample, measure it to obtain its mean, and use that mean to estimate the population mean.

We find the mean by adding all of the scores and dividing the sum by N, the number of scores. The statistical symbol used to represent "sum of" is Σ (the Greek capital letter sigma). Thus, the mean is calculated using the following formula:

$$\bar{X} = \frac{\Sigma x}{n} \quad \text{-\# of scores} \qquad \text{or} \qquad \mu = \frac{\Sigma x}{N}$$

sample

To obtain ΣX, we need to add up all the scores. In symbols it looks like this: $\Sigma X = X_1 + X_2 + ... X_n$. This means that we have to add up the first score, the second score, etc., all the way to the last score. (With $n = 10$, the X_n score is the 10th score.) Consider the following scores (Table 4.5):

Table 4.5   Test Scores of Five Students

Score
10
9
8
6
2

The sum of these scores is 35, and the mean is 7:

$$\Sigma X = 10 + 9 + 8 + 6 + 2 = 35 \quad and \quad \bar{X} = \frac{\Sigma x}{n} = \frac{35}{5} = 7$$

The mean serves as the best measure when we have to estimate the unknown value of any score in the distribution (for both a sample and a population). That is, if the exact value of a particular score is unknown, the mean may be used to estimate that score.

In a symmetrical distribution, the majority of the scores cluster around the mean, and the mean then serves as an appropriate representative score (Figure 4.2, part a). However, in a skewed distribution, the mean is pulled toward the "tail" and it does not represent a point around which scores tend to cluster (Figure 4.2, part b and c).

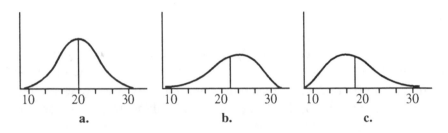

Figure 4.2 Symmetrical distribution (part a), negatively skewed distribution (part b), and positively skewed distribution (part c)

Part b (Figure 4.2) shows a negatively skewed distribution, where the "tail" points at the low scores; and part c shows a positively skewed distribution, where the "tail" points at the high scores. Note that in a positively skewed distribution the scores tend to cluster *below* the mean, and in a negatively skewed distribution the scores tend to cluster *above* the mean.

Comparing the Mode, Median and Mean

The mean is affected by every score in the distribution, because it is calculated by first adding up all the scores, and then dividing the sum by N, the number of scores. Changing even one score in the distribution will result in a change in the mean. By contrast,

[handwritten annotations in top margin: "median ordinal R½", "mode N o R", "mean X̄"]

the mode and the median may, or may not, be changed as a result
of a change in one score. This characteristic of the mean can be
both an advantage and a disadvantage. It is an advantage because
it accounts for every score in the distribution. However, it is a
disadvantage when there are extreme scores in a skewed
distribution. Let's look, for example, at these scores: 10, 12, 13,
13, 15, and 16. The mode is 13, the median is 13, and the mean
is 13.17. Changing the last score from 16 to another score, say 30,
will not bring about a change in the mode or in the median, but
will change the mean to 15.83.

Mode can be used with nominal, ordinal, interval, and ratio
scales. Scores do not need to be rank-ordered to calculate the
mode; therefore, it can be used with a nominal scale.[2] For a
median, we need to order the scores first to find the top and bottom
50%. A nominal scale has no order; therefore, we need at least an
ordinal scale. Median can also be computed, of course, for the
more advanced interval and ratio scales. To calculate the mean, we
need to add the scores and divide the sum by the number of scores.
The mean can be computed only for interval and ratio scales. The
comparison of scales reveals one reason for requiring more than
one type of measure of central tendency. Although the mean is
used the most, it is inappropriate with an ordinal or a nominal
scale.

Mode and median are most often used for descriptive statistics.
The mean is used for descriptive statistics, as well as for inferential
statistics. It is also used extensively in subsequent computations,
as we will see later (e.g., in the computation of variance, Chapter
5; and *t*-test, Chapter 10). In certain cases, even though the data
comprise an interval scale, we prefer using the median rather than
the mean. The following example will help to explain the reason
behind the decision to use the median instead of the mean.

[handwritten: mean = descriptive & inferential]
[handwritten: mode & median = mostly descriptive]

---

[2] **A HINT:** If we state that a certain statistic can be used with a
nominal scale, it is also understood that it can be used with a more sophisticated
scale (i.e., ordinal, interval, and ratio).

Assume there is an office with four secretaries and one supervisor. The secretaries make $15,000, $17,000, $18,000, and $10,000. The supervisor makes $60,000. A casual visitor might ask: How much do you make here, on the average? The median is $17,000 and the mean is $24,000. Presented with the decision of whether to choose the median or the mean as a representative score, you would probably choose the median, because it is a good representation of four out of five workers. The mean of $24,000 is too high for the four secretaries, and too low for the supervisor; thus, it does not represent the salary of any of the five office employees.

Another example underscores the same point. You may recall that we hear reports about the median housing price and median income (as opposed to *mean* housing price and *mean* income). If there are a few very expensive houses in an area, using the mean as a measure of average price may cause potential buyers to think that all the houses in this area are too expensive for them.

The examples above illustrate cases where the mean is not appropriate as a representative score. When there are extreme scores, they tend to pull the mean toward them, making it an inappropriate representation of the vast majority of the scores. This happens because the mean is the measure of central tendency most affected by extreme scores.

For your convenience, a summary of the steps used in the computations of the mode, median, and mean is included at the end of this chapter.

The Mean of Combined Groups

Occasionally, we want to find the overall mean for two or more groups combined when only individual group means are available. For example, suppose we have a mean for a group of boys and a mean for a group of girls, and we want to find the overall mean of the two combined. If there is an *equal* number of boys and girls, then we can simply add up the two means and divide them by 2

weighted mean

(the number of means) in order to find the mean of the two means. However, when the number of girls is different from the number of boys, a procedure for finding the **weighted mean** is required. This procedure takes into consideration the unequal number of observations in each group, as well as the means of the groups. The following general formula is used to compute the weighted mean:

$$\overline{X}_{TOTAL} = \frac{\Sigma \, (n_i \overline{X}_i)}{N}$$

# of observ. *mean of group*

N — total observations

Where $\overline{X}_{TOTAL}$ = the weighted mean

n_i = the number of observations in a group

$\overline{X}_i$ = the mean of a group

N = the total number of observations in all the groups

The Greek letter Σ (sigma), which is used as a symbol for summation, indicates that we repeat what follows it (in the numerator, in parentheses) for each group we have. For example, when there are three groups, we first multiply the number of observations (n) by the mean for each group. Next, we add the products from all three groups, and divide the sum by the combined number of observations in all the groups. A numerical example may help to illustrate how the weighted mean is computed.

Glen Grove school has two sixth-grade classes, one with 25 students, and the other with 28 students. Both classes took an achievement test in social studies, and the two sixth-grade teachers calculated the mean of the students in their own respective classes. They found that the mean of the first class is 83.6, and the mean of the second class is 90.2. The School Board asked the principal to report on the overall mean score of all the sixth graders in the school, without disclosing the exact means of each of the two classes. To find the overall mean, the principal needs to take into consideration the different number of students in each of the two classes as well as the different means. For each of the two classes, the principal multiplies the number of students by the class mean, adds up these products, and divides the sum by the combined number of students (N=53). In the calculations which follow, n_1 and n_2 represent the number of students in each of the two sixth-grade classes, and they are added to obtain N (the combined number of students in both classes). X_1 and X_2 are the means of the two classes.

$$\overline{X}_{TOTAL} = \frac{(n_1)(\overline{X}_1) + (n_2)(\overline{X}_2)}{n_1 + n_2} =$$

# of students × class mean

# of class mean × class

$$= \frac{(25)(83.6) + (28)(90.2)}{25 + 28} =$$

Class 1   Class 2   — total # of students in both classes

$$= \frac{(2090.0) + (2525.6)}{53} = \frac{4615.6}{53} = 87.09$$

The resulting weighted mean of 87.09 represents the social studies test scores of the two sixth-grade classes. This mean also accounts for the different means and for the different number of students in each of the two classes. Note that the weighted mean is not simply the mean of the two means (83.6 and 90.2) divided by 2; rather, it is closer to the higher mean of the second class because this class is larger.

Calculating the Mode, Median and Mean:
A Summary of the Steps

The calculations of the mode, median, and mean are summarized next, using the following scores: 9, 15, 12, 11, 12, 9, 7, 13, 12, 8, 8 (Table 4.6).

Table 4.6   A Frequency Distribution

Score	Frequency
15	1
13	1
12	3
11	1
9	2
8	2
7	1

Frequency = 12 = mode
11 = midpoint = median

Step 1:   Create a frequency distribution by ordering and tallying the scores (Table 4.6).

Step 2:   Check which score occurs most frequently. The score is 12, which is the mode.

Step 3:   Find the midpoint of the distribution which is the score of 11. There are 5 scores above it and 5 scores below it. The score of 11 is the median.

Step 4:   Add up all the scores and divide by 11, the number of scores in the distribution. The sum of the scores is 116, divided by 11, and we get 10.55, which is the mean.[3]

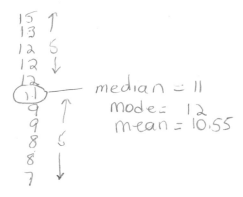

15 ↑
13
12 5
12 ↓
12
(11) ── median = 11
9   ↑   mode = 12
9   mean = 10.55
8   5
8   ↓
7

---

[3] **A HINT:** Unless told otherwise, always carry your computations to two decimal places.

Summary

1. A **measure of central tendency** is a summary score that represents a set of scores.

2. The **mode** is the score that occurs most frequently in a distribution.

3. A distribution of scores may have one mode, two modes (**bimodal**), three or more modes (**multimodal**), or no mode (**amodal**).

4. The **median** is the point in a distribution where 50% of the scores are above it and 50% of the scores are below it.

5. The exact median can always be computed, although the computations may be lengthy at times. An estimated median is sometimes used when the exact one is not readily apparent.

6. The **mean**, which is also called the **arithmetic mean**, is calculated by dividing the total sum of the scores by the number of scores. The symbol for the population mean is the Greek letter mu (μ); and the symbol for the sample mean is $\bar{X}$ ("ex bar").

7. The mean is the measure of central tendency which is used the most.

8. If the value of a score in the distribution is unknown, the mean can be used to estimate that score.

9. Mode can be used with nominal, ordinal, interval, and ratio scales. Median can be used with ordinal, interval, and ratio scales. Mean can be used with interval and ratio scales.

10. The mean is not an appropriate measure of central tendency when the interval or ratio scales have extreme scores, because it may yield a skewed measure. In such cases, the median, which is not affected by extreme scores, should be used.

11. Mode and median are most often used for descriptive statistics. The mean is used for both descriptive and inferential statistics.

— page 87

12. A **weighted mean** is computed when we want to find the overall mean of two or more combined groups. This procedure takes into consideration the different group sizes, as well as the different means.

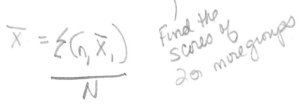

$$\overline{X} = \frac{\Sigma (n_i \overline{X}_i)}{N}$$

Find the scores of 2 or more groups

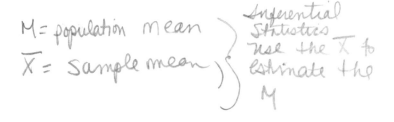

M = population mean

$\overline{X}$ = Sample mean

Inferential Statistics — use the $\overline{X}$ to estimate the M

X =

Σ = sigma or sum

Chapter 5
MEASURES OF VARIABILITY

We have described a measure of central tendency (a mode, a median, or a mean) as a representative score; that is, a single number that represents a set of scores. These measures indicate the center of the distribution. The graphs in Figure 5.1 will attempt to convince you that, in addition to central tendency measures, we also need an index of the **variability** of the group. Compare part a to part b in Figure 5.1. What are the similarities and differences between them?

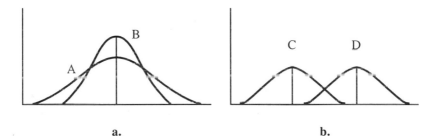

a.   b.

Figure 5.1 A graph showing two groups with the same mean, but different spread (part a); and a graph showing two groups with different means, but the same spread (part b)

After studying part a, you will probably conclude that Group A and Group B share the same mean, but Group A has a larger spread (i.e., Group A is more heterogeneous than Group B). In Group B, scores tend to cluster closer to the mean. Now, examine part b: Notice that both Group C and Group D have the same spread, or variability, but Group D has a higher mean than Group C.[1]

Suppose part a in Figure 5.1 represents test scores of two third-grade classes, and you were asked to choose the one you would prefer to teach next year. If the only information available to you was the mean for each class, you would probably flip a coin to choose between Group A and Group B, because they have the same mean. However, if the graphic representation was available to you, you would probably choose the third grade represented by B, which is more homogeneous and, therefore, easier to teach.

Looking at part b, if the same question were asked and only the means for both Group C and Group D were provided, you would probably choose the third-grade class depicted by D which has a higher mean. In fact, teaching either Group C or Group D would involve about the same amount of work for the teacher.

The examples depicted in Figure 5.1 were given to convince you that in order to present an accurate and complete description of a group, in addition to the mean, another index is needed: that of the variability of the group.

The Range

A very simple and easy measure of variability is the **range**. It indicates the distance between the highest and the lowest score in the distribution. The range is used mainly for descriptive purposes (a descriptive statistic). It does not give us much information about the variability *within* the distribution.

---

[1] **A HINT:** How can you tell which mean is higher if there are no numbers along the horizontal axis?   Remember the rule about drawing a frequency polygon: The numbers are lowest at the intersection on the left side, and increase as you move to the right on the horizontal axis. Since the mean of Group D is farther to the right, it is higher than the mean of Group C.

The range has a limited usefulness as a measure of variability. It is simply the distance between the two extreme scores in a distribution, but we know nothing about what is in between. To illustrate, compare the two sets of numbers: 10, 10, 10, 9, 1; and 10, 2, 1, 1, 1. Both have the same range, yet they represent a very different combination of scores.

It is interesting to note that there is a disagreement as to how to calculate the range. The statistics textbooks are divided between two approaches. One approach says: Subtract the lowest score from the highest score. For example, for the scores 25, 23, 22, 19, 18, 16, the range is: 25 - 16 = 9.

The other approach, and the one which this author supports, suggests that to find the range, subtract the lowest score from the highest score, and add 1. For the example above, the range is: 25 - 16 + 1 = 10. The rationale for adding 1 is: if both 25 and 16 (the extreme scores) are included, then the range is 10.

Variance and Standard Deviation

Since the range is not a satisfactory measure of the variability within the group, we are looking for another index of variability. Let's look at the following two graphs, a and b (See Figure 5.2).

The distances of the scores from the mean in part a (Figure 5.2) are larger than the distances of the scores from the mean in part b. In part a, some scores are up to 5 points above or below the mean. In part b, the scores cluster together, and they are no more than 1 point above or below the mean. Thus, it would make sense to be able to calculate an index of the mean (average) distance from the mean, expressed as absolute numbers (disregarding the plus or minus sign). The index showing the mean distance from the mean is called the **standard deviation**. In a distribution with a high spread of scores, that index value is high; and when the scores cluster closer to each other, that number is low. The standard deviation (*SD*) can be calculated using two methods, the **deviation**

score method and the **raw score method**. The computation of the deviation score method is easier to understand and it is discussed next.

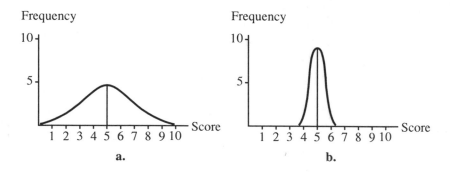

Figure 5.2 Two graphs with the same mean, but different spread

The Deviation Score Method

Let's look at the computational steps for calculating the standard deviation, using the deviation score method. In the first example these scores are used: 6, 5, 4, 3, 2 (see Table 5.1). We will find their mean, and then the deviation (distance) of each score from the mean. The deviation score is indicated in this book by $X\text{-}\overline{X}$ (i.e., score minus the mean).[2] Next, we will try to add up the deviation scores to find their mean (the mean of the distance of all scores from the mean).

---

[2] **A HINT:**   The deviation score is sometimes indicated by a lower case x.

Table 5.1   Raw Scores and Deviation Scores

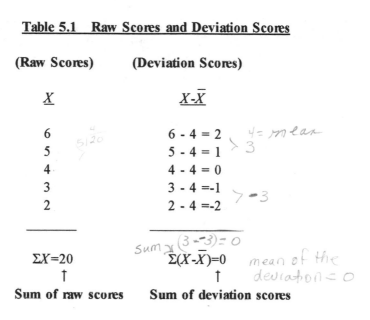

(Raw Scores)	(Deviation Scores)
$\underline{X}$	$\underline{X-\bar{X}}$
6	6 - 4 = 2
5	5 - 4 = 1
4	4 - 4 = 0
3	3 - 4 =-1
2	2 - 4 =-2

$\Sigma X=20$ $\Sigma(X-\bar{X})=0$

↑   ↑

Sum of raw scores   **Sum of deviation scores**

$$Mean = \bar{X} = \frac{\Sigma X}{N} = \frac{20}{5} = 4$$

You probably noticed that the sum of the deviation scores is zero; therefore, the mean of the deviations is also zero. To convince you that you were not set up by a selection of a particular set of numbers which are likely to end up with a deviation scores mean of zero, we can try another set (Table 5.2).

Table 5.2   Raw Scores and Deviation Scores

X	$X-\overline{X}$
10	10 - 7 = 3
9	9 - 7 = 2
8	8 - 7 = 1
1	1 - 7 =-6
$\Sigma X=28$	$\Sigma(X-\overline{X})=0$

$$\overline{X} = \frac{\Sigma X}{N} = \frac{28}{4} = 7$$

You may try creating your own set of numbers, but the end result will always be $\Sigma(X-\overline{X}) = 0$. The reason is this: The mean is defined as a point where the sum of deviations around it always adds up to zero.

Clearly, this is a dead end.   But we can bypass this phenomenon by employing two procedures: (a) using the absolute value of the deviation scores (absolute value is the number itself, disregarding the + or - sign); or (b) squaring the deviation scores. Each procedure will result in positive values, avoiding the problem of the negative deviation scores canceling the positive ones. Researchers, experimenting with both procedures, found out that the second procedure provided them with a more useful measure. Therefore, we will proceed using that method.

The next step, then, is to square the deviation scores, add up the squared scores, divide the sum by N (the number of scores), and then get the mean of the squared deviation scores. That mean is called the **variance**. The variance is defined as the **mean squared**

deviation.[3] To indicate the variance we use the following statistical symbols: σ^2 for the population variance (lower case Greek letter sigma, squared) and S^2 for the sample variance.[4] The formula for the population variance is:

$$VARIANCE = \sigma^2 = \frac{\Sigma(X - \bar{X})^2}{N}$$

(handwritten annotations: "Population variance", "sum", "score", "mean", "# of scores")

Where $\sigma^2 =$ the population variance

        $\Sigma(X-\bar{X})^2 =$ the sum of the squared deviations from the mean

        $N =$ the number of scores

The following numerical examples (Tables 5.3 and 5.4) will help to show the computational steps needed to find the variance, using the deviation score method.

In the discussion of the rationale for using a measure of variability, we stated that such a measure will give us an index of the mean (average) distance from the mean. But, if you look at the variances we obtained in both examples, and compare them to the actual deviations (the second column, $X-\bar{X}$, in Tables 5.3 and 5.4), you would realize that the variance is an *overestimate* of the mean

---

[3] **A HINT:** To remember how to find the variance, take the definition above (mean squared deviation), and read it backward: first you find the deviations, then you square them, and then you find their mean.

[4] **A HINT:** To understand the difference between the population and the sample variance, see the discussion in this chapter about "Comparing the Variance and SD for Populations and Samples".

Table 5.3   Raw Scores, Deviation Scores, and Squared Deviation Scores (The Same Numbers as in Table 5.1)

X	$X-\bar{X}$	$(X-\bar{X})^2$
6	2 ×	4 2^2
5	1	1 1^2
4	0	0 0^2
3	-1	1 -1^2
2	-2	4 -2^2
$\Sigma X=20$	$\Sigma(X-\bar{X})=0$	$\Sigma(X-\bar{X})^2=10$

score — mean

$$VARIANCE = \sigma^2 = \frac{\Sigma(X-\bar{X})^2}{N} = \frac{10}{5} = 2$$

variance *square root 151.41*

# of scores   SD

Table 5.4   Raw Scores, Deviation Scores, and Squared Deviation Scores (The Same Numbers as in Table 5.2)

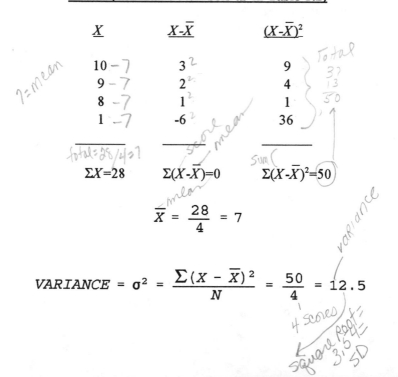

X	$X-\bar{X}$	$(X-\bar{X})^2$
10 −7	3 ^{2}	9
9 −7	2 ^{2}	4
8 −7	1 ^{2}	1
1 −7	-6 ^{2}	36
$\Sigma X=28$	$\Sigma(X-\bar{X})=0$	$\Sigma(X-\bar{X})^2=50$

7=mean

total=28/4=7

score — mean

sum

Total
37
13
50

$$\bar{X} = \frac{28}{4} = 7$$

mean

$$VARIANCE = \sigma^2 = \frac{\Sigma(X-\bar{X})^2}{N} = \frac{50}{4} = 12.5$$

variance

4 scores
square root=
3.54
SD

of these deviations. For example, in Table 5.4, the variance of 12.5 is not a good representation of the deviation scores 3, 2, 1, and -6.

The reason for that is simple: In order to find the variance, we squared the deviation scores. Consequently, the variance, which is the mean of the squared deviations is higher than the deviation scores it is supposed to represent. Therefore, the next logical step is to find the square root of the variance to bring us back to the original units. In our first example (Tables 5.1 and 5.3), the variance is 2, and its square root is 1.41, which is called the **standard deviation**. The standard deviation, abbreviated as SD, is simply the positive square root of the variance. In our second example (Tables 5.2 and 5.4), the variance is 12.5, and the standard deviation is $\sqrt{12.5} = 3.54$. Now, if you compare the SD in both examples to the deviation scores, you would agree that in each case the SD is a good average of the deviation scores in that distribution.

The symbol used for the population SD is σ (sigma) and for the sample SD the symbol is S. There is a slight difference in the computations of these two variances (population and sample), as explained later on in this chapter.

As you may have noticed, in the two numerical examples given before, the mean was a whole number. In real life, however, there is a greater probability that the mean is not going to be a whole number. In such cases, the computation of the variance and SD is going to be very time consuming, and you are more likely to make errors entering the numbers on the calculator. For example (Table 5.5):

Table 5.5 Raw Scores, Deviation Scores, and Squared Deviation Scores

X	$X-\bar{X}$	$(X-\bar{X})^2$
7	2.25	5.0625
6	1.25	1.5625
5	0.25	0.0625
1	-3.75	14.0625

$$\Sigma X=19 \qquad \Sigma(X-\bar{X})=0 \qquad \Sigma(X-\bar{X})^2=20.75$$

4.75=mean

$$\bar{X} = \frac{\Sigma X}{N} = \frac{19}{4} = 4.75 \quad \text{mean}$$

$$\sigma^2 \ (variance) = \frac{\Sigma(X-\bar{X})^2}{N} = \frac{20.75}{4} = 5.19$$

$$\sigma \ (SD) = \sqrt{\sigma^2} = \sqrt{5.19} = 2.20 \quad \text{square root of 5.19}$$

This was not too bad, because we had only four numbers in the distribution, but with a larger set this can become quite tedious and frustrating.[5]

----

[5] **A HINT:** In most cases, both variance and standard deviation are reported within 2 decimal places. For your computation, you may want to carry it to the 3rd decimal place, rounding off to 2 for the final answer, or simply round off to 2 decimal places throughout your computations.

The method we have used so far is called the **deviation score method**, for the simple reason that we had to find first the deviation scores before being able to compute the variance and *SD*. There is a second method used to calculate variance and *SD*, called the **raw score method**. This method is usually easier to compute, especially when the mean is not a whole number, because there is no need to use the mean or the deviation scores with this method. (The computations of the raw score method are presented later in this chapter, under "Additional Notes.")

[handwritten: Standard Deviation is square root of the variance]

[handwritten: variance = average distance from mean in square units — measured in sq. units]

Using the Variance and *SD*

The variance is used mostly as an intermediate step in order to find the *SD*, or for further computations in procedures such as *t*-test (see Chapter 10), and analysis of variance (ANOVA) (see Chapter 11). Standard deviation, on the other hand, is used in reporting data. When describing a distribution, in addition to a measure of central tendency, the *SD* is also used. For example, in reporting results of tests, summary scores, such as mean and standard deviation, are most likely to be used. Checking technical manuals of tests will show an extensive use of these two indexes (mean and *SD*). Scales of tests are usually described in terms of their mean and *SD*. For example, we are told that a certain IQ test has a mean of 100 and a *SD* of 15. (Chapter 6, which discusses the normal curve, and Chapter 7, which discusses test scores, explain this point further.)

While the variance can be used to indicate the variability of a group, it is measured in *squared* units. You may recall that to find the variance (using the deviation score method), we first squared and then averaged the distances of all scores from the mean. Therefore, the variance represents the average distances from the mean in squared units. The standard deviation, on the other hand, is the square root of the variance and can be used to represent the average distance from the mean.

A higher variance may show higher variability in a group, compared with a lower variance. However, these values are difficult to interpret, because they are measured in squared units. The *SD*, on the other hand, is measured in the same units as the original data, and is easier to interpret.   For example, when measuring height, a *SD* of 6 means that, on the average, the height of the members of the group deviate 6 inches from the mean.

The variance and the *SD* are sensitive to extreme scores. Having even one extreme score in a group may substantially increase the variance and *SD*.   Consider these two sets of scores, Set 1 and Set 2.   Note that they are the same with the exception of one extreme score in Set 1.

Table 5.6   Two Sets of Scores, with an Extreme Score in Set 1

	Set 1	Set 2
	40	11
	10	10
	9	9
	8	8
	7	7
	6	6
	5	5
	4	4
	3	3
	2	2
$\Sigma X =$	94.00	65.00
$\overline{X} =$	9.40	6.50
$VAR =$	110.04	8.24
$SD =$	10.49	2.87

The mean in Set 1 is higher than most of the scores it is supposed to represent.   The extreme score of 40 pulls the mean toward it. The variance and *SD* in Set 1 are also much higher than in Set 2, due to the extreme score of 40. In this case, using the *SD* of 10.49 to represent the average deviation from the mean will give misleading information, because all scores (with the exception of 40) are fairly close together, and none of them deviates as much as 10.49 around the mean.

larger range = higher variance + SD

Factors Affecting the Variance and *SD*

As you probably have noticed, there is a relationship between the range, the variance, and the *SD*; the larger the range, the higher the variance and *SD*. The range is larger when there is a big difference, or distance, between the highest and the lowest scores; that is, when the group is more heterogeneous regarding the characteristic being measured. This characteristic can be, for example, height, IQ, reading scores, and age. The range, variance, and *SD* will be high when there is one or more extreme scores, even if most scores cluster together (see Table 5.6).

A second factor which can affect the variance and *SD* is the test level of difficulty. When the test is very easy, most students answer all the questions correctly; therefore, there is no variability in the scores, and they cluster together. Mastery tests (or criterion-referenced tests) tend to be easier, as opposed to norm-referenced tests, which are designed to spread the scores widely. (See Chapter 7.) Similarly, tests which are very difficult for all examinees tend to yield scores which cluster together at the low end.

The length of a test also affects the variance and *SD*. A longer test has the potential to spread the scores more widely than does a shorter test. Compare, for example, two tests: Test A which includes 100 items, and Test B, which includes 10 items. Let's assume the mean of Test A is 50, and that of Test B is 5. In test A, people might score up to 50 points above or below the mean. In Test B, people might score only up to 5 points above or below the mean. Since the *SD* is a measure of the mean (average) distance of the scores from the mean, clearly this mean distance is likely to be higher in Test A than in Test B. Thus, a long test usually has a higher *SD* (and variance) than does a short test.

SD for a population is a fixed #

Comparing the Variance and *SD* for Populations and Samples

You may recall that we use Greek letters for population parameters, and English (or Latin) letters for sample statistics. The symbol for the population variance is σ^2, the Greek letter lower case sigma, squared; and for the population *SD* it is simply σ. The sample variance is represented by the symbol S^2, and the sample *SD* is *S*. *Sample SD (S) can vary depending on S.*

The standard deviation of a population (σ) is a fixed number, but the sample standard deviation (*S*) varies, depending on the sample.   When several samples are selected from the same population, they are likely to have somewhat different standard deviations.[6] When researchers started comparing such samples to the population from which they were selected, they realized that the samples' variances and standard deviations were consistently lower than the variance and standard deviation of the population, especially when the sample size was small (under 30).   Since the numerical values (for example, the mean and *SD*) of the sample are used to estimate the population values, and to avoid making a consistent error, the formula for sample variance was modified, resulting in a slightly larger variance. This larger variance provides a better estimate of the population variance.

The formula we introduced earlier for calculating the variance using the deviation score method is:

$$VARIANCE = \sigma^2 = \frac{\Sigma (X - \overline{X})^2}{N}$$

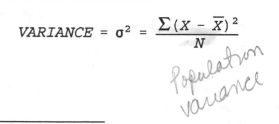

Population variance

---

[6] **A HINT:** The same applies to means: means from different samples selected from the same population are likely to differ, whereas the mean of the population (μ) is a fixed number.

This is the appropriate formula for the population variance (σ^2). When we need to calculate the sample variance (S^2), the formula is (note the change in the denominator):

$$S^2 = \frac{\Sigma(X - \overline{X})^2}{n-1} \quad \text{sample variance}$$

Dividing the numerator, $\Sigma(X-\overline{X})^2$, by n-1 (instead of dividing by N) will result in a bigger number, which is a more accurate estimate of the population variance.

Additional Notes:
Computations of Variance and Standard Deviation

Computations of the Raw Score Method

The variance and standard deviation can also be calculated using the **raw score method** which involves less computational steps and is simpler than the deviation score method. The main disadvantage of this formula is that it might seem complicated and intimidating when you look at it for the first time. To help you learn how to use this computational method, we will walk you step-by-step through the process. The formula for computing the variance using the raw score method is:

$$VARIANCE = \sigma^2 = \frac{N\,\Sigma X^2 - (\Sigma X)^2}{N^2}$$

Where $N =$ the number of the scores

$\Sigma X^2 =$ the sum of the squared scores

$(\Sigma X)^2 =$ the sum of the scores, squared

It is important to differentiate between two similar expressions: ΣX^2 and $(\Sigma X)^2$. To obtain ΣX^2, first we square every raw score (X), and then add the squared X's. To get $(\Sigma X)^2$, first we add all the X's (the sum of the scores' column), then square that sum. For example (Table 5.7):

Table 5.7   Raw Scores and Squared Raw Scores

X	X^2	
		$\Sigma X = 9$
2	4	
4	16	$(\Sigma X)^2 = 9^2 = 81$
3	9	
		$\Sigma X^2 = 29$
$\Sigma X=9$	$\Sigma X^2=29$	

Now let's take the same set of numbers we used earlier (in Table 5.3) when we computed the variance using the deviation score method and compute it again using the raw score method (Table 5.8):

Table 5.8   Raw Scores and Squared Raw Scores

X	X^2
6^2	36
5^1	25
4^2	16
3^2	9
2^2	4
$\Sigma X=20$	$\Sigma X^2=90$

$$\sigma^2 = \frac{N\Sigma X^2 - (\Sigma X)^2}{N^2} = \frac{(5)(90) - (20)^2}{5^2} =$$

$$= \frac{450 - 400}{25} = \frac{50}{25} = 2$$

The variance, as in the deviation score method, is 2, and the standard deviation is the square root of that number.

$$SD = \sqrt{VARIANCE} = \sqrt{2} = 1.41$$

Now let's try the raw score method one more time, using the second set of numbers (presented in Table 5.4) which we used with the deviation score method (Table 5.9).

Table 5.9   Raw Scores and Squared Raw Scores

X	X^2
10	100
9	81
8	64
1	1
$\Sigma X=28$	$\Sigma X^2=246$

$$\sigma^2 = \frac{(4)(246) - (28)^2}{4^2} = \frac{984 - 784}{16} =$$

$$= \frac{200}{16} = 12.5$$

We obtain a variance of 12.5, which is the same as the variance obtained using the deviation score method (see the computations which follow Table 5.4). The SD is the square root of the variance:

$$SD = \sqrt{12.5} = 3.54$$

Table 5.10 summarizes the methods which may be used for the computations of variances for populations and samples.[7] There are different denominators in the formulas for computing the sample variance (S^2) and the population variance (σ^2), for both the deviation score and the raw score methods. To find sample variance we use a denominator of n-1, and to find the population variance we use a denominator of N.

---

[7] **A HINT:** Note that there are two formulas for the computation of the population variance using the raw score method. Both formulas should give you the exact same answer. In this chapter, we have introduced the first one, which is easier to use than the second one. The formula for sample variance using the raw score method is not discussed in this book.

**Table 5.10   A Summary of the Computational Methods for Variances:
Deviation Score and Raw Score Methods for Populations and Samples**

	Deviation Score Method	Raw Score Method
POPULATION	$$\sigma^2 = \frac{\sum (X - \overline{X})^2}{N}$$	$$\sigma^2 = \frac{N\sum X^2 - (\sum X)^2}{N^2} = \frac{\sum X^2 - \frac{\sum X^2}{N}}{N}$$
SAMPLE	$$S^2 = \frac{\sum X - \overline{X})^2}{n - 1}$$	$$S^2 = \frac{\sum X^2 - \frac{(\sum X)^2}{n}}{n - 1}$$

Computations of Variance and Standard Deviation
For a Population:
A Summary of the Steps

A. The Deviation Score Method

Table 5.11 Raw Scores, Deviation Scores, and Squared Deviation
Scores

(Col. 1)	(Col. 2)	(Col. 3)
X	$X-\bar{X}$	$(X-\bar{X})^2$
6	2	4
4	0	0
3	-1	1
3	-1	1
$\Sigma X=16$	$\Sigma(X-\bar{X})=0$	$\Sigma(X-\bar{X})^2=6$

$$\bar{X} = \frac{16}{4} = 4 = mean$$

$$VAR = \sigma^2 = \frac{\Sigma(X-\bar{X})^2}{N} = \frac{6}{4} = 1.5$$

$$SD = \sigma = \sqrt{VAR} = \sqrt{1.5} = 1.22$$

Steps

1. Find the mean $(\overline{X})$

2. Subtract the mean from each score; enter that number (the deviation score) in the $X\text{-}\overline{X}$ column (col. 2).

3. Square each deviation score; enter in the $(X\text{-}\overline{X})^2$ column (col. 3).

4. Sum up the $(X\text{-}\overline{X})^2$ column to get $\Sigma(X\text{-}\overline{X})^2$.

5. Divide $\Sigma(X\text{-}\overline{X})^2$ (sum of squared deviations) by N (the number of scores) to find the variance (σ^2).

6. Find the square root of the variance to get the standard deviation (σ).

B. The Raw Score Method

Table 5.12   Raw Scores and Squared Raw Scores

X	X^2
6	36
4	16
3	9
3	9
$\Sigma X=16$	$\Sigma X^2=70$

$$\sigma^2 = \frac{N\Sigma X^2 - (\Sigma X)^2}{N^2} = \frac{(4)(70) - (16)^2}{4^2} =$$

$$= \frac{280 - 256}{16} = \frac{24}{16} = 1.5$$

$$SD = \sqrt{\sigma^2} = \sqrt{1.5} = 1.22$$

Steps

1. Square each score; enter the squared scores in the X^2 column.

2. Add up the two columns.

3. Enter ΣX^2 and $(\Sigma X)^2$ in the formula and compute.

Σ = sum

X = scores

$\bar{X}$ = mean

σ^2 = population variance

N = number of Scores

Summary

1. To describe a distribution of scores, an index of **variability**, as well as a measure of central tendency, is needed.

2. The **range** is the distance between the highest and the lowest scores in the distribution. To calculate the range, subtract the lowest score from the highest score and add 1.

3. The range is not a useful index of the variability of the group, and it is used mostly for descriptive purposes.

4. The **deviation score** is the distance of the raw score from the mean, indicated by $X\text{-}\bar{X}$ (i.e., the score minus the mean).

5. The **variance** is the **mean squared deviation**. To calculate it, square each deviation score, add all squared deviations, and

divide their sum by the number of scores (N) for a population, or by the number of scores minus 1 (n - 1) for a sample.

6. The **standard deviation** (SD) is the square root of the variance and it indicates the average (mean) distance of scores from the mean.

7. There are two methods to calculate the variance and SD: the **deviation score** and the **raw score** method.

8. The variance is not commonly used when describing a distribution of scores; rather, it is used in subsequent computations (e.g. SD, t-test, and ANOVA).

9. Standard deviation is used extensively to describe a distribution of scores. It is also used heavily in reporting test results.

10. In groups with a wide spread of scores (heterogeneous groups) the range, variance, and SD are higher than in groups where scores cluster together (homogeneous groups).

11. Variance and SD of a longer test (with more items) are higher than those of a shorter test (with less items) when the level of difficulty of items in the two tests is similar.

Variance - average distance from
mean in square units = measured in
square units
Standard Deviation = Square Root of variance

Variance in most cases is large
than standard deviation

SD = 94 es =

scores				square scores
		$X - \bar{X}$		
10		3	+3	9
9			+2	
8				
		-6	$X - 6$	36
28				50

Part Three

THE NORMAL CURVE
AND STANDARD SCORES

Chapter 6
THE NORMAL CURVE
AND STANDARD SCORES

The Normal Curve

For years, scientists have noted that many variables in the behavioral and physical sciences are distributed in a bell shape. These variables are said to be **normally distributed**, and their graphic representation is referred to as the **normal curve**. For example, if the IQ scores of a group of 10,000 randomly selected adults are graphed using a frequency polygon, the graph is going to be bell-shaped, with the majority of people clustering just above or below the mean of 100, and increasingly fewer people as the IQ scores get higher or lower.

The development of the mathematical equation for the normal distribution is credited, according to some sources, to the French mathematician Abraham Demoivre (1667-1754). According to other sources, it was the German mathematician Karl Friedrich Gauss (1777-1855) who developed the equation. Thus, the normal curve is also called the "Gaussian Model".

The normal curve is a theoretical, mathematical model that can be represented by a mathematical formula. However, since many behavioral measures are distributed in a shape like the normal curve, it has not only theoretical importance, but it also has practical implications in the behavioral sciences. The normal distribution is actually a group of distributions, each determined by a mean and a standard deviation. Some of these distributions are wider and more "flat," while others are narrower, with more of a "peak" (see Figure 6.1).[1]

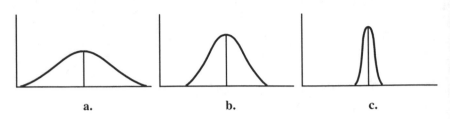

a.   b.   c.

Figure 6.1 Three normal distributions with
different levels of "peakedness" (or "flatness")

Regardless of the exact shape of the normal distributions, all share four characteristics:

1. The curve is symmetrical around the vertical axis; that is, half the scores are on the right side of the axis, and half the scores are on its left.

2. The scores tend to cluster around the center (i.e., around the mean, or the vertical axis).

3. The mode, median, and mean have the same value.

4. The curve has no boundaries on either side. That is, the tails of the distribution are getting very close to the horizontal axis, but never quite touch it.[2]

---

[1] **A HINT:** The level of "peakedness" or "flatness" of the curves is called **kurtosis**.

[2] **A HINT:** Remember that this is a *theoretical* model. In reality, for a given distribution the number of scores is finite, and certain scores are the highest and the lowest points of the distribution.

Most people who talk about the normal curve, or bell-shape distribution, usually refer to the **standard,** or **unit, normal curve,** which is the one we will be using. The standard normal curve is divided into segments, and each segment contains a certain percentage of the area under the curve (Figure 6.2). The distances between the various points on the horizontal axis are equal, but the segments closer to the center contain more scores than the segments farther away from the center.

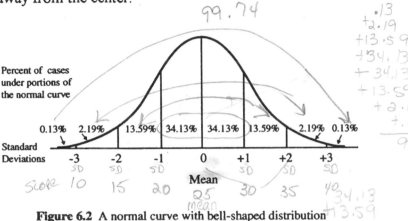

Percent of cases under portions of the normal curve

0.13%   2.19%   13.59%   34.13%   34.13%   13.59%   2.19%   0.13%

Standard Deviations   -3 SD   -2 SD   -1 SD   0   +1 SD   +2 SD   +3 SD

Score   10   15   20   25   30   35   40

Mean

Figure 6.2 A normal curve with bell-shaped distribution

The z-score distribution has a mean of 0 and a standard deviation (*SD*) of 1. The units on the left of the mean (below the mean) are considered negative (e.g., -1, -2), and the units to the right of the mean (above the mean) are considered positive (e.g., +1, +2). In a test with a mean of 25 and a *SD* of 5, 34.13% of the scores are between the mean and ± 1 SD; that is, between 25 and 30, or between 20 and 25. Similarly, the area between the mean and 2 *SD* above the mean includes 47.72% (34.13+13.59 = 47.72) of the scores. The area between 3 *SD* above and 3 *SD* below the mean includes almost all the cases in the distribution, 99.74% (Figure 6.3).

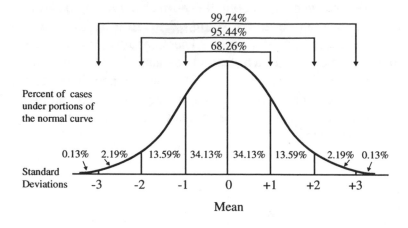

Figure 6.3 The percentages of area under the normal curve

Although many characteristics are normally distributed in the population, measuring and graphing these characteristics for a small number of cases will not necessarily look like the normal curve. Part a (Figure 6.4) shows a graph of scores obtained for a small sample size (less than 30), and part b shows the graph of scores obtained for a large sample size. Note that the graph in part b looks "smoother" than the graph in part a. As the number of cases increases, the shape of the distribution approximates more closely the normal curve.

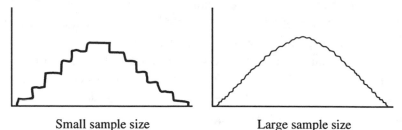

Small sample size   Large sample size

a.   b.

Figure 6.4 Normal curve distributions with a small sample size (part a) and a large sample size (part b)

The normal curve can be used to describe, predict, and estimate many types of variables which are normally distributed. We will use the example of IQ scores, which have a mean of 100 and a standard deviation of 15 (see Figure 6.5).

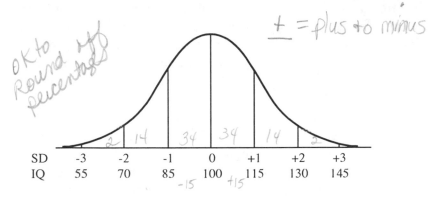

(handwritten annotations: "$\pm$ = plus to minus", "OK to Round off percentage", values written above curve sections: "2", "14", "34", "34", "14", "2")

SD	-3	-2	-1	0	+1	+2	+3
IQ	55	70	85	100	115	130	145

(handwritten: "-15" and "+15" near 100 and 115)

Figure 6.5 A normal distribution of IQ scores

Using Figure 6.5, we can ask and answer a variety of questions. For example: (1) What percent of people have an IQ between 100 and 115? Find the area between the mean and 1 *SD* and round it off. Our answer is 34%. (2) What percent of people have an IQ of ±1 *SD*? Add 34%+34% to get 68%, or approximately two-thirds of the population. (3) What percent of the scores lies between the mean and +2 *SD*? Add 34%+14% to get 48%. (4) A person with an IQ of 115 has an IQ higher than what percent of the population? Knowing that an IQ of 115 is +1 *SD* above the mean (that is, 34% above the mean), we add 50% (the percent of people below the mean) to 34%, for a total of 84%. (5) A person with an IQ of 85 has an IQ higher than what percent of the population? An IQ of 85 is 1 *SD* (or 34%) below the mean; therefore, we subtract 34% from 50% and get 16%.

z score is always 0
SD is always

Standard Scores

Until now, you have been introduced to two types of measures: **individual scores** (raw scores and deviation scores) and **group scores** (mode, median, mean, range, variance, and standard deviation). Suppose Kenneth, a student in your class, took two achievement tests, one in English and one in mathematics, and you want to compare this student's performance on the two tests. Knowing the student's score on each test will not allow you to determine on which test the student performed better, compared with the other students in the class. Let's say that Kenneth received a score of 50 in English and 68 in mathematics. Would you say that Kenneth performed better in mathematics than in English? Of course not. We do not know how many items were on each test, how difficult the tests were, and how well the other students did on the tests. Two scores from two different tests, with two different means and standard deviations, are not comparable.

Standard scores allow us to compare scores from different tests by converting these scores into the same scale, into a "common denominator". Once the scores are measured using the same units, they can then be compared to each other.

Z Scores

The first step, then, is to convert the test raw scores into standard scores called z **scores**. The z score is a type of standard score that tells us how many standard deviation units a given score is above or below the mean for that group. For example, in a test with a mean of 20 and a SD of 4, a score of 24 is 1 SD unit above the mean (20+4=24), and is said to correspond to a z score of +1.

The theoretical range of the z scores is $\pm\infty$ ("plus/minus infinity"). However, since the area above a z score of +3 or below a z score of -3 includes only 0.13% of the cases, for practical purposes we will use the scale of -3 to +3. The z scores create a scale with a mean of 0 and a SD of 1. The shape of the z score distribution is the same as that of the raw scores used to calculate the z scores, when the following conversion formula is used:

$$Z = \frac{raw\ score - mean}{SD} \quad OR \quad Z = \frac{X - \overline{X}}{S}$$

Let's practice the conversion of raw scores to z scores, using the scores obtained by Kenneth. Kenneth had a score of 50 in English and a score of 68 in mathematics. Suppose that in English the class mean and SD were 45 and 5, respectively; and in mathematics, 56 and 6, respectively. Now we can find out on which test Kenneth scored better, in comparison to his classmates. First, we convert his raw scores in English and in mathematics into z scores (Table 6.1):

Table 6.1   Student's Scores, Class Means, and Class Standard Deviations on English and Mathematics Tests

Subject	Kenneth's score	Class mean	Class SD
English	50	45	5
Mathematics	68	56	6

$$Z_{English} = \frac{score - mean}{SD} = \frac{50 - 45}{5} = \frac{5}{5} = +1.00$$

$$Z_{math} = \frac{score - mean}{SD} = \frac{68 - 56}{6} = \frac{12}{6} = +2.00$$

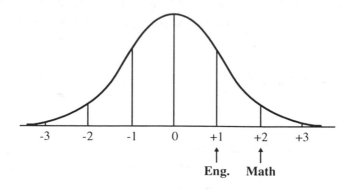

Figure 6.6 A normal distribution showing the
z scores of Kenneth in English and mathematics

Since both the English and the mathematics scores were
converted into the same units (z scores), they can be depicted on
the same graph (Figure 6.6).

Conclusion: The z score of +2.00 in mathematics is farther
above the mean, compared with the z of +1.00 in English. So,
although in comparison to his classmates, Kenneth performed above
the mean on both tests, he did better on the mathematics test than
on the English test.

Table 6.2 presents the raw scores of one student on four tests,
and the means and *SD* scores of the student's classmates on these
tests. The computations which follow the table demonstrate the
conversion of raw scores into z scores.

**Table 6.2   Student's Scores, Class Means, Class Standard Deviations,
and *Z* Scores on Four Tests**

Subject	Raw score	Mean	SD	Z
Social Studies	93	70	14	**+1.64**
Language Arts	57	63	12	**-0.50**
Mathematics	45	72	16	**-1.69**
Reading	80	50	15	**+2.00**

$$\text{Social Studies} \quad Z = \frac{93 - 70}{14} = +1.64$$

$$\text{Language Arts} \quad Z = \frac{57 - 63}{12} = -0.50$$

$$\text{Mathematics} \quad Z = \frac{45 - 72}{16} = -1.69$$

$$\text{Reading} \quad Z = \frac{80 - 50}{15} = +2.00$$

The raw scores which are *above* the mean convert into *positive* z scores; and the raw scores which are *below* the mean convert into *negative* z scores. A person who scores exactly at the mean, the most "average" student, is assigned a z score of 0.00. It is clear that for reporting purposes, z scores are not very appealing. A student may answer 93 questions correctly, yet get a z score of 1.64. Also, some of the students may bring home a negative score!

To overcome some of the problems associated with z scores (e.g., negative scores, scores of 0, and scores with decimals), these scores can be converted into another scale, such as the commonly-used T-score scale.

T Scores

In order to convert scores from z to T, we multiply each z score by 10, and add to it a constant of 50, as follows:

$$T = 10 \, (z) \, + \, 50$$

For example, a z score of 1.50 becomes a T score of 65:

$$T = 10 \, (1.50) \, + \, 50 \, = \, 15 \, + \, 50 \, = \, 65$$

The *T*-score scale has a mean of 50 and a *SD* of 10 (Figure 6.7). Scores are usually rounded off and reported in whole numbers. In order to calculate *T* scores, *z* scores have to be calculated first. Now, let's practice by converting the *z* scores listed in Table 6.2 to *T* scores, recording them in Table 6.3.

first calculate z score then T score

Scores rounded off & reported in whole numbers

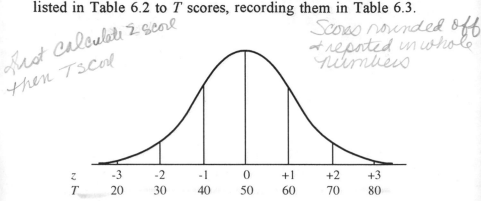

z	-3	-2	-1	0	+1	+2	+3
T	20	30	40	50	60	70	80

Figure 6.7 A normal curve showing *z* scores and the corresponding *T* scores

Table 6.3   Conversion of *Z* Scores to *T* Scores

z Score	*T* Score
+1.64	10 (+1.64) + 50 =66.4 or 66
-0.50	10 (-0.50) + 50 =45.0 or 45
-1.69	10 (-1.69) + 50 =33.1 or 33
+2.00	10 (+2.00) + 50 =70.0 or 70

As you can see, a *z* score of -0.50 is converted to a *T* score of 45 (below the mean), and a *z* score of +2.00 is converted to a *T* score of 70 (above the mean).

Other Converted Scores

Many measures used for educational and psychological testing indicate the position of an individual in relation to the population. The Wechsler IQ test has a mean of 100 and a *SD* of 15. The Stanford-Binet IQ test has a mean of 100 and a *SD* of 16. The College Entrance Examination Board (CEEB) scale has a mean of

500 and a *SD* of 100. The Scholastic Aptitude Test (SAT) has a mean of 500 and a *SD* of 100, and the ACT test is reported to have a mean of 20.6 and a *SD* of 4.5.

The Normal Curve and Percentile Ranks

A **percentile rank** of a score indicates the percentage of examinees who scored *at* or *below* that score. For example, a percentile rank of 65 (P_{65}) means that 65% of the examinees scored at or below that score. Another definition of percentile rank omits the "at", stating that it indicates the percentage of examinees who scored *below* that score. Yet another definition states that it includes the percentage of scores below a given score, plus half of those who have obtained that same score.

Percentiles are used to describe various points in a distribution. For example, a percentile rank of 70 (P_{70}) is said to be at the 70th percentile. Since percentiles represent an ordinal, rather than interval or ratio scale, they should not be manipulated (e.g., added or multiplied). If manipulation is desired, percentiles should first be converted to *z* scores, which have equal intervals.

The normal curve can be used to calculate percentiles assuming that the distribution of scores is normally distributed. For example, a *z* score of +1 corresponds to a percentile rank of 84 (50│34.13=84.13 or 84), and a *z* score of -2 corresponds to a percentile rank of 2 (50-34.13-13.59=2.28 or 2) (Figure 6.8).[3] In real life, obtained *z* scores are not likely to be whole numbers; rather, we probably have to find percentiles for *z* scores such as +1.53 or -1.69. A special table which lists *z* scores and the area under the normal curve corresponding to these scores may be used in such cases. The percentile score which corresponds to each *z* score can be found by calculating the area under the normal curve corresponding to that *z* score.

---

[3] **A HINT:** To find these percentiles, add up all the percentages under the normal curve left of the *z* score. Since the percentages to the left of a +1.00 *z* score add up to 84, this will be the reported percentile score.

ad

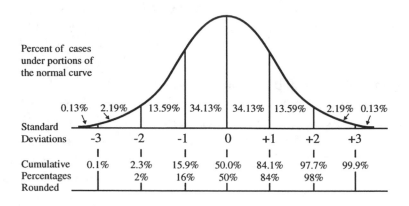

Percent of cases
under portions of
the normal curve

0.13%	2.19%	13.59%	34.13%	34.13%	13.59%	2.19%	0.13%

Standard
Deviations   -3   -2   -1   0   +1   +2   +3

Cumulative   0.1%   2.3%   15.9%   50.0%   84.1%   97.7%   99.9%
Percentages   2%   16%   50%   84%   98%
Rounded

Figure 6.8 The normal curve with standard deviations
and cumulative percentages

To use the table (Appendix Table A), locate the *z* score on the left hand column (column 1). Moving to column 2 marked "Area from the Mean," locate the number corresponding to the *z* score. This number indicates the area between the mean and the *z* score. The 4 decimals can be converted to percentages by rounding down to 2 digits. For example, .4574 is converted to 46%, and .0319 is converted to 3%. For positive *z* scores, we add these percentages to 50%, and for negative *z* scores, we subtract these percentages from 50%. To convert *z* scores to percentiles, we need to use only the two left columns of this table. Let's practice the conversion process by finding percentiles for the *z* scores we recorded earlier in Table 6.3.

For a *z* score of +1.64: the corresponding number in column 2 is .4495, which is converted to 45% and added to 50%, resulting in a percentile of 95. For a *z* score of -0.50: the corresponding number of .1915 in column 2 is converted to 19%, which we then subtract from 50% (because the *z* score is negative), resulting in a percentile of 31. For a *z* score of -1.69: we subtract 45% from 50%, to get a percentile of 5. And a *z* score of +2.00 is converted to a percentile of 98 (50%+48%).

Using the normal curve to find percentiles is justified when normal distributions are studied. However, suppose a classroom teacher wants to convert the teacher-made test scores to percentiles in order to report the scores to the students' parents. The teacher can first use the test scores to create a frequency polygon. Then, the teacher can examine the graph to ascertain whether the distribution of scores is "normal". In most instances when we have small group size ($n < 30$), the shape of the distribution will not approximate the normal curve. When the shape of the distribution is not normal, it is inappropriate to use the normal curve model as a means to calculate percentiles. Instead, the teacher can use a frequency distribution to which cumulative frequencies are added (Table 6.4). (For a complete explanation of cumulative frequencies see Chapter 3.)

Table 6.4   Cumulative Distribution of Scores of 30 Students

(Col. 1)	(Col. 2)	(Col. 3)	(Col. 4)
		Cumulative	Cumulative
Score	Frequency	Frequency	Percentage
25	1	30	100
23	1	29	97
20	1	28	93
19	2	27	90
18	2	25	83
17	3	23	77
15	4	20	67
14	5	16	53
11	4	11	37
9	3	7	23
6	2	4	13
5	1	2	7
2	1	1	3

$n=30$

Using Table 6.4, we can determine that a person with a score of 23 (second from the top in col. 1) scored better than 97% (second from the top in col. 4) of those who took the test. Or that a person with a score of 9 (fourth from the bottom in col. 1) scored as well as or better than 23% (fourth from the bottom in col. 4) of the examinees.

In practice, a percentile rank of 100 is not reported. We cannot say that a person with a score of 25 scored better than 100% of the people in the group. Instead, 99% (or in some cases, 99.9%) is considered the highest percentile.

Summary

1. The **normal curve** is the graphic representation of normally distributed variables in the behavioral and physical sciences.

2. The graph of the normal curve is bell-shaped, with the majority of scores clustering just above or below the mean and increasingly fewer scores at either ends of the curve.

3. The **normal distribution** consists of a group of distributions, each determined by a mean and a standard deviation.

4. The normal distribution has four characteristics:

    a. It is symmetrical around the vertical axis.
    b. The scores tend to cluster around the center.
    c. The mode, median and mean have the same value.
    d. Theoretically, the curve has no boundaries on either side.

5. Converting scores into **standard scores** enables us to make comparisons between tests by using the same units of measurement.

6. A *z* **score** is a type of standard score that tells us how many standard deviation units a given score is above or below the mean for that group.

7. *T* **scores** overcome some of the problems associated with *z* scores (e.g., negative scores, scores of 0, and scores with decimal places) and are, therefore, often used for reporting purposes.

8. Scores from many educational and psychological tests are used to indicate the relative position of an individual in relation to the population.

9. The **percentile rank** of a score indicates the percentage of examinees who scored *at* or *below* that score. Other definitions of percentile rank state that it includes the percentage of examinees who scored *below* a given score; or that it includes the percentage of examinees who scored *below* a given score, *plus half* the percentage of those who had obtained that same score.

10. When the distribution is assumed to be normal, the table listing the area under the normal curve can be used to convert *z* scores into percentiles.

11. When the shape of the distribution is not normal, **cumulative frequencies** and **cumulative percentages** may be added to a frequency distribution in order to calculate percentiles.

Chapter 7
INTERPRETING TEST SCORES

Tests are used in all areas of life. They are sometimes given to job applicants and to people seeking certifications. They may also be used to determine placement and admission into programs, to diagnose and evaluate patients, to monitor progress, to assign grades, and more. Tests may be constructed by individuals, such as the classroom teacher, or by commercial corporations. Some of the biggest designers of tests are companies which produce school-related standardized achievement tests, such as the California Achievement Test (CAT) or the Iowa Test of Basic Skills (ITBS). Our discussion in this chapter will focus exclusively on school-related tests, particularly achievement tests.

There are several ways to report test scores. Some of the most common ways are: raw scores, percent correct, standard scores (z and T), percentile ranks, stanines, grade equivalents, and scale scores. Raw scores derived from teacher-made tests are used extensively by classroom teachers who generally convert them into percent correct and letter grades. Raw scores derived from standardized tests constructed by commercial test companies are usually converted into norms. In and of itself, a raw score does not have much meaning without having additional information about the test, such as the number of items and their level of difficulty, as well as the scores of the other examinees who took the test. Test scores can be classified into two major categories: norm-referenced and criterion-referenced.

Norm-Referenced Tests

Norm-referenced (NR) tests include norms which allow the test user to compare the performance of an individual taking the test to that of similar examinees who have taken the test previously. These examinees comprise the norming group. The norming group is a sample taken from the population of all potential examinees. Stratified random sampling procedure is usually employed to select the sample used for norming. Stratification is done on characteristics such as sex, age, socioeconomic status, race, and geographic region. The norming group should be large enough and represent demographically the characteristics of the potential test takers. The test is first given to the norming group and then the scores on the test are used to generate the norms. Later, when new examinees take the test, their scores are usually compared to the scores of the norming group, rather than to the scores of others taking the test with them.

Commercial achievement test companies describe in their technical manual how the norming group was selected, its demographic characteristics, and when the norms were obtained. Other technical aspects of the test, such as its reliability and validity, are likely to be discussed in the manual as well. Norms are usually included in standardized commercially-constructed tests. Standardized tests are used extensively in grade school (and to a lesser extent, in high school) to measure achievement. In standardized tests, items have been first pilot-tested and revised, and the test administration procedures are uniform.

Occasionally, test companies develop two types of norms: national and local. This is especially common with standardized achievement tests, which are given annually to many students in the U.S. In a typical school, students and their parents receive a computer-generated report which lists the raw scores, as well as national and local norms. The **national norms** compare the student to similar students in the population at large. The **local norms** compare the student to others with the same demographic characteristics, such as other students in the district or the school. Several tests, such as college admission tests, are designed for a particular purpose. The norming group, although more specific, is still comprised of examinees with characteristics similar to those of the potential test users. For example, the Scholastic Aptitude Test (SAT) is normed on college-bound high school juniors or seniors, and the Graduate Record Examination (GRE) is normed on students who plan to attend graduate schools. Test publishers report several types of scores. A typical student report includes raw scores on each subtest, as well as norms. Standardized scores, such as z and T scores, also help place students' performance in relation to others who took the same test. When the scores reported by standardized test publishers include z and T scores, these scores are first **normalized** to conform to the shape of the normal curve (rather than using the simple transformation described in Chapter 6). Three of the most commonly used norms are percentile ranks, stanines, and grade equivalents.

Percentile Ranks

Percentile ranks are easy to understand by lay people, which may be one of the reasons they are popular as norm-referenced scores. All major standardized achievement test companies include percentile ranks in their reports to school personnel and parents. Percentile ranks describe the percentage of people who scored below that score.[1] For example, when a raw score of 58 is converted to a percentile rank of 82, it means that a student with that raw score performed better than 82% of those in the test norming group. Commercial testing companies provide tables to convert raw scores to percentile ranks. The conversion can be done

---

[1] **A HINT:** Another definition of percentile rank includes those who scored *equal* to, in addition to *below*, a given score. In practice, however, with a large-scale testing and a large sample size in the norming group, there is not much difference between the two definitions. The first one presented is easier to understand and is used most often.

commercially by sending the answer sheets to the company or manually by the test user. (For an additional discussion of percentile ranks and percentiles, see Chapter 6.)

Standardized test reports may include **percentile bands**, in addition to percentile ranks. Since the tests are not completely reliable and include a certain level of error, the band gives an estimated range of the true percentile rank. The bands are usually represented by a series of X's or by a shaded area.

After a commercial norm-referenced achievement test is administered in school, the parents or guardians of the students are likely to receive reports describing their children's performance on the tests. Although the reports produced by various testing companies may differ from each other, most of them include information about the student's national percentile ranks and percentile bands on the subject areas covered by the test. The following is a sample test report (Figure 7.1):

Table 7.1   A Sample Report of a Norm-Referenced Test

Name_____Grade_____Teacher_____School_____ Date____

Subject Area	National Percentile Rank	National Percentile Band 1 2 3 4 5 6 7 8 9
Composite (3 R)	76	XXXXX
Reading	75	XXXX
Mathematics	77	XXXXX
Language Arts	76	XXXX
Reference Skills	68	XXX
Science	71	XXXX
Social Studies	66	XXXX

Additional information provided on test reports may include: local percentile ranks, national norms, a breakdown of the various subject areas into subscales, the total number of items for each subscale, and the number of items answered correctly by the student. To help the parents understand the report, an explanation of the information is usually provided. In addition, parents are encouraged to meet with their children's teachers who can provide further explanation of the report.

Stanines

Stanines comprise a scale with 9 points, a mean of 5, and a SD of 2. The word *stanine* is derived from the words "standard nine." In a normal curve distribution, stanines allow the conversion of percentile ranks into nine larger units. (See Figure 7.1) Thus, the middle stanine, 5, includes the middle 20% of the distribution; stanines 4 and 6, each includes 17%; stanines 3 and 7, each includes 12%; stanines 2 and 8, each includes 7%; and stanines 1 and 9, each includes 4% of the distribution. Approximately one-fourth of the distribution of scores (23%, to be exact) is in stanines 1-3, and 23% of the scores are in stanines 7-9. Approximately one-half (54%) of the distribution is in the three middle stanines, 4-6. Educators may need to pay special attention to students scoring at the bottom 3 stanines by providing remediation programs, and to students scoring at the top 3 stanines by providing enrichment programs.

Grade Equivalents

Grade equivalents (GE) allow the conversion of raw scores to grade level norms, expressed in terms of years and months. For example, if a student obtained a GE of 4.2, it means that in the norming group, the average fourth grader in November obtained the same score. A GE of 4.0 corresponds to the average performance of fourth graders in the norming group in September, and a GE of 4.9 corresponds to the average performance of fourth graders in June. "Typical" students are expected to gain 1 GE a year to maintain their position in relation to their age-mates.

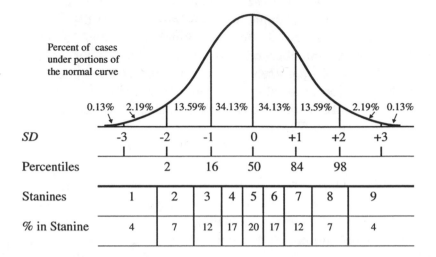

Figure 7.1 A graph showing standard deviations, percentiles, stanines, and percentages of individuals in each.

Many schools do not use GE scores in their reports to parents, because these scores are often misunderstood and misinterpreted. As an example, parents of a fifth grader whose child receives a GE of 6.5 in reading may request that their child be promoted to sixth grade. This request is misguided for several reasons: (a) the other students in the fifth grade class may also be performing above grade level; (b) the student may be above grade level in reading, but not in other subjects; (c) a fifth grader may have difficulties adjusting socially to peers in sixth grade; and (d) a GE of 6.5 means only that the average student in sixth grade would have received that score, not that a fifth grader is likely to succeed in sixth grade. We are actually speculating on how well a sixth grader would have performed on the fifth grade test, because the sixth graders in the norming group did not actually take the fifth grade test. In addition, since the fifth grader has not actually taken the sixth grade test, we should not assume that this student is likely to succeed in sixth grade.

Test items constructed for NR tests are written specifically to maximize differences among the examinees. Some items have a high level of difficulty in order to differentiate among the top students, while some other items are easy in order to distinguish among the low scoring students. Easy items may also be placed at the beginning of the test or section to encourage all students. The majority of the items are of average difficulty and are designed to be answered correctly by 30-80% of the examinees.

Criterion-Referenced Tests

Criterion-referenced (CR) tests enable us to compare the performance of an individual to certain criteria. (CR tests may also be called **domain-referenced** or **content-referenced** tests.)   By contrast, NR tests compare the examinee to other people in the norming group who took the test. The criteria, which should be specific and clear, are based on skills or objectives, as set forth by educators (e.g., teachers, curriculum specialists, and content experts). After specifying criteria, a task is designed to measure the level to which the criteria have been met. The task may be a pencil-and-paper achievement test, or it may be performance-based, such as identifying countries on a world map.

Two types of scores are used with CR tests: percent correct and mastery/nonmastery. Reporting scores in terms of **percent correct** is easy to do and to understand. It is often used by the classroom teachers to generate letter grades. For example, a teacher may inform the class that to get an "A" on a test, one must score at least 90% correct, and to get a "B", one must score 80-89% correct. This type of score does not take into consideration that the whole test may be too difficult or too easy. The **mastery/nonmastery** score is based on the theory of mastery learning which advocates mastery of the present material before moving on to new material. There are several approaches which can be used to set the standards for mastery and to determine the point separating mastery from nonmastery. For example, content specialists can help establish a cutoff score to separate mastery from nonmastery, or it may be decided that students have to get at least 80% of the items correct in order to demonstrate mastery.

While several published CR tests are available in specific areas such as mathematics or reading, many publishers also include CR interpretation in their NR tests. In addition to listing information about norms, such as percentiles and stanines, the computer-generated report sent to the school for each student may also show the total number of items in each section of each subtest and the number of items answered correctly by the student. This service helps the teacher diagnose the strengths and weaknesses of individual students, as well as the whole class.

Summary

1. Raw scores derived from teacher-made tests are usually converted into letter grades. Raw scores derived from standardized tests are usually converted into norms.

2. **Norm-referenced tests** include norms which allow the test user to compare the performance of an individual taking the test to that of similar examinees who have taken that same test previously.

3. The **norming group** is a sufficiently large sample of all potential examinees who represent the demographic characteristics of the total group. Norms may be local or national.

4. In standardized tests, items are pilot-tested and revised and the test administration procedures are uniform.

5. Scores are **normalized** to conform to the shape of the normal curve.

6. **Percentile ranks** describe the percentage of people who scored below a given score. A **percentile band** gives an estimated range of the true percentile rank.

7. **Stanines** allow the conversion of percentile ranks into 9 larger units.

8. **Grade equivalents** allow for the conversion of raw scores to grade level norms, which are expressed in terms of years and months.

9. **Criterion-referenced tests** enable us to compare the performance of an individual to certain criteria and are sometimes referred to as **domain-referenced** or **content-referenced** tests. The criteria should be specific and clear and be based on skills or objectives set forth by educators.

10. The task designed to measure achievement in relation to the established criteria may be paper-and-pencil or performance-based.

11. The **percent correct** method of reporting scores is generally used to generate letter grades based on a predetermined scale.

12. The **mastery/nonmastery** score is based on the theory which advocates mastery of present material before moving on to new material.

Part Four

MEASURING RELATIONSHIPS

Chapter 8
CORRELATION

Correlation may be defined as the relationship or association between two or more variables. These variables have to be related to each other or paired. The most common way to use correlation in the field of education is to administer two measures to the same group of people and then correlate their scores on one measure with their scores on the other measure.

The strength, or degree of correlation, is indicated by a **correlation coefficient.** The coefficient can range from -1.00, indicating a perfect negative correlation; to 0.00, indicating no correlation, to +1.00, indicating a perfect positive correlation.

Graphing Correlation

Correlation between two measures obtained from the same group of people can be shown graphically through the use of a **scattergram** (Figure 8.1).

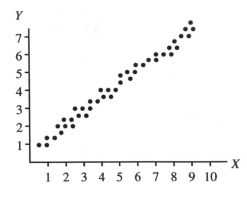

Figure 8.1 A scattergram showing the correlation
between two variables, X and Y

    The convention is to plot one variable on the horizontal axis (X axis), and the other one on the vertical axis (Y axis). Each person in the group is represented by a single point which is located above this person's score on the X variable and across from the person's score on the Y variable. For example, suppose we want to plot the scores of seven fourth-grade students on two tests, mathematics computation (X) and mathematics concepts (Y) (Table 8.1).

Table 8.1   Scores of Seven Students on Two Mathematics Tests

Student Number	Math Computation X	Math Concepts Y
A	18	20
B	17	15
C	11	12
D	19	18
E	13	12
F	15	16
G	?	?

Drawing the scattergram: First, draw the X and Y axes, recording all the data points (Figure 8.2). Be sure you include all the scores on X and on Y. (Check the lowest and the highest score on each variable.)

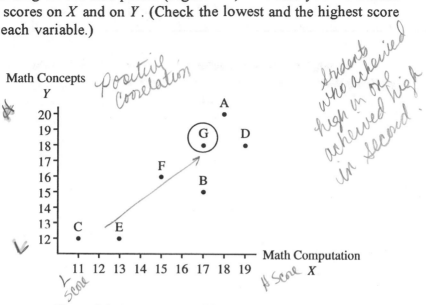

Figure 8.2 A scattergram of the data in Table 8.1

To plot the location of each student, draw an imaginary vertical line upward starting at the student's score on X, and an imaginary horizontal line starting at the student's score on Y, parallel to the X axis. The intersection of the two lines should be a point indicating the location of that student. For example, for student A, draw the imaginary vertical line starting at $X=18$; and the imaginary horizontal line starting at $Y=20$. The intersection of these two lines shows the location of student A (Figure 8.2). Do the same for students B through F. To read the X and Y scores of the seventh student (G), locate the letter G on the scattergram. This intersection corresponds to $X=17$ and $Y=18$.

Notice that the points on the scattergram create a pattern that goes from bottom left upward to top right. This is typical of a *positive* correlation, in which an *increase* in one variable is associated with an *increase* in the other variable. In our example, students who achieved high scores on the mathematics computation test generally achieved high scores on the mathematics concepts test. Those who obtained low scores on the mathematics computation test generally had low scores on the mathematics concepts test.

In a **negative** correlation, an *increase* in one variable is associated with a *decrease* in the other variable. For example, there is probably a negative correlation between days per year students are absent from school and their grade point average (GPA). That is, as students are absent more and more days (an increase in X), their GPA falls lower and lower (a decrease in Y). The scattergram in Figure 8.3 shows the hypothetical relationship between the two variables. Note that the direction of the points is from top left downward to bottom right.

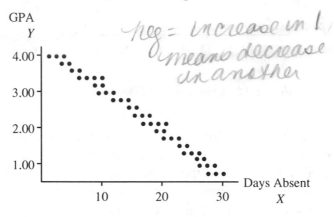

Figure 8.3 A scattergram showing negative correlation between the number of days students are absent from school and their grade point average (GPA)

If you were to draw an imaginary line around the points on a scattergram, you would notice that as the correlation (positive or negative) gets higher, the points tend to cluster closer to the line (Figure 8.4). Thus, an inspection of the scattergram can indicate the approximate strength (or degree) of the correlation. For example, the scattergram in part a shows a higher correlation than that in part b.

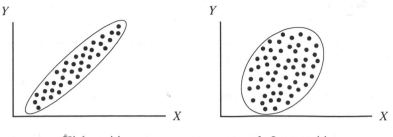

a. High positive   **b.** Low positive

Figure 8.4 Scattergrams of a high positive correlation (part a)
and a low positive correlation (part b)

When there is a very low correlation, or no correlation, between
two variables, the scattergram contains points that do not form any
clear pattern, and are scattered widely (Figure 8.5).

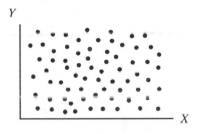

No correlation

Figure 8.5 A scattergram showing no correlation
between two variables, X and Y

Pearson Product Moment

The most commonly used correlation procedure is the Pearson
product moment, whose coefficient is represented by the letter r.
The **Pearson product-moment coefficient** (often referred to as

Pearson *r*) is named in honor of Karl Pearson (1857-1936), a British scientist who contributed a great deal to the development of statistics. Pearson was a student of Sir Francis Galton who studied, among other subjects, heredity and relationships. In 1896, Pearson developed the product-moment coefficient, which became quite popular within a short period of time. In order to use Pearson's correlation, the following requirements should be satisfied:

1. The scores are measured on an interval or ratio scale. If the scores comprise an ordinal or a nominal scale, Pearson's correlation should not be used. (Spearman rank-order correlation which is used with ordinal scales is described at the end of this chapter. For information about correlation of other types of data, consult other textbooks.)

2. The two variables to be correlated should have a linear relationship (as opposed to a curvilinear relationship). To illustrate the difference between linear and curvilinear relationships, examine Figure 8.6. Part a shows a linear relationship between height and weight, where the points form a pattern going in one direction. Part b shows a curvilinear relationship where the age of individuals is correlated with their strength. Notice that the direction of the points is not consistent. In this example, the trend starts as a positive correlation and ends up as a negative correlation. For example, newborns are very weak, and get stronger with age. They then reach an age when they are the strongest, and as they age, they become weaker. When Pearson *r* is used with variables that have a curvilinear relationship, the resulting correlation is an underestimate of the true relationship between these variables.

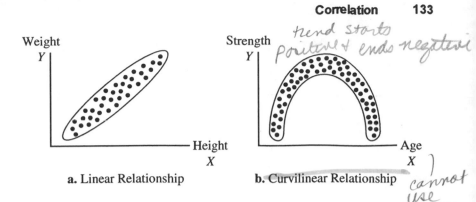

[handwritten annotations: "trend starts positive + ends negative" above part b; "cannot use Pearson because it underestimates the true relationship of the variables" to the right of part b]

Figure 8.6 Scattergrams showing linear relationship between height and weight (part a), and curvilinear relationship between age and strength (part b)

Evaluating the Correlation Coefficient

After obtaining the correlation coefficient, the next step is to evaluate it. It is important to remember that the *sign* of the correlation (negative or positive) is not indicative of the *strength* of the correlation. A negative correlation is not something negative. What matters is the absolute value of the correlation. Thus, a correlation of -.93 is higher and indicates a stronger relationship than a correlation of +.85.

Table 8.2 lists guidelines for the interpretation of the strength of the correlation coefficients. Note that the various categories in the table are not mutually exclusive, and a given coefficient may be found in two categories (e.g., a coefficient of .65 may be defined as *moderate* or as *substantial*). This is due to the fact that there is no complete agreement among researchers as to what the range of each category should be. When in doubt, you can use combinations such as: "*r*=.70 is a moderate to substantial correlation."

[handwritten note at bottom: "most important is the absolute value of the correlation. -93 is higher + indicates a stronger relationship than +85."]

Table 8.2	An Interpretation of Correlation Coefficients

Correlation	Interpretation
.00 - .30	negligible to low
.20 - .50	low to moderate
.40 - .70	moderate
.60 - .90	substantial
.80 -1.00	high to very high

In addition to being used to describe the relationship between variables, correlation can also be used for prediction (in a statistical procedure called regression, described in Chapter 9). Additionally, correlation can be used in assessing reliability (e.g., test-retest reliability, discussed in Chapter 13) and in assessing validity (e.g., concurrent validity, discussed in Chapter 14).

Hypotheses for Correlation

The null hypothesis (H_O) in correlation states that the correlation coefficient is zero:

$$H_O: r = 0$$

The alternative hypothesis (H_A) states that the population correlation is not equal to zero:

$$H_A: r \neq 0$$

After we obtain the correlation coefficient, we then consult the table of critical values (Appendix Table B). The degrees of freedom (df) in correlation are the number of pairs of scores minus 2 ($df = n - 2$). If the obtained coefficient r exceeds the critical value, the null hypothesis is rejected. Rejecting the null hypothesis means that the chance that $r=0$ is very small, and that r is large enough to be considered different from zero. When the null hypothesis is rejected, the level of significance (p level) is reported (e.g., $p < .05$ or $p < .01$).

level of significance = p level

p > p∠

Computing Pearson Correlation

Since the correlation coefficient is reflective of the relative position of scores in their group, we can calculate the correlation using z scores, which are a measure of the relative position of individuals in their group. (See Chapter 6.) The Pearson product-moment correlation coefficient can be computed using this z score formula:

$$r = \frac{\Sigma z_x\, z_y}{N}$$

Where $r =$ Pearson product-moment coefficient

$z_x =$ the z score of an individual on variable X

$z_y =$ the z score of an individual on variable Y

$\Sigma z_x z_y =$ the sum of the cross products of z_x and z_y

$N =$ the number of pairs of scores

Z scores show the relative position of a person in the group. When a person scores below the mean, the z score is negative; when the person scores above the mean, the z score is positive. If the relative positions of individuals on both X and Y are the same (for example, on both tests they scored above the mean, or on both tests they scored below the mean), then both of their z scores are either positive, or both are negative. Multiplying these two z

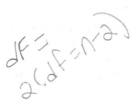

df =
2(.df = N-2)

scores (z_x and z_y) yields a positive number.[1] Consequently, the sum of all the products is high, resulting in a high r value. However, when individuals score above the mean on one variable and below the mean on the other variable, then multiplying their z scores on X by their z scores on Y yields a negative number, resulting in a lower r value.

To compute r, we find the z score for each person on X (z_x), and on Y (z_y), and then multiply z_x by z_y for each individual in order to find the product ($z_x z_y$). Next, we add up all the products, and divide the sum by N, the number of individuals (i.e., pairs). To show the computation of Pearson r, let's look at the following example. Suppose we want to find the correlation of the scores of six students on two tests, Reading Vocabulary (X) and Reading Comprehension (Y) (Table 8.3). The means of X and Y are 9.16 and 13.50, respectively; and the standard deviations of X and Y are 1.34 and 1.50, respectively. For your convenience, we have already computed the students' z scores on the X and Y variables.

Table 8.3   Raw Scores, Z Scores, and Cross Products of Six Students on Reading Vocabulary Test (X) and Reading Comprehension Test (Y)

Student	Reading Vocab. X	Reading Comp. Y	Z_x	Z_y	$Z_x Z_y$
A	9	14	-0.124	0.333	-0.041
B	8	12	-0.868	-1.000	0.868
C	10	14	0.620	0.333	0.206
D	11	15	1.364	1.000	1.364
E	10	15	0.620	1.000	0.620
F	7	11	-1.612	-1.667	2.687

$\Sigma Z_x Z_y = 5.704$

mean 9.16 13.5
SD 1.34 1.50

---

[1] **A HINT:** To remind those of you who may have forgotten: when we multiply two positive numbers, we get a positive number; when we multiply two negative numbers, we get a positive number; when one of the numbers is positive and the other is negative, we get a negative number.

$$r = \frac{\sum z_x z_y}{N} = \frac{5.7044}{6} = .95$$

Note that for all pairs, with the exception of the first one, a positive z score on X is associated with a positive score on Y, and a negative z score on X is associated with a negative score on Y. The consistency in the relative position of individuals in their group, expressed as z scores, has resulted in a high positive correlation of .95.

After the correlation coefficient is calculated, you may want to ascertain whether it is statistically significant. Appendix Table B lists the critical values of the Pearson r coefficient. In our example, the degrees of freedom (df) are 4 (number of pairs minus 2). The critical values are .811 for a p of .05, .882 for a p of .02, and .917 for a p of .01. These critical values can be listed as: $r_{(.05,4)}$ = .811, $r_{(.02,4)}$ = .882, and $r_{(.01,4)}$ = .917; where .05, .02, and .01 indicate the p level and 4 indicates the degrees of freedom. Our calculated r value of .95 exceeds the .05, .02, and .01 level of significance. Consequently, we reject the null hypothesis at $p < .01$ level. We conclude that a correlation coefficient of this magnitude ($r=.95$) could have occurred by chance alone less that 1 time in 100. (See Chapter 1 for a discussion of the statistical hypothesis testing.)

Pearson r can be computed using another formula, called the raw score formula. Although this formula may look complicated, it is actually easier to use than the z score formula, because there is no need to convert the raw scores into z scores. The formula is:

$$r = \frac{N\sum XY - (\sum X)(\sum Y)}{\sqrt{N\sum X^2 - (\sum X)^2} \sqrt{N\sum Y^2 - (\sum Y)^2}}$$

Where	$r =$	the correlation between X and Y
	$N =$	the number of pairs of scores
	$\Sigma XY =$	the sum of the cross products of X and Y
	$\Sigma X =$	the sum of the scores on X
	$\Sigma Y =$	the sum of the scores on Y
	$\Sigma X^2 =$	the sum of the squared X scores
	$\Sigma Y^2 =$	the sum of the squared Y scores

Table 8.4 lists the same scores of the six students on the two tests of Reading Vocabulary (X) and Reading Comprehension (Y), which were presented in Table 8.3. These scores are used to demonstrate the computation of Pearson r, using the raw score formula.

Table 8.4   Raw Scores, Squared Raw Scores, and Cross Products of Six Students on Reading Vocabulary (X) and Reading Comprehension Test (Y)

Student	Test X	Test Y	X^2	Y^2	XY
A	9	14	81	196	126
B	8	12	64	144	96
C	10	14	100	196	140
D	11	15	121	225	165
E	10	15	100	225	150
F	7	11	49	121	77

$$\Sigma X = 55 \quad \Sigma Y = 81 \quad \Sigma X^2 = 515 \quad \Sigma Y^2 = 1107 \quad \Sigma XY = 754$$

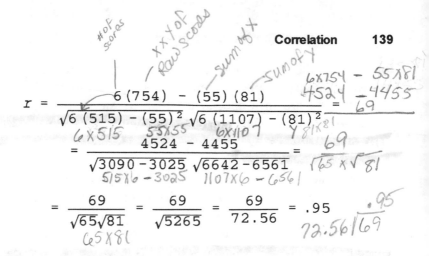

$$r = \frac{6(754) - (55)(81)}{\sqrt{6(515) - (55)^2}\,\sqrt{6(1107) - (81)^2}}$$

$$= \frac{4524 - 4455}{\sqrt{3090 - 3025}\,\sqrt{6642 - 6561}}$$

$$= \frac{69}{\sqrt{65}\sqrt{81}} = \frac{69}{\sqrt{5265}} = \frac{69}{72.56} = .95$$

Using the raw score method we obtain the same correlation coefficient as that obtained using the z-score method. In the future, when you will need to compute correlation, chances are that you will use a computer to do the computations. However, if you would need to compute the correlation coefficient by hand, we suggest that you use the raw score method.

Factors Affecting Correlation

When the position of individuals on one variable, in relation to other individuals in their group, is similar to their position on the other variable, the resulting correlation is high. In other words, the correlation is high if the following occurs: those who score high on X also score high on Y; those who score low on X also score low on Y; and those who score in the middle on X also score in the middle on Y. The actual scores on X and on Y do not have to be the same, only the *relative position* of scores in their group.

The reliability of the instruments used to collect data also affects the correlation. The correlation coefficient may underestimate the true relationship between two variables if the measurement instrument is not reliable. (See Chapter 13 for a discussion of reliability.)

The correlation obtained may also underestimate the real relationship between the variables if one or both variables have a **restricted range** (i.e., low variance). For example, suppose we want to measure the correlation between IQ scores and mathematics scores, and our sample is comprised only of junior high school students who are in a special gifted program, and who have IQ scores of 130-145. The correlation obtained would probably be lower than if we had used all the students in the school, whose IQ scores have a wider range.

To demonstrate an extreme case, suppose all the students receive the same score on test X. (This may happen if the test was too easy.) If we try to correlate their scores on X with their scores on another test, Y, we will get a correlation of zero ($r=.00$). Knowing the score on one test will not allow us to predict the score on the other test. To illustrate this point, the following are scores of four students on two tests, X and Y (Table 8.5). Notice that all the students received the same score on X ($X=25$); therefore, there is no variability, and the variance of the X scores is zero. The correlation between the two variables cannot be defined using these test scores. If the z score method were to be used, the z scores could not have been computed for the scores on the X variable, because the standard deviation (which is used to compute z scores) would have been zero.

Table 8.5   Raw Scores, Squared Raw Scores, and Cross Products of Four Students on Two Tests

Student	Test X	Test Y	X^2	Y^2	XY
A	25	15	625	225	375
B	25	18	625	324	450
C	25	17	625	289	425
D	25	14	625	196	350

$\Sigma X = 100$ $\Sigma Y = 64$ $\Sigma X^2 = 2500$ $\Sigma Y^2 = 1034$ $\Sigma XY = 1600$

$$r = \frac{N \sum XY - (\sum X)(\sum Y)}{\sqrt{N \sum X^2 - (\sum X)^2}\ \sqrt{N \sum Y^2 - (\sum Y)^2}} =$$

$$= \frac{(4)(1600) - (100)(64)}{\sqrt{4(2500) - (100)^2}\ \sqrt{4(1034)(64)^2}} =$$

$$= \frac{6400 - 6400}{\sqrt{10000 - 10000}\ \sqrt{4136 - 4096}} =$$

$$= \frac{0}{\sqrt{0}\ \sqrt{40}} = \frac{0}{0} = .00$$

The scattergram showing this correlation (Figure 8.7) shows that the points form a vertical line, as all the scores on the X variable have the same value.

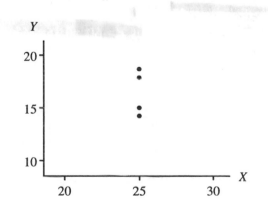

Figure 8.7 A scattergram of the data in Table 8.5 showing $r = .00$, when all the scores on the X variable are the same

Further Interpretation of the Correlation Coefficient

The correlation coefficient may be evaluated and interpreted using three approaches:

1. Describing the correlation as low, moderate, substantial, or very high, using the guidelines provided in Table 8.2.

2. Stating whether the coefficient is statistically significant (i.e., stating the probability of obtaining such results by chance alone), by reading the computer printout, or by consulting the table of critical values (Appendix Table B).

3. Calculating the amount of variance shared by the two variables being correlated. The **shared variance**, also known as the **coefficient of determination**, is an index which describes how much individual differences in one variable are associated with individual differences in the other variable.[2] To compute the shared variance, square the correlation coefficient. For example, if two variables correlate .60, the shared variance is $r^2 = .60^2 = 0.36 = 36\%$. Figure 8.8 shows a graph of this shared variance.

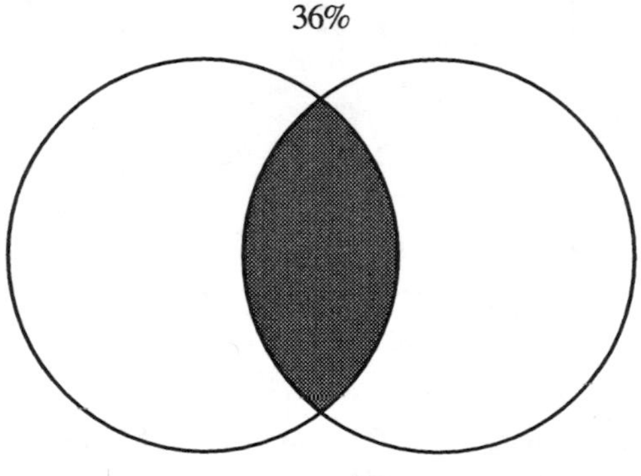

36%

Figure 8.8 A graph of the shared variance when $r = .60$

---

[2] **A HINT:** This shared variance is a *group* index and it says nothing about an *individual* score.

The variables overlap 36%, or a little more than one-third. Knowing a person's performance on X (or on Y), one can predict 36% of this person's performance on Y (or on X). Two-thirds are still unknown and unaccounted for by the predictor variable.

If two variables correlate .90, the shared variance is 81% ($r^2=.90^2=0.81=81\%$). Figure 8.9 illustrates the overlapping of the two variables when $r = .90$.

81%

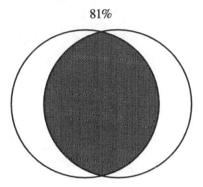

Figure 8.9 A graphic presentation of the shared variance when $r = .90$

A correlation of .60 may look quite low, but it is not uncommon in real-life studies. Correlations of this magnitude are acceptable for research studies and for group prediction. For individual prediction, the correlation should be .80 or higher.

Intercorrelation Tables

Occasionally, a number of variables are correlated with each other. The results of these correlations are displayed in a table, called an **intercorrelation table,** rather than being embedded in the text. For example, a researcher may want to intercorrelate five achievement tests: Spelling, Phonics, Vocabulary, Language Mechanics, and Total Battery. We will number these tests 1 through 5, respectively. After obtaining the intercorrelations, we present them in a table (Table 8.6).

Table 8.6   Intercorrelations of Five Tests

	1	2	3	4	5
1. Spelling	1.00	.63	.45	.57	.82
2. Phonics	.63	1.00	.39	.68	.78
3. Vocabulary	.45	.39	1.00	.85	.86
4. Language Mechanics	.57	.68	.85	1.00	.91
5. Total Battery	.82	.78	.86	.91	1.00

If you inspect Table 8.6 you would see that it has two distinct features:

1. All the correlations presented on the diagonal are perfect ($r=1.00$). The reason is obvious: these are all correlations of a variable with itself (e.g., 1 & 1, 2 & 2).

2. The correlations recorded in the two areas marked by the two triangles are a mirror-image of each other.

Considering these two features, it is clear that the table as presented has *duplicate* information (one of the triangles) and *unnecessary* information (the correlations of 1.00 on the diagonal). Thus, the table can be reorganized to present the results more efficiently. Table 8.7 may look as if it lacks some information, but, in fact, it contains all the information needed.

Table 8.7   **An Abbreviated Intercorrelation Table**

	2	3	4	5
1. Spelling	r= .63	.45	.57	.82
2. Phonics		.39	.68	.78
3. Vocabulary			.85	.86
4. Language Mechanics				.91
5. Total Battery				

[handwritten annotations: "p value = level of significance", "P < .05 = by chance alone less than in 5% of the time", "Correlation coefficient of this magnitude occuring"]

Reading intercorrelation tables: You may need some practice reading these tables, because they are presented in an abbreviated form. Suppose you try to find the correlation of tests 4 and 5, and have difficulty locating it. You should simply look for tests 5 and 4. For practice, let's follow the correlation of the Vocabulary test (test 3) with all the other four tests.

Start by reading the correlations listed in the column marked 3: 3 & 1, r=.45; 3 & 2, r=.39. The direction is down vertically. Next comes 3 & 4. In order to locate this correlation, take a 90^0 angle to your right, from where the correlation of 3 & 3 might have been, and start reading horizontally *across* from test 3. This will lead you to r=.85, the correlation of 3 & 4; and then to .86, the correlation of 3 & 5.

When intercorrelation tables are presented in a research report, several correlations may be identified as statistically significant. The significance levels may be indicated by asterisks corresponding to certain levels (e.g.,* p <.05 or ** p <.01); or by listing the exact level of significance next to each correlation coefficient (e.g., r=.56, p <.046). A level of significance of p <.05 means that correlation coefficients of that magnitude could have been obtained by chance alone less than 5% of the time, and we are quite confident that the correlation is different from zero.   When the level of significance is p <.01, we are saying that similar results could have been obtained by chance alone no more than 1% of the time.

Correlation Tables

   Correlation tables differ from **intercorrelation** tables in the type of information they convey and in the way they look. Suppose we want to correlate the IQ level of parents and their children. The children are divided into three groups, those with low, medium, and high IQ scores.   In addition, IQ scores are available for these children's fathers and mothers (Table 8.8).[3]   Incidently, in this example we do not have two scores for each participant; rather, each child is paired with his/her parents.

Table 8.8   <u>Correlations of Mothers and Fathers and Their Daughters or Sons With Different IQ Level</u>

	Low IQ		Medium IQ		High IQ	
	Daughter	Son	Daughter	Son	Daughter	Son
Mother	r=.56* n= 15	r=.62† n= 20	r=.55† n= 22	r=.44* n= 21	r=.48 n= 16	r=.58* n= 15
Father	r=.52 n= 14	r=.45 n= 18	r=.54† n= 23	r=.48* n= 20	r=.49* n= 17	r=.50 n= 15

* p <.05   † p <.01

---

[3]   **A HINT**: As with any continuous variable that is divided into categories (such as high, medium, and low), the criterion used for creating the categories has to be logical.

In Table 8.8, the correlation (r), the statistical significance, and the number of pairs at each combination of children and parents (n), are specified for each cell.   For example, according to this table, there are 20 boys with low IQ (n=20) who are paired with their mothers. The correlation of the IQ scores of these boys and their mothers is .62 (r=.62), significant at the .01 level (†p<.01).

The correlation table (Table 8.8) is also different from the intercorrelation table (Table 8.7) in its layout. It does not contain a triangle of blank space, and it does not have the same variables serving as both column *and* row headings.   Both types of tables provide an efficient way to present a large number of correlation coefficients.

Spearman Rank-Order Correlation

When observations on the variables to be correlated are rank-ordered, the statistic known as **Spearman rank-order correlation** is used.   The correlation coefficient is represented by r_s.[4]   This rank-order correlation coefficient is easy to compute and is interpreted in the same way as the Pearson coefficient r.[5]   The formula for the Spearman coefficient is:

$$r_s = 1 - \frac{6 \sum D^2}{N(N^2 - 1)}$$

---

[4] **A HINT:** The Greek letter ρ (rho) may also be used to indicate a rank-order correlation coefficient.

[5] **A HINT:**   Although Spearman rank-order correlation (r_s) is easy to compute, even by hand, we do not recommend (as several textbooks do) converting interval or ratio scale scores to ranks just so r_s can be computed. When *both* variables are measured on an interval or ratio scale, Pearson correlation should be used. With computers readily available, Pearson product-moment correlation is just as easy to calculate as the Spearman rank-order correlation.

Where $r_s =$ the Spearman coefficient

$\Sigma D^2 =$ the sum of squared differences between the two ranks assigned to each individual

$N =$ the number of individuals (number of pairs of rankings)

In cases where one set of scores is rank-ordered and the other set includes scores measured on an interval or ratio scale, the latter should first be converted to ranks. The following example helps demonstrate the computations of Spearman rank-order correlation:

A teacher wants to determine if academic achievement correlates with the social skills of 10 second-grade students. Spearman rank-order correlation is used to determine whether students who obtain high achievement scores are also ranked high on social skills; and whether those who are low achievers are also ranked low on social skills.   The total battery scores on a standardized achievement test administered annually to all second graders in the school serve as a measure of academic achievement. Based on classroom and playground observations, the teacher rank-orders the students on their social skills (Table 8.9).   Since the achievement scores are measured on an interval scale, the first step is to convert them to ranks.

Tied ranks. Student number 4 and student number 6 have the same achievement test score of 69. There are three students who scored below the score of 69. The two students who scored 69 are ranked fourth and fifth, so the ranks of 4 and 5 are added together, and then divided by 2 (the number of students who had obtained the same score). Thus, both students are assigned a rank of 4.5. The next rank after 4.5 is 6 (student #2).

Table 8.9   Ranking Scores of 10 Students on Achievement and Social Measures

Student No.	Achievement Score	Rank	Social Rank	D	D^2
1	67	3	2	1	1
2	75	6	10	-4	16
3	55	2	1	1	1
4	69	4.5	5	-0.5	0.25
5	86	7	9	-2	4
6	69	4.5	3	1.5	2.25
7	99	10	8	2	4
8	44	1	4	-3	9
9	97	9	6	3	9
10	88	8	7	1	1

$$\Sigma D^2 = 47.5$$

Next, the difference between the two ranks assigned to each student is computed and recorded in the column marked D. The next step is to square these differences, and add them up to obtain ΣD^2. Once this is completed, the appropriate numbers are plugged into the formula, and r_s is computed.

$$r_s = 1 - \frac{6\Sigma D^2}{N(N^2 - 1)} = 1 - \frac{6(47.5)}{10(10^2 - 1)} =$$

$$= 1 - \frac{285}{10(100 - 1)} = 1 - \frac{285}{990} = 1 - .29 = .71$$

The teacher finds a moderate-to-substantial positive correlation of .71 between the second graders' achievement scores and their social skills. In other words, it seems that in most cases the students who are high achievers are also ranked high on their social skills, and the low achievers are ranked low on their social skills.

Summary

1. **Correlation** is defined as the relationship or association between two or more paired variables. The most common way to pair variables is to administer the measures of these variables to the same group of people.

2. The **correlation coefficient** indicates the strength (or degree) of correlation. The coefficient can range from 1.00 (perfect positive correlation) to -1.00 (perfect negative correlation). A coefficient of 0.00 indicates no correlation.

3. The **scattergram** is used to show graphically the correlation between two variables. The direction of the points on the scattergram and the degree to which they cluster indicate the strength of the correlation and whether the correlation is positive or negative.

4. In a **positive** correlation, an increase in one variable is associated with an increase in the other variable. In a **negative** correlation, an increase in one variable is associated with a decrease in the other variable.

5. A negative correlation is as useful as a positive correlation.

6. The most commonly used correlation procedure is the **Pearson product moment**, whose coefficient is represented by the letter r. Pearson r is used with data measured on an interval or a ratio scale, when the variables to be correlated have a linear relationship.

7.   Correlation coefficients can be described as ranging from negligible to very high (or perfect, which is very uncommon).

8.   Correlation is used in several ways: (a) in describing relationships between variables, (b) in prediction, and (c) in the assessment of reliability and validity.

9.   The **null hypothesis** in correlation states that the correlation coefficient is zero; and the **alternative hypothesis** states that in the population, the correlation is not equal to zero.

10.   Correlation is high and positive when the relative position of individuals on one variable is similar to their position on the other variable.

11.   Pearson r can be computed using the z **score** method or the **raw score** method.

12.   Correlation is underestimated if the measurements being used to derive the scores have low reliability and if the variables being measured have a low variance.

13.   The square of the correlation coefficient shows, in percentages, how much the two variables have in common.

14.   Correlations between three or more variables are presented in an **intercorrelation** or **correlation** table.

15.   **Spearman rank-order correlation** is used to correlate variables that are rank ordered (i.e., measured on an ordinal scale). This correlation coefficient is represented by r_s. Spearman rank-order correlation coefficient is interpreted in the same way as Pearson r correlation.

Chapter 9
PREDICTION AND REGRESSION

In our daily life, prediction is quite common. When we hear thunder and see lightning, we often predict they will be followed by rain. We might also predict the relationship between the day of the week and the expected crowd at the movie theater. In education, we also use prediction. For example, we might predict that a bright elementary school student will do well in high school, or that a student who is having difficulties on the midterm examination is probably going to get a low grade on the final examination.

From our personal experience we know that our predictions do not always materialize, and people and events continue to surprise us. We also know that when there is a strong relationship between the predictor variable and the predicted variable, our prediction is likely to be more accurate. There are exceptions, of course. Sometimes rain does not follow thunder and lightning, and occasionally, bright young children drop out of high school. Nevertheless, knowing something about the relationship between the variables allows us to make a prediction that is better than a chance guess.

In this book, the discussion of prediction will focus on educational settings, using scores on one variable to predict scores on another variable. The variable used as a predictor is called the **predictor variable**, or the **independent variable**, and is represented by the letter X. The predicted variable, represented by the letter Y, is called the **criterion variable** or the **dependent variable**. For example, Scholastic Aptitude Test (SAT) scores may be used as the predictor variable, and college freshman grade point average (GPA) scores as the criterion variable.

The technique used for prediction is called **regression**. At the heart of the rationale for prediction is the notion that the predictor and the criterion variables are correlated. The higher the correlation between these variables, the more accurate the prediction. When only one variable is used to predict another, the procedure is called **simple regression**, and when two or more variables are used as predictors, the procedure is called **multiple regression**.

The theory of regression was developed by Sir Francis Galton (1822-1911), a friend and mentor of Karl Pearson (who developed the Pearson product moment correlation). Galton attempted to use the heights of fathers to predict the heights of their sons. He noticed that, when using the prediction equation, sons of tall parents were predicted to be shorter than their fathers, and sons of short fathers were predicted to be taller than their fathers. Galton realized that the predicted Y score is closer to the mean of the Y distribution, compared with its corresponding predictor value, X, and the mean of its distribution. This phenomenon was not observed when the correlation between X and Y was perfect.

The discussion which follows will focus on simple linear regression, where the predictor variable (X) and the criterion variable (Y) have a linear relationship.[1] Our numerical example demonstrates the computations involved in simple regression. Additionally, the concept of multiple regression will be introduced briefly without using a numerical example.

---

[1] **A HINT:** You may want to read again the chapter on correlation (Chapter 8) which discusses the idea of linear relationship.

Simple Regression

After observing a significant correlation between two variables, a researcher may want to use one variable to predict the other one. For example, PSAT scores may be used to predict SAT scores. The prediction can be achieved by developing a regression equation. In order to develop the equation, we first need to have both predictor and criterion scores for a group of people *similar* to those whose criterion scores we would like later to be able to predict. Once the equation is available, it can be used to predict criterion (dependent) scores for a new group of people for whom only the predictor scores are available.

For example, educators may be interested in finding out if scores obtained on a measure of academic self-concept (ASC) can be used to predict the GPA of high school students. Scores on the ACS test obtained by a randomly-selected group of high-school students may be correlated with the students' GPAs. Using the scores on the two measures, ASC and GPA, we can calculate the regression equation. If the ASC test is shown to be a good predictor of GPA, teachers may use this information in planning individualized instruction and course work for their students. Of course, correlation and prediction do not imply causation. We cannot conclude from the regression study that ASC *affects* GPA. Quite likely, both variables are related to ability as able students have higher academic self-concepts, and they also get higher grades on their course work. To ascertain whether ASC affects GPA, an *experimental* study should be conducted in which academic self-concept is being manipulated.

The regression equation can be used to draw a line through a scattergram of the two variables involved, designated as X and Y. This line is called the **regression line**, or the **line of best fit** (Figure 9.1).

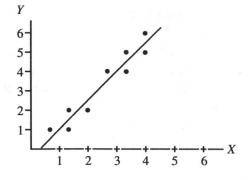

Figure 9.1 A scattergram showing the regression line

The position of the line is determined by the **slope** (the angle), represented by the letter b; and by the **intercept** (the point where the line intersects the vertical axis, Y), represented by the letter a.[2] The prediction equation is:

$$\hat{Y} = bX + a$$

Where $\hat{Y} =$ the predicted Y score (pronounced "Y hat"; also represented by the symbol Y')

$b =$ the slope

$X =$ a score on the independent variable

$a =$ the intercept

The prediction equation demonstrates that in order to compute the $\hat{Y}$ (predicted Y) scores, we first need to calculate the values of b and a. The formula for computing b is:

---

[2] **A HINT:**   Computer printouts of statistical programs usually refer to b as the **coefficient**, and to a as the **constant**.

$$b = r \frac{S_y}{S_x}$$

Where $b =$ the slope of the line

$r =$ the correlation between the X and Y variables

$S_y =$ the standard deviation of the Y variable

$S_x =$ the standard deviation of the X variable

The formula for the computation of a is:

$$a = \overline{Y} - b\overline{X}$$

Where $a =$ the regression line intercept

$\overline{Y} =$ the mean of the Y variable

$\overline{X} =$ the mean of the X variable

$b =$ the slope (the coefficient)

If you were to inspect regression lines and their slopes (b), you would realize that the higher the value of b, the steeper the line; and the lower the value of b, the more flat the line. For example when $b=0.25$, for every increase of 1 unit in X there is an increase of 0.25 unit in Y. When $b=0.5$, for every increase of 1 unit in X there is an increase of 0.5 units in Y. When $b=1$, for every increase of 1 unit in X there is an increase of 1 unit in Y. When $b=2$, for every increase of 1 unit in X there is an increase of 2 units in Y. Parts a, b, c, and d in Figure 9.2 show four regression lines when the intercept is zero (i.e., the regression line passes through the point where both axes are at zero).

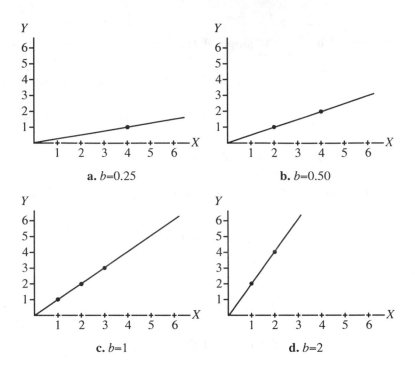

Figure 9.2 Four regression lines with different slopes

The Standard Error of Estimate, S_E

Unless the predictor and the criterion variables have a perfect correlation, any attempt to use X (the predictor) to predict $\hat{Y}$ (the criterion) is likely to result in a certain degree of error. Consequently, for some individuals the $\hat{Y}$ score is an overestimate of their "true" Y score; and for others, the $\hat{Y}$ score is an underestimate of their "true" Y score. The difference between the actual Y score and the $\hat{Y}$ score for each individual is called **the error score**. (This may also be called the **residual**). The standard deviation of the error scores, across all individuals, is called the **standard error of estimate** (S_E).[3] More specifically, assuming a normal distribution of error scores, the actual Y score would lie within $\pm 1 S_E$ of the $\hat{Y}$ score about 68% of the time, and within $\pm 2 S_E$ about 95% of the time. The S_E is calculated by using the scores from the group used to generate the regression equation. The formula for S_E is:

$$S_E = S_Y \sqrt{1 - r^2}$$

Where S_E = the standard error of estimate

S_Y = the standard deviation of the Y variable

r^2 = the square of the correlation [4]

Holding S_Y constant, S_E decreases as r increases. Thus, the higher the correlation, the lower the S_E, and the prediction is more accurate. The following formula demonstrates that when X and Y have a perfect correlation ($r=1.00$), there is no error in prediction ($S_E = 0$):

$$S_E = S_Y \sqrt{1 - 1.00^2} = S_Y \sqrt{1 - 1.00} =$$
$$= S_Y \sqrt{0.00} = 0.00$$

When $r=0.00$ (no correlation), S_E is equal to the SD of the Y variable (S_Y):

---

[3] **A HINT:** The standard error of estimate may also be represented by the symbol $S_{y \cdot x}$.

[4] **A HINT:** You may recall that in the chapter about correlation (Chapter 8) we discussed the concept of r^2 (the shared variance or coefficient of determination), which refers to the proportion of the variability (or information) of Y that is contained in X.

$$S_E = S_Y \sqrt{1 - 0.00} = S_Y \sqrt{1} =$$
$$= S_Y (1) = S_Y$$

Suppose from our experience as high school teachers we hypothesize that students' academic self-concept is a good predictor of students' grade point average (GPA). Assume we have our students' scores on an Academic Self-Concept (ASC) measure, as well as their GPAs. The scores on both of these measures for five randomly-selected students are listed in Table 9.1.

Table 9.1   Obtained Scores on Academic Self-Concept (ASC), GPA, and Predicted GPA Scores for Five Students

Person No.	ASC X	GPA Y	(Predicted Y) $\hat{Y}$
A	23	3.50	3.80
B	25	3.83	3.93
C	15	2.89	3.27
D	18	3.75	3.47
E	20	4.10	3.60

Using the ASC and GPA scores (X and Y scores) of these five students, we find a correlation of .56 between ASC and GPA. The standard deviation of the X variable (S_X) is 3.96 and the standard deviation of the Y variable (S_Y) is 0.46.

We can now calculate the standard error of estimate (S_E):

$$S_E = S_Y \sqrt{1 - r^2} = 0.46 \sqrt{1 - .56^2} =$$
$$= 0.46 \sqrt{0.31} = (0.46)(0.83) = 0.38$$

In the future, if we have ASC scores for students similar to those in our example, we can use these scores to predict the students' GPAs. On the average, the predicted GPA scores ($\hat{Y}$) will be off the "true" GPA scores by about 0.38 points.

An Example of Simple Regression

Ms. Wright, an eighth-grade language arts teacher, wants to know whether she could use a practice test she constructed to predict the scores of her students on the state-mandated end-of-year language arts examination. The teacher hypothesizes that the practice test administered at the beginning of the second semester is a good predictor of the state-mandated test. Thus, she might want to administer to her students the practice test, then use the test results to design early intervention and remediation for students who are expected to do poorly on the state-mandated test. To ascertain whether the practice test is a good predictor of the state-mandated test, the teacher uses the scores from the practice test (the predictor, or independent variable) and the scores from the state-mandated test (the criterion, or dependent variable) from last year's students to generate the regression equation. Since the state-mandated language arts test is scored on a scale of 1-50, the teacher has designed her test to use the same scale.[5] Although the teacher uses the scores of all the students from last year's class, in this computational example, only the scores of 10 students will be used to demonstrate how to generate the regression equation (Table 9.2). The first step is to find the correlation between the two tests, then the b coefficient (the slope), followed by a (the intercept).

---

[5] **A HINT:** In this example, we use numbers in a range of 1-50 for both the predictor (the practice test) and the criterion (the eighth grade end-of-year state-mandated test); however, the regression procedure allows for any range of scores to be used for any of the two variables.

Table 9.2   Raw Scores, Squared Raw Scores, and Cross Products of 10 Students on Practice Test and on State Test

Student	Practice Test X	State Test Y	X^2	Y^2	XY
A	45	40	2025	1600	1800
B	45	46	2025	2116	2070
C	46	37	2116	1369	1702
D	50	49	2500	2401	2450
E	35	31	1225	961	1085
F	47	50	2209	2500	2350
G	23	32	529	1024	736
H	46	48	2116	2304	2208
I	40	44	1600	1936	1760
J	41	39	1681	1521	1599

$\Sigma X=418$ $\Sigma Y=416$ $\Sigma X^2=18026$ $\Sigma Y^2=17732$ $\Sigma XY=17760$

$$r = \frac{N\Sigma XY - (\Sigma X)(\Sigma Y)}{\sqrt{N\Sigma X^2 - (\Sigma X)^2} \sqrt{N\Sigma Y^2 - (\Sigma Y)^2}}$$

$$r = \frac{10(17760) - (418)(416)}{\sqrt{10(18026) - 418^2} \sqrt{10(17732)\, 416^2}} =$$

$$= \frac{177600 - 173888}{\sqrt{180260 - 174724} \sqrt{177320 - 173056}} =$$

$$= \frac{3712}{\sqrt{5536} \sqrt{4264}} = \frac{3712}{\sqrt{23605504}} = \frac{3712}{4858.55} = .76$$

Once the correlation is found, the b coefficient can be computed, followed by the computation of the value of a. After we have r, b, and a, the regression equation can be calculated. Using the data in our example, we first compute the b coefficient:

$$b = (r)\frac{S_Y}{S_X} = .76\ \frac{6.88}{7.84} = (.76)(.88) = 0.67$$

The b coefficient can also be found using a formula which may be easier to use, because there is no need to first compute the variances of the predictor variable and the criterion. The formula is:

$$b = \frac{N\Sigma XY - (\Sigma X)(\Sigma Y)}{N\Sigma X^2 - (\Sigma X)^2}$$

$$b = \frac{10(17760) - (418)(416)}{10(18026) - (418)^2} =$$

$$= \frac{177600 - 173888}{180260 - 174724} = \frac{3712}{5536} = 0.67$$

Using the scores in Table 9.2, b is computed using this second formula. Note that this formula yields the same b value ($b=0.67$) as that obtained using the first formula. Once we have the value of b, we can then calculate a:

$$a = \overline{Y} - b\overline{X} = 41.60 - (0.67)(41.80) =$$

$$= 41.60 - 28.03 = 13.57$$

After finding the values of b (the slope) and a (the intercept), they are entered in the regression equation:

$$\hat{Y} = bX + a = 0.67\,(X) + 13.57$$

Now, for every X score we can predict $\hat{Y}$, using this regression equation.

Standard error of estimate. With the regression equation, we can compute the state-mandated language arts score (the predicted criterion score, $\hat{Y}$) for each student in a new group of eighth graders.   These predicted scores would be calculated after administering students the language arts practice test (the predictor, X) and before the actual state-mandated language arts test scores are available. Table 9.3 lists the $\hat{Y}$ scores for the 10 students. To compare our $\hat{Y}$ scores to the actual Y scores, we create a fourth column where we record the difference between the two Y scores (obtained Y scores minus $\hat{Y}$ scores). This column lists the *error score*.

Table 9.3   Obtained Scores, Predicted Scores, and Error Scores of 10 Students

Student	X	Y	(Predicted Score) $\hat{Y}$	(Error Score) $E=Y-\hat{Y}$	E^2
A	45	40	43.75	-3.75	14.03
B	45	46	43.75	2.25	5.08
C	46	37	44.42	-7.42	55.00
D	50	49	47.10	1.92	3.62
E	35	31	37.04	-6.04	36.49
F	47	50	45.09	4.91	24.14
G	23	32	28.99	3.01	9.03
H	46	48	44.42	3.58	12.84
I	40	44	40.39	-3.61	13.01
J	41	39	41.06	-2.06	4.26
				$\Sigma E=0.00$	$\Sigma E^2=177.50$

For some of the scores, the predicted score is an overestimate, resulting in a negative error score; for others, the predicted score is an underestimate, resulting in a positive error score. Checking the computation, you may notice that in the "Error" column, the negative error scores cancel the positive error scores resulting in a sum of zero for that column.

Next, we compute the standard error of estimate (S_E):

$$S_E = S_Y \sqrt{1 - r^2} = 6.88 \sqrt{1 - .76^2} =$$

$$= 6.88 \sqrt{1 - .58} = 6.88 \sqrt{.42} =$$

$$= 6.88 (.65) = 4.44$$

A S_E of 4.44 means that for each student, on the average, we overestimate or underestimate the state-mandated language arts score by close to 4.5 points. For example, for a student whose $\hat{Y}$ score is 42, about 68% of the time the actual Y score will lie within 4.44 above or below the $\hat{Y}$ score (i.e., between approximately 37.5 and 46.5). You may think that this is quite a wide margin of error. You may also think that because of the potential of error we may fail to identify those who need help, or provide remediation to those who do not need it. Remember, though, that without having this information, it may be even more difficult to predict students' scores!

Graphing the Regression Equation

As was mentioned before, the regression equation can be graphed. Figure 9.4 shows a scattergram of the scores obtained on the practice test (X) and the scores obtained on the state-mandated test (Y), with the regression line added. We can use two pairs of X scores and their corresponding predicted Y scores to draw the line. It is easier to draw the line if we choose one low and one high X score. In our example, we will use $X=23$ with a $\hat{Y}$ of 28.99, and $X=50$ with a $\hat{Y}$ of 47.10. The intercept (a) is 13.57, the point where the regression line intersects the Y axis.[6] If you were to graph the rest of the $\hat{Y}$ scores, they would all lie on the regression line.

The regression line goes through the intersection of the means of the two variables ($\bar{X}$= 41.80 and $\bar{Y}$=41.60). Figure 9.3 shows the actual scores of all 10 students. For several students, the $\hat{Y}$ score is an overestimate (i.e., the $\hat{Y}$ score is above the actual Y score); and for several students, the $\hat{Y}$ score is an underestimate (i.e., the $\hat{Y}$ score is below the actual Y score).

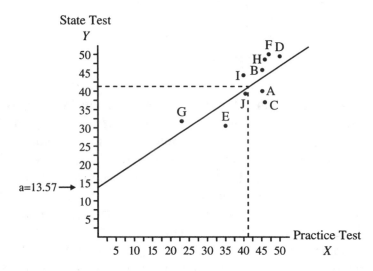

Figure 9.3 A regression line for predictiong scores on the state-madated test using the practice test scores (data in Table 9.3)

The Coefficient of Determination, r^2

The **coefficient of determination**, r^2 (also called **the percent of shared variance**), can be used to describe the relationship between

---

[6] **A HINT:** On a graph of the regression line, the Y intercept, a, is the same value as the one obtained by computation *only* when the X and Y axes are drawn with an origin of zero (i.e., both start at the zero point).

the variables.[7] Our computation yielded a correlation of .76 between the teacher-constructed language arts practice test and the end-of-year state-mandated language arts test. The coefficient of determination is the square of the correlation (r^2). With r=.76, r^2 = $.76^2$ = .5897, which means that about 59% of the variation in performance on the state test (Y) is associated with changes in performance on the practice test (X); 41% of the variation is due to other factors.

Multiple Regression

When two or more variables are used to predict one criterion variable, the **multiple regression** procedure is employed. For example, scores on a kindergarten readiness test, combined with teacher assessment, may be used to predict first graders' scores on a standardized achievement test. A researcher is likely to consider using several variables as predictors when there is no single variable that has a high correlation with the criterion, so as to serve as a satisfactory predictor. In such cases, additional predictor variables may be used, to predict more accurately the criterion variable.

The regression equation in multiple regression is an extension of the equation for simple regression. In addition to the intercept (a), the equation contains a regression coefficient (b) for each of the predictor variables (X). The combined correlation of the predictor variables with the criterion variable is called **multiple R**. With two predictors, the regression equation is:

$$\hat{Y} = b_1 X_1 + b_2 X_2 + a$$

---

[7] **A HINT:** This concept was also discussed in Chapter 8 (correlation).

Where $\hat{Y}$ = the predicted Y score

b_1 =   the slope (coefficient) of predictor X_1

X_1 =   the score on predictor X_1

b_2 =   the slope (coefficient) of predictor X_2

X_2 =   the score on predictor X_2

a =   the intercept (i.e., the constant)

In multiple regression, we can calculate R^2 which is similar to r^2 in simple regression, and can range from 0 to 1.00. It indicates the proportion of the variation in Y that can be accounted for by the variation of the combined predictor variables.

For any level of correlation between the predictor variables and the criterion, when the predictor variables have a low correlation with each other, R^2 is greater than when the predictor variables correlate highly with each other. To illustrate this point, let's look at Figure 9.4. Part a shows two predictor variables, X_1 and X_2, which correlate highly with the criterion variable Y, and in addition, correlate highly with each other. The high correlation between the two predictor variables is evidenced by the fact that they overlap a great deal. Adding a second predictor (X_2) to the first predictor (X_1) has not significantly increased R^2, the amount of variation in Y (the criterion) that can be accounted for by the predictors. That is, adding a second predictor does not account for a much greater proportion of the criterion Y. Part b shows two predictor variables, X_3 and X_4, and a criterion variable. Each of the two predictors has a high correlation with the criterion variable, and a low correlation with each other (they overlap very little). In comparison with part a, part b shows that the two predictor variables combined overlap more with the criterion variable and can account for more of the variation in Y.

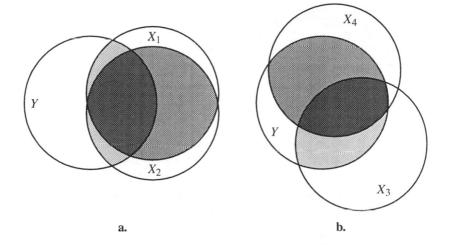

Figure 9.4 Two graphs showing different levels of correlation between the two predictors, and between the predictors and the criterion: the two predictors, X_1 and X_2, correlate highly with each other (part a); and the two predictors, X_3 and X_4, have a low correlation with each other (part b)

Summary

1. Regression is a technique used for prediction. The variable used as a predictor is called the **independent variable** and is represented by the letter X. The predicted variable is called the **criterion** or the **dependent variable**, and is represented by Y.

2. Regression is based on the assumption that the predictor (or predictors) and the criterion variables correlate with each other. The higher the correlation, the more accurate the prediction.

3.   When one variable is used to predict another variable, the procedure is called **simple regression**. When two or more variables are used as predictors, the procedure is called **multiple regression**.

4.   The prediction of Y scores for a given group of individuals for whom the X scores are available can be accomplished by using the **regression equation**. A predicted Y score is represented by $\hat{Y}$ ("Y hat").

5.   The regression equation can be used to draw a line. The position of the line is determined by its **slope**, represented by the letter b; and by its **intercept** (the point where the regression line intersects the vertical axis), represented by the letter a. The prediction equation is:

$$\hat{Y} = bX + a$$

6.   The slope (b) may also be identified as the **coefficient**, and the intercept may be identified as the **constant**.

7.   The sample used to derive the regression equation should be similar to the sample for whom we want to predict future scores.

8.   Unless the predictor and the criterion variables have a perfect correlation, any attempt to use the predictor variable (X) to predict the criterion variable ($\hat{Y}$) is likely to result in a certain degree of error. The **error score** is the difference between actual Y and $\hat{Y}$ scores.

9.   The standard deviation of the error scores across all individuals is called the **standard error of estimate** (S_E). The higher the correlation between the predictor variable and the criterion variable, the lower the S_E, making the prediction more accurate.

10. S_E indicates how much, on the average, $\hat{Y}$ scores overestimate or underestimate the actual Y scores.

11. The regression equation for multiple regression is an extension of the equation for simple regression. It includes an intercept a (the constant), and a slope b (the regression coefficient) for each of the predictor variables.

12. The combined correlation of the predictor variables with the criterion variable is called **multiple R**.

13. R^2 (which is similar to r^2 in simple regression) indicates the proportion of the variation in Y (the criterion variable) that can be accounted for by the variation of the combined predictor variables.

Part Five

INFERENTIAL STATISTICS

Chapter 10
T-TEST

Many researchers are concerned with comparing groups to each other. Their studies test hypotheses that predict whether the differences between groups are statistically significant, or whether they could have occurred simply by chance. When two means are being compared with each other, the statistic used is a *t*-test. For example, research studies may involve comparing an experimental group to a control group, boys to girls, or pretest to posttest scores. The numbers used for the comparison are the means of the two groups derived from interval or ratio-scale measures, and both means are derived from the same measure. As we analyze research data, we should keep in mind that small differences are expected even among members of the same group. These differences may occur due to sampling error and are considered chance differences.

You might ask, How can we distinguish between differences due to sampling error and "real" differences? At what point do we say that the difference is too large to be attributed to sampling error, and that it probably indicates a real difference? Unfortunately, there are no standards or cutoff scores. After obtaining the means, we cannot simply "eyeball" them and determine whether they are similar or different. A difference of 2 points between means may be defined as statistically significant in some cases, but not in others. The group means and variances, in addition to the sample size, all play a role in determining whether the difference between the means is a "real" difference.

The t-test is based on the t distribution which was developed in 1908 by W. S. Gosset, who worked for a brewery in Dublin. Since employees were not allowed to publish in journals, Gosset used the pseudonym "Student" in an article he sent to a journal, and the t distribution became known as "Student's t distribution".

Hypotheses for T-Test

Predictions of outcomes in studies which are using the t-test state the expected relationship between two means. These predictions are the research hypotheses and they reflect what the researcher hypothesizes about the nature of the relationship between the means. (The research hypothesis is also called the alternative hypothesis and is represented by the symbol H_A or H_1; see Chapter 1.) A study is then designed in order to test these hypotheses. When the direction of the outcome is stated before the start of the study, it is called a **directional hypothesis**. For example, we may predict that a group of first graders using the whole language approach (experimental group, E) would score higher on an end-of-year reading test, compared with a similar group of first graders using basal readers (control group, C). The directional hypothesis is:

$$H_A : Mean_E > Mean_C$$

Where H_A =   the research hypothesis (the alternative hypothesis)

$Mean_E$ =   the mean of the experimental group

$Mean_C$ =   the mean of the control group

When we predict a difference between the two groups, but the direction of the outcome is not specified, the research hypothesis is called **nondirectional**. The nondirectional hypothesis is:

$$H_A : Mean_1 \neq Mean_2$$

For example, we may predict differences in attitudes toward computers between junior high boys and girls, but due to inconclusive results in previous studies, we are unable to predict which of the two groups will have a more positive attitude.

Occasionally, the research hypothesis is not stated as directional or nondirectional, but in a null form. That is, we predict that there will be no difference between the means. This is not very common in educational research, but in cases where the research hypothesis is stated as null, that hypothesis is considered nondirectional.

Another type of hypothesis that is central to statistical testing is the null (statistical) hypothesis, symbolized by H_0 (see Chapter 1). The null hypothesis states that any observed difference between the means is too small to indicate a real difference between them and that such difference is probably due to sampling error. In other words, the null hypothesis always predicts no difference between the means.[1] In symbols, the null hypothesis is:

$$H_O : Mean_1 = Mean_2$$

The null hypothesis is submitted to a statistical test. Based on the results of this statistical test, we decide whether to retain or to reject the null hypothesis. Since the null hypothesis always predicts no difference, there is no need to formally state it when the research hypotheses are presented.

In order to calculate the t-test value, a score should be obtained for each person. The scores are then used to calculate the t value. After calculating a t value, the next step is to consult the table of critical values for the t distribution (Appendix Table C). In order

---

[1] **A HINT:** This is true when we use the t-test. You may remember that in correlational studies, the null hypothesis always predicts no relationship between the variables being correlated (i.e., it predicts a correlation that does not significantly differ from zero). (See Chapter 8.)

to use the table, the researcher needs to know whether to use the critical values listed under the **one-tailed** or **two-tailed test**. Without going into a lengthy explanation about what the tails are, remember the following rule: If your research hypothesis is *directional*, use the one-tailed test. If your research hypothesis is *nondirectional* or is stated as *null* (i.e., you predict no difference between the means), use the two-tailed test. When in doubt, use the two-tailed test which is more conservative.[2]

Using the *T*-Test

A *t*-test is used to compare two means in three different situations:

1. *T-test for independent samples.* The two groups whose means are being compared are independent of each other. A typical example is a comparison of experimental and control groups.

2. *T-test for paired samples* (also called *t*-test for dependent, matched, or correlated samples). The two means represent two sets of scores which are paired. A typical example is a comparison of pretest and posttest scores obtained from one group of people.

3. *T-test for a single sample*. This *t*-test is used when the mean of a sample is compared to the mean of a population. For example, we may use the Graduate Record Examination (GRE) scores of psychology graduate students (the sample) to test whether they are significantly different from the overall mean GRE in the university (the population).

---

[2] **A HINT:** A conservative test or a conservative decision generally reduces the chance of making a Type I error.

T-Test for Independent Samples

This *t*-test is used extensively in experimental designs and in causal-comparative (ex-post facto) designs when means from two groups are being compared. There are several assumptions underlying this test:

a. The groups are independent of each other.

b. A subject may appear in only one group.

c. The two groups represent a random sample of their respective populations.

d. The two groups come from two populations whose variances are approximately the same. This assumption is called the assumption of the **homogeneity of variances**. We compare the two variances to check if they are not significantly different from each other.

The *t*-test is considered a **robust** statistic; that is, even if assumptions c and d listed above are not met, the researcher can still safely use the test to analyze the data. As a general rule, it is desirable to have similar group sizes, especially when the groups are small.[3]

An example of an independent *t*-test. A new test preparation company, called Bright Future (BF), wants to convince high school students studying for the American College Testing (ACT) assessment test that enrolling in their test preparation course would significantly improve the students' ACT scores. BF selects 10 students at random and assigns five to the experimental group and

---

[3] **A HINT:** As in several other statistical tests, researchers usually try to have a group size of at least 30. Larger samples are more stable and require a smaller *t*-value (compared with smaller samples) to reject the null hypothesis.

five to the control group.[4]   The experimental group students
participate in the test preparation course conducted by BF. At the
conclusion of the course, both groups of students take the ACT test
form which was given to high school students the previous year.
BF conducts a *t*-test for independent samples to compare the scores
of Group 1 (Experimental, E) to those of Group 2 (Control, C).

The study's research (alternative) hypothesis (H_A) is directional
and can be described as:

$$H_A : \mu_E > \mu_C$$

Note that μ, the symbol for the population mean, is used in
writing hypotheses. Remember that although we may conduct our
studies using *samples*, we are testing hypotheses about *populations*.

The null hypothesis states that there is no significant difference
between the two means. A study is then designed to test the null
hypothesis and to decide whether it is tenable. The null hypothesis
is:

$$H_0 : \mu_E = \mu_C$$

The *t*-value is computed using this formula:

$$t = \frac{\overline{X}_1 - \overline{X}_2}{\sqrt{\dfrac{(n_1 - 1)\,S_1^2 + (n_2 - 1)\,S_2^2}{n_1 + n_2 - 2}\left(\dfrac{1}{n_1} + \dfrac{1}{n_2}\right)}}$$

[handwritten annotations: "mean-Group 1", "mean of group 2", "# of people in group1", "#in group1", "#in group2", "variance of group1", "variance of group2", "# people in group1", "# people group2"]

----

[4] **A HINT:** Although in real-life studies researchers try to have larger
sample sizes, in this chapter (as well as in other chapters) we are using small
sample sizes to simplify the computations in the examples given.

Where $\overline{X}_1 =$ the mean of Group 1 (Experimental)

$\overline{X}_2 =$ the mean of Group 2 (Control)

$S_1^2 =$ the variance of Group 1

$S_2^2 =$ the variance of Group 2

$n_1 =$ the number of people in Group 1

$n_2 =$ the number of people in Group 2

Note that in addition to the difference between the two means (the numerator), the formula also includes the two sample sizes and the two variances (the denominator). We cannot simply look at the difference between the two means and decide whether that difference is statistically significant. The number of the scores in each group and the variability of these scores also play a role in the t-test calculations. The difference between the means is viewed in relation to the spread of the scores. When the spread is small (a low variance), even a small difference between the means may lead to results that are considered statistically significant. With a larger spread (a higher variance), a relatively large difference between the means may be required in order to obtain results that are considered statistically significant.

After finding the t-value, it is then compared to appropriate critical values in the t-test table of critical values. When the obtained t-test exceeds its appropriate critical value, the null hypothesis is rejected. This allows us to conclude that there is a high level of probability that the difference between the means is notably greater than zero and that a difference of this magnitude is unlikely to have occurred by chance alone. The following are ACT scores and the computations of the t-value for students in experimental and control groups who participated in the study conducted by BF (Table 10.1):

Table 10.1   ACT Scores of Experimental and Control Groups

(Experimental) Group 1	(Control) Group 2
23	17
18	19
26	21
32	14
21	19
$\Sigma X_1 = 120$	$\Sigma X_2 = 90$

$\overline{X}_1 = 24 \qquad S_1^2 = 28.5 \qquad n_1 = 5$

$\overline{X}_2 = 18 \qquad S_2^2 = 7.0 \qquad n_2 = 5$

$$t = \frac{24-18}{\sqrt{\frac{(4)(28.5)+(4)(7.0)}{5+5-2}\left(\frac{1}{5}+\frac{1}{5}\right)}} =$$

$$= \frac{6}{\sqrt{\frac{114+28}{8}(0.40)}} = \frac{6}{\sqrt{7.1}} = 2.26$$

When the two groups have the same number of scores (i.e., $n_1 = n_2$), a simpler formula can be used to compute the t-value:

$$t = \frac{\overline{X}_1 - \overline{X}_2}{\sqrt{\frac{S_1^2}{n_1}+\frac{S_2^2}{n_2}}} = \frac{6}{\sqrt{5.7+1.4}} = \frac{6}{\sqrt{7.1}} = 2.26$$

Next, we consult the table of critical values (Appendix Table C). To do so, we need to determine the appropriate degrees of freedom (*df*). As was described before (see Chapter 1), *df* are typically *n*-1. With two groups, *df* are:

Independent degrees of freedom

$$(n_1 - 1) + (n_2 - 1) \qquad OR \qquad n_1 + n_2 - 2$$

The hypothesis for this study was directional; therefore, we use the one-tailed test. With *df* of 8 (5+5-2), the critical value under *p* of .05 is 1.86. (This is listed as: $t_{crit(.05,8)} = 1.86$, with .05 showing the *p* level, and 8 indicating the *df*.) We find the critical value by locating *p* of .05 under the one-tailed test, and *df* of 8. The intersection of *p*=.05 and *df*=8 gives us the value of 1.86, called the **critical value**. Our obtained *t* value of 2.26 exceeds the corresponding critical value; therefore, we move on to the right to the next column and check the critical value at *p*=.025, which is 2.306 ($t_{crit(.025,8)} = 2.306$). (In tables where *p*=.025 column is not included, move directly to *p*=.01 column.) Our obtained value of 2.26 does not exceed the critical value of 2.306. Thus, we report our results to be significant at the *p* <.05 level, which is the last critical value we did exceed.

Our decision is to reject the null hypothesis. Such a large difference between the two groups could have occurred by chance alone less than 5% of the time.[5] The hypothesis stated by BF Company is confirmed: students who participated in the test-taking course scored significantly higher on the practice form of the ACT than the control group students . Based on the result of this study, we can be at least 95% confident that the course offered by BF is indeed helpful to students similar to those who participated in the

---

[5] **A HINT:** You should remember, though, that we are making our statistical decision in terms of *probability*, not *certainty*. Rejecting the null hypothesis at *p* <.05 means that there is a possible error associated with this decision.

study. Of course, this was a small sample size, and BF may need to repeat the study with larger samples to really convince students and their parents!

T-Test for Paired (Dependent) Samples

When the two means compared are from two sets of scores which are related to each other, the t-test for paired (dependent) samples is used. It is used, for example, in experimental research to measure the effect of an intervention by comparing the posttest to the pretest scores. The most important requirement for conducting this t-test is that the two scores are *paired*. In studies using a pretest-posttest design, it is easy to see how the scores are paired: they belong to the same individuals. Another way of pairing may be by family. For example, we may want to investigate if, as several researchers claim, the IQ scores of the oldest children in a family are higher than those of the younger siblings. One set of scores would be the IQ scores of the older siblings and the second set of scores would be the IQ scores of their younger siblings. The computation of t-test for paired samples, which is different from that of t-test for independent samples, is explained in the example which follows.

An example of a paired (dependent) t-test. A special program, developed to enhance children's self-concept, is implemented with four- and five-year-old children in Sunny Days Preschool. The intervention lasts six weeks and involves various activities in the class and at home. All the children in the program are pretested and posttested using the Purdue Self-Concept Scale for Preschool Children (PSCS). The test is comprised of a series of 40 pairs of pictures, and scores can range from 0 to 40. The t-test for paired samples is used to test the hypothesis that students would improve significantly on the posttest, compared with their pretest scores. The hypothesis is:

$$H_A : Mean_{POST} > Mean_{PRE}$$

To compute the t value, we find the difference between each pair of scores and record this difference in the column marked D (see Table 10.2). Next, we square each D score and record it in the column marked D^2. The sums of these two columns (ΣD and ΣD^2) are then used in the formula. The t-value is computed using this formula:

$$t = \frac{\Sigma D}{\sqrt{\dfrac{n\Sigma D^2 - (\Sigma D)^2}{n-1}}}$$

Where ΣD = the sum of the D column

ΣD^2 = the sum of the D^2 column

n = the number of pairs

Table 10.2 lists the pretest and posttest scores of six students, selected at random from the experimental group. The computations of the t-value follow the table.

Table 10.2   Pretest and Posttest Scores of Six Students

Pretest X_1	Posttest X_2	$X_2-X_1=D$	D^2
31	34	+3	9
30	31	+1	1
33	33	0	0
35	40	+5	25
32	36	+4	16
34	39	+5	25
ΣX_1=195	ΣX_2=213	ΣD=18	ΣD^2= 76

$$t = \cfrac{\sum D}{\sqrt{\cfrac{n\sum D^2 - (\sum D)^2}{n-1}}} = \cfrac{18}{\sqrt{\cfrac{(6)(76) - 18^2}{6-1}}} =$$

$$= \frac{18}{\sqrt{26.4}} = \frac{18}{5.14} = 3.50$$

$t_{crit(.05,5)} = 2.015 \quad t_{crit(.025,5)} = 2.571 \quad t_{crit(.01,5)} = 3.365$

obtained $t = 3.50$ $df = 6\text{-}1 = 5$ reject null at $p < .01$

Our obtained t value is 3.50, which exceeds the critical values under $p=.05$, $p=.25$, and $p=.01$ (see Appendix Table C). Therefore, we reject the null hypothesis which states that there is no difference between the pretest and the posttest scores. The chance that the means are the same is less than 1% (i.e., $p < .01$). We conclude that the research hypothesis which predicted that the posttest scores will be significantly higher than the pretest scores is confirmed. According to this study, the self-concept enhancement intervention was effective in increasing the self-concept of preschool children.

T-Test for a Single Sample

Occasionally, the researcher is interested in comparing a single group (a sample) to a larger group (a population). For example, a high school teacher of a freshmen accelerated English class may want to confirm that the students in that class had obtained higher scores on an English placement test compared with their peers. In order to carry out this kind of a study the researcher *must* know prior to the start of the study the mean value of the population. In our example, the mean score of the population is the overall mean of the scores of all freshmen on the English placement test.

An example of a single sample _t_-test. A first grade teacher in a school commented to her colleague, a kindergarten teacher, that the students in her class this year seem to be less bright than those she usually has in first grade. Her colleague disagreed with her, and to test whether the first graders this year are really different from those in previous years, they conduct a _t_-test for a single sample. The scores used are from the Wechsler Preschool and Primary Scale for Intelligence - Revised (WPPSI-R), which is given every year to all kindergarten students in the district. In this example, we consider the district to be the population to which we compare the mean of the class. Although the mean IQ score of the population at large is 100 (μ=100), this district's mean IQ score is 110 (μ = 110), and this mean is used in the analysis. The teachers' hypothesis states that there is no difference in IQ scores between the sample (this year's first grade students) and the average first graders in the district (based on past years' data).

$$H_A = Mean_{CLASS} = Mean_{DISTRICT}$$

The formula for _t_-test of a single sample is:

$$t = \frac{\overline{X} - \mu}{S_{\overline{X}}}$$

Where $\overline{X}$ = the sample mean

μ = the population mean

$S_{\overline{X}}$ = the standard error of the mean

To find $S_{\bar{X}}$ we use this formula:

$$S_{(\bar{X})} = \frac{S}{\sqrt{n}}$$

Where $S_{\bar{X}}$ = the standard error of the mean

S = the sample standard deviation

n = the number of individuals in the sample

In order to test their hypothesis, the two teachers randomly select IQ scores of 10 students from this year's first grade class. These IQ scores are listed in Table 10.3, followed by the computation of the t-value.

Table 10.3   IQ Scores of 10 Students

Scores
115
135
105
100
112
118
103
98
140
99

$\overline{}$
$\Sigma X=1125$

$\bar{X} =112.5$

$S =14.89$

$$S_{\overline{x}} = \frac{S}{\sqrt{n}} = \frac{14.89}{\sqrt{10}} = \frac{14.89}{3.16} = 4.71$$

$$t = \frac{\overline{X} - \mu}{S_{\overline{x}}} = \frac{112.5 - 110}{4.71} = \frac{2.5}{4.71} = 0.53$$

$df = 9$;   use two-tailed test

$t_{crit(.05,9)} = 2.262$;   obtained $t = 0.53$;   retain null hypothesis

The obtained t-value of 0.53 does not exceed the critical value under $p=.05$, which is 2.262. (See Appendix Table C.) Thus, the null hypothesis is retained.[6]   Based on these results, the two teachers conclude that there is no significant difference between this year's first graders and the "typical" first graders in the district. The research hypothesis which was stated in a null form (i.e., predicting no difference between the two means) was confirmed.

Summary

1.   *T-test* is used to compare two means to determine whether the difference between them is statistically significant.

2.   *T*-test requires data measured on an **interval** or a **ratio** scale.

---

[6] **A HINT:** There is a certain level of error in any statistical decision. When we decide to retain the null hypothesis we risk making a Type II error (see Chapter 1), where we retain the null hypothesis when, in fact, it should be rejected. In our particular example, however, t-value is very small ($t = 0.53$) and our decision to retain the null hypothesis is likely to be the proper decision.

3. A **directional** hypothesis predicts which of the two means is going to be higher.

4. A **nondirectional** hypothesis predicts a difference between the two means, but does not specify which mean will be higher.

5. When using the table of **critical values**, directional hypotheses are tested using the **one-tailed** test, and nondirectional hypotheses are tested using the **two-tailed** test. When in doubt, use the two-tailed test, which is more conservative.

6. T-test can be used to compare means from: (a) two independent groups; (b) two paired (dependent) groups; and (c) a single sample and a population.

7. *T*-test for independent samples is used when the two groups whose means are being compared are independent of each other. For example, this *t*-test may be used to compare the means of experimental and control groups.

8. *T*-test for paired samples (also called *t*-test for **dependent, matched,** or **correlated** samples) is used when the means come from two sets of paired scores. For example, posttest scores may be compared to pretest scores, where both are obtained for the same group of students.

9. *T*-test for a single sample is used when the mean of a sample of individuals is compared to the mean of a population. For example, we may compare the mean grade point average (GPA) of high school students who participate in extra-curricular activities to the GPA of the total student body.

Chapter 11
ANALYSIS OF VARIANCE

Analysis of variance (ANOVA) is used to compare the means of two or more independent samples and to test whether the differences between the means are statistically significant. ANOVA, which was developed by R. A. Fisher in the early 1920s, can be thought of as an extension of the t-test for independent samples. However, the t-test can compare only two means, whereas ANOVA can compare two or more means simultaneously.

Suppose, for example, we want to compare five groups. If a t-test is used, we have to repeat it 10 times (i.e, compare the mean from group 1 with the means from groups 2, 3, 4, and 5; and the mean from group 2 with the means from groups 3, 4, and 5, and so on). There is a certain level of error every time we do a t-test, and the error is compounded as we repeat the test. The main risk is that we may make a Type I error; that is, reject the null hypothesis when in fact it is true and should be retained (see Chapter 1). However, when we use ANOVA to compare five means simultaneously, the error level can be kept at the .05 level, and thus is not higher than using a t-test one time. ANOVA, then, reduces the potential error which might be made if the researcher had used a series of t-tests and were to reject the null hypothesis based on these multiple comparisons, when in fact it should be retained. In addition, performing one ANOVA procedure is more efficient than doing a series of t-tests.

In ANOVA, the **independent variable** is the categorical variable which defines the groups being compared (e.g., instructional procedures, grade level, or marital status). The **dependent variable** is the measured variable whose means are being compared (for example, reading scores, level of job satisfaction, or blood pressure).

There are several assumptions for ANOVA: (a) the groups are independent of each other; (b) the dependent variable is measured on an interval or ratio scale; (c) the dependent variable being measured is normally distributed in the population; (d) the scores are random samples from their respective populations; and (e) the variances of the populations from which the samples were drawn are equal (the assumption of the **homogeneity of variances**). Assumptions a and b must always be satisfied. Assumption e can be tested using special tests, such as the F test in which the largest variance is divided by the smallest variance. Assumptions c and d are often difficult to satisfy in education and behavioral sciences; however, even if we cannot ascertain that random sampling was used, we can generally satisfy the requirement that the samples are not biased. ANOVA is considered a *robust* statistic which can stand some violation of these assumptions, and empirical studies show that there are no serious negative consequences if these assumptions are not met.

When only one independent variable is used in ANOVA, the procedure is called **one-way ANOVA**. When two independent variables are used, the procedure is called **two-way ANOVA**. For example, one-way ANOVA is used when we want to compare the reading scores (the dependent variable) of first graders taught reading using three instructional methods (the independent variable): phonics, whole language, and a combination of phonics-whole language. When, in addition to dividing the students into three groups based on the reading instructional method, we also divide them by gender, we would use a two-way ANOVA. This is because two independent variables (method and gender) are studied. This design allows us to further explore whether there is a difference between boys and girls within each reading instructional method. For example, we may find out that the phonics method is better for boys, while the whole language method is better for girls. In general, when more than one independent variable is used in ANOVA, the design is called a **factorial ANOVA**.

Although ANOVA is designed to compare means, it also studies *variances* which are measures of variability. In fact, in ANOVA, both variances and means play a role. Similarly, you may recall that the means were used in the computation of the variance. When we used the deviation score method to compute the variance, we first found the mean, then added the deviations (or distances) of all scores around the mean, and then divided that sum by the number of scores.[1] (See Chapter 5 for the deviation score method for computing the variance).

One-Way ANOVA

Hypotheses for One-Way ANOVA

One-way ANOVA tests the null hypothesis (H_o) which states that all the groups represent populations which have the same means. When there are three means, the null hypothesis is[2]

$$H_O : \mu_1 = \mu_2 = \mu_3$$

---

[1] **A HINT:** You may recall that in computing a *t*-test for independent samples (Chapter 10), variances were also included in the computational formula.

[2] **A HINT:** Although *samples* are studied, as with other statistical tests, we are interested in the *populations* which are represented by these samples. Therefore, in the null and alternative hypotheses, μ (the Greek letter **mu**) is used for the population means.

The alternative hypothesis, H_A (also called the research hypothesis) states that there is a statistically significant difference between at least two means. When there are three groups, the alternative hypothesis is:

$$H_A: \mu_1 \neq \mu_2 \quad \text{and/or} \quad \mu_1 \neq \mu_3 \quad \text{and/or} \quad \mu_2 \neq \mu_3$$

Conceptualizing One-Way ANOVA

ANOVA studies three types of variability which are called the **sum of squares** and are abbreviated as **SS**. They are:

1. **Within group (SS_W)** - the variability within the groups which is found by computing the variability for each group and adding these variabilities across all groups.

2. **Between** (or **among**) **groups** (SS_B or SS_A) - the average variability of the means of the groups around the total mean. The total mean is the mean of all the scores, combined.

3. **Total (SS_T)** - the variability of all the scores around the total mean.[3]

The total sum of squares is equal to the combined *within* sum of squares and the *between* sum of squares:

$$SS_T = SS_W + SS_B$$

This can be shown visually (Figure 11.1) and algebraically (see computations in the example that follows). In Figure 11.1, X_1 is

---

[3] **A HINT:** Think of it as combining the scores from all the groups to create one large group, and computing the variability of this group around the total mean.

the score of an individual in group 1; $\overline{X}_1$ is the mean of group 1; and $\overline{X}_T$ is the total mean. An inspection of this figure confirms that SS_T equals SS_W and SS_B combined.

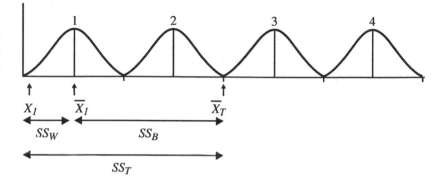

Figure 11.1 A graph showing the three sums of squares: SS_W, SS_B, and SS_T

Another way to look at the variability is to examine the distances (or deviations) of the scores from the mean. Assume we have test scores for four groups of students. Suppose the total mean ($\overline{X}_T$) is 10; the mean of group 3 ($\overline{X}_3$) is 12; and Jim (X_1), who is a member of group 3, has a score of 14 (Figure 11.2). Jim's distance from the total mean is 4 ($X_1-\overline{X}_T=14-10=4$). This distance can be partitioned into two components: Jim's distance from his group mean ($X_1-\overline{X}_3=14-12=2$) and the distance of Jim's group from the total mean ($\overline{X}_3-\overline{X}_T=12-10=2$).

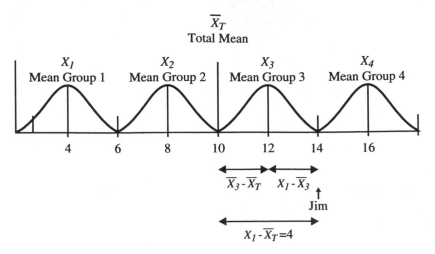

Figure 11.2 A graph showing that Jim's distance from the total mean $(X_1 - \overline{X}_T)$ is equal to his distance from his group's mean $(X_1 - \overline{X}_3)$ plus the distance of his group's mean from the total mean $(\overline{X}_3 - \overline{X}_T)$

Steps in the Computation of ANOVA

1. The first step in the computation of ANOVA is to find the three sums of squares: SS_W (within), SS_B (between), and SS_T (total).

2. The second step is to find the **variance estimates**, which are also called the **mean squares** and are abbreviated as **MS**. To do so, the sums of squares (SS) are divided by the appropriate degrees of freedom (*df*). To find the mean square within (MS_W), SS_W is divided by the appropriate *df* (df_W), which are calculated as *N-K* (the number of individuals minus the number of groups). To find the mean square between (MS_B), SS_B is divided by the appropriate degrees of freedom (df_B), which are calculated as *K*-1 (the number of groups minus 1). The degrees of freedom for within and the

degrees of freedom for between (df_W and df_B) should equal the total degrees of freedom (df_T) which are calculated as N-1 (the total number of individuals minus 1).[4] For example, when there are three groups with five individuals in each group, the degrees of freedom are:

$$df_W = N - K = 15 - 3 = 12$$

$$df_B = K - 1 = 3 - 1 = 2$$

$$df_T = N - 1 = 15 - 1 = 14$$

The formulas for MS_W and MS_B are:

$$MS_W = \frac{SS_W}{N-K} \qquad\qquad MS_B = \frac{SS_B}{K-1}$$

MS_W (also called the **error term**) can be thought of as the average variance to be expected in any normally distributed group.

3. The next computational step is to divide the between-group mean square (MS_B) by the within-group mean square (MS_W). This division results in an **F-ratio**. The formula for the F-ratio is:

$$F = \frac{MS_B}{MS_W}$$

MS_B, the numerator, increases as the differences between the group means increase; therefore, greater differences between the means also result in a higher F-ratio. Additionally, since the

---

[4] **A HINT:** If you do your computations by hand, you may want to make sure that df_W and df_B are equal to df_T.

denominator is the within-group mean square, when the groups are homogeneous and have low variances, MS_W is also small and the F-ratio is likely to be higher. Figures 11.3 and 11.4 help to clarify these points.

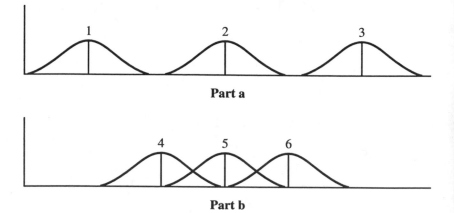

Part a

Part b

Figure 11.3 A graph showing three groups with different means and
similar variances (part a), and a graph showing three groups
with similar means and similar variances (part b)

Parts a and b in Figure 11.3 show the distributions of scores of several groups. The variances of the three groups in part a (groups 1, 2, and 3) are about the same as the variances of the three groups in part b (groups 4, 5, and 6). However, the means of the three groups in part a are farther apart from each other, compared with the means of the three groups in part b. If asked to predict which part of Figure 11.3 would yield a higher F-ratio, we would probably choose part a, where the three groups do not overlap and the means are quite different from each other. By contrast, the means of groups 4, 5, and 6 are closer to each other, and the three distributions overlap. The distances between the means are related to MS_B, which is the numerator in the computation of the F-ratio.

Part a in Figure 11.4 shows three groups (A, B, and C), and part b shows three other groups (D, E, and F). Notice that the three groups in part a have the same means as the three groups in part b, but the variances are different. The variances of the three groups depicted in part a are very low (that is, the groups are homogeneous with regard to the characteristic being measured); and the variances of the three groups depicted in part b are high, with a wide spread of scores in each group. We can predict that the F-ratio computed for the three groups in part a would probably be high and statistically significant, whereas the F-ratio computed for the three groups in part b would probably be low and not statistically significant. This prediction would be based on the knowledge that the variances are related to MS_W, the denominator in the F-ratio computation. Thus, when the group variances are lower, MS_W is lower, and we are more likely to get a significant F-ratio.

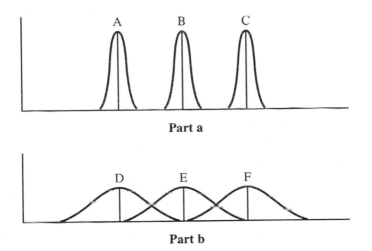

Part a

Part b

Figure 11.4 A graph showing three distributions with small variances (part a) and a graph showing three distributions with the same means as the groups in part a, by with higher variances (part b)

4. Once the F-ratio is obtained, the table of critical values for the F-distribution (Appendix Table D) is consulted to determine whether to retain or reject the null hypothesis. Retaining the null hypothesis means that the sample means are not significantly different from each other, and we consider them as coming from the same population. Rejecting the null hypothesis means that at least two sample means differ significantly from each other.

5. If the null hypothesis is rejected, the next step is to conduct a **post hoc comparison** in which all possible pairs of means are compared to each other in order to find out which pair(s) of means differ(s). When the researcher predicts which means are expected to differ *before* starting the investigation, a method of **a priori** (or **planned) comparison** is used to test this prediction. A priori comparisons are appropriate when the researcher has a sound basis for predicting the outcomes before starting the study, while post hoc comparisons are appropriate in exploratory studies. In this book we demonstrate the computations of one post hoc comparison method only.

Further Interpretation of the F-Ratio

Each of the following three graphs (Figure 11.5, parts a, b, and c) represents visually three hypothetical samples and their F-ratios.

Part a in Figure 11.5 depicts group scores on a seventh-grade reading test, from three neighboring school districts. Note that the three group distributions overlap a great deal and the means are not very different from each other. The F-ratio is probably small and not significant. Part b shows mean scores from a third-grade mathematics test given to second, third, and fourth grade classes. It is expected that the second graders would score the lowest, and that the fourth graders would score the highest. The difference between the second graders and the fourth graders is probably significant. The differences between the second and the third graders, and between the third and the fourth graders, may also be significant. Consequently, the F-ratio in this one-way ANOVA is probably significant. Part c shows mean scores on an aggression scale, given to three groups after an intervention designed to decrease aggression. The three groups are: control (C), placebo (P), and experimental (E). Note that after the intervention the experimental group had the lowest aggression mean score, followed by the placebo group, while the control group scored the highest. The difference between the experimental group and the placebo group may be significant, and quite likely, there is a significant difference between the experimental and control groups. The difference between the placebo and the control groups is probably not significant. We can speculate that in this hypothetical example, the F-ratio is probably large enough to exceed the corresponding critical value, leading us to reject the null hypothesis.

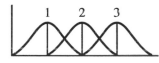

a. *F*-ratio is probably not significant (retain null)

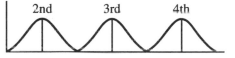

b. *F*-ratio is probably significant (reject null)

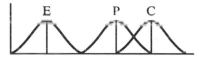

c. *F*-ratio is probably significant (reject null)

Figure 11.5 Reading mean scores of seventh-graders from three neighboring districts (part a); mathematics mean scores of second, third, and fourth graders (part b); and mean scores on an aggression scale given to three groups in an experimental study (part c)

An Example of One-Way ANOVA

Professor Learner, the statistics course instructor at Midwestern State University, wants to test four instructional methods for teaching statistics. Students who signed up to take the statistics course are assigned at random to four sections: section 1 is taught using computer-aided instruction (CAI); section 2 is taught using lectures; section 3 is taught using independent study; and section 4 is taught using cooperative learning. In this study, the instructional methods are the independent variable. Students in all four sections have to take five quizzes and a comprehensive final examination. The scores on each quiz can range from 1 to 15. To illustrate the computations of ANOVA, we choose at random the scores of five students from each section on one of the quizzes. These quiz scores are the dependent variable. With four groups, the null hypothesis (H_o) and the alternative hypothesis (H_A) are:

$$H_O : \mu_1 = \mu_2 = \mu_3 = \mu_4$$

$$H_A : \mu_i \neq \mu_j$$

The subscripts i and j can represent any two of the four groups. In other words, the alternative hypothesis predicts that there will be a significant difference between at least two of the four means.

Table 11.1 lists the scores of the randomly selected students, followed by group summary scores (e.g., ΣX, and ΣX^2). The summary scores are used in the computations of SS_T, SS_B, and SS_W.

Table 11.1   **Raw Scores and Summary Scores of Four Groups on a Statistics Quiz**

	Section				
1	2	3	4		
14	14	11	15		
15	13	10	14		
13	11	11	15		
13	13	14	14		
14	15	10	15		
Summary Scores:					**TOTAL**
ΣX 69	66	56	73	$\Sigma X_T =$	264
ΣX^2 955	880	638	1067	$\Sigma X_T^2 =$	3540
n 5	5	5	5	$N_T =$	20
$\overline{X}$ 13.8	13.2	11.2	14.6	$\overline{X}_T =$	13.2

The formulas for computing SS_T, SS_B, and SS_W are listed next, followed by the computations for our numerical example:

$$SS_T = \Sigma X_T^2 - \frac{(\Sigma X_T)^2}{N_T}$$

$$SS_B = \sum \left[\frac{(\Sigma X)^2}{n} \right] - \frac{(\Sigma X_T)^2}{N_T} =$$

$$= \left[\frac{(\Sigma X_1)^2}{n_1} + \frac{(\Sigma X_2)^2}{n_2} + \frac{(\Sigma X_3)^2}{n_3} + \frac{(\Sigma X_4)^2}{n_4} \right] - \frac{(\Sigma X_T)^2}{N_T}$$

$$SS_W = \sum [\Sigma X^2 - \frac{(\Sigma X)^2}{n}] =$$

$$= [\Sigma X_1^2 - \frac{(\Sigma X_1)^2}{n_1}] + [\Sigma X_2^2 - \frac{(\Sigma X_2)^2}{n_2}] +$$

$$+ [\Sigma X_3^2 - \frac{(\Sigma X_3)^2}{n_3}] + [\Sigma X_4^2 - \frac{(\Sigma X_4)^2}{n_4}]$$

$$SS_T = 3540 - \frac{(264)^2}{20} = 3540 - \frac{(69696)}{20} =$$

$$= 3540 - 3484.8 = 55.2$$

$$SS_B = (\frac{69^2}{5} + \frac{66^2}{5} + \frac{56^2}{5} + \frac{73^2}{5}) - (\frac{264^2}{20}) =$$

$$= (952.2 + 871.2 + 627.2 + 1065.8) - 3484.8 =$$

$$= 3516.4 - 3484.8 = 31.6$$

$$SS_W = (955 - \frac{69^2}{5}) + (880 - \frac{66^2}{5}) +$$

$$+ (638 - \frac{56^2}{5}) + (1067 - \frac{73^2}{5}) =$$

$$= (955 - 952.2) + (880 - 871.2) + (638 - 627.2) +$$

$$+ (1067 - 1065.8) = 2.8 + 8.8 + 10.8 + 1.2 = 23.6$$

$$SS_B + SS_W = SS_T$$
$$31.6 + 23.6 = 55.2$$

Our computations result in: $SS_T=55.2$, $SS_B=31.6$, and $SS_W=23.6$. The next step is to find MS_B and MS_W by dividing each SS by the appropriate df. Then, the F-ratio is found by dividing MS_B by

$$F = \frac{MS_B}{MS_W} = \frac{10.53}{1.48} = 7.14 \qquad p<.01$$

MS_W. In our example, $MS_B=10.53$; $MS_W=1.48$; and $F=7.14$.

$$MS_B = \frac{31.6}{3} = 10.53 \qquad\qquad MS_W = \frac{23.6}{16} = 1.48$$

Using Table D in the Appendix, we find the appropriate critical values. The critical level at the $p = .05$ level, with dfB of 3 and dfW of 16, is 3.24. For the $p = .01$, the critical value is 5.29. These critical values can be listed as:

$$F_{crit(.05,3,16)} = 3.24 \qquad\qquad F_{crit(.01,3,16)} = 5.29$$

Since we exceed the .01 probability level, we report the results as: $p<.01$. The significant F-ratio ($p <.01$) indicates that there is a significant difference between at least one pair of means and the null hypothesis (H_O) is rejected in favor of the alternative hypothesis (H_A). In making the decision to reject the null hypothesis, there is less than 1% chance of making a Type I error (i.e., rejecting the null hypothesis when, in fact, it should be retained).

The One-Way ANOVA Summary Table
The results of an ANOVA computation are likely to be
displayed in a summary table (Table 11.2). This table lists the sum
of squares (SS), degrees of freedom (*df*), mean squares (MS), *F*-
ratio (*F*), and the level of significance (*p* level). The results may
also be incorporated into the text, in place of a table, listing the *F*-
ratio, degrees of freedom for numerator (*df*B) and denominator
(*df*W) as follows: $F_{(dfB,dfW)}$. The level of significance (*p* level) may
also be indicated in the text. The general format of the ANOVA
summary table is:

**Table 11.2   The General Format of the One-Way ANOVA
Summary Table**

Source	SS	*df*	MS	*F*	*p*
Between	SS_B	*K*-1	MS_B	*F*-ratio	<.05>
Within	SS_W	*N-K*	MS_W		
Total	SS_T	*N*-1			

The results of our computational example are presented in
Table 11.3, which follows the format for an ANOVA summary
table (as shown in Table 11.2).

**Table 11.3   One-Way ANOVA Summary Table for the
Data in Table 11.1**

Source	SS	*df*	MS	*F*	*p*
Between	31.6	3	10.53	7.14	<.01
Within	23.5	16	1.48		
Total	55.2	19			

After obtaining a significant F-ratio, our next step is to conduct a post hoc comparison to find out which means are significantly different from each other.

Post Hoc Comparisons

There are several methods for post hoc comparisons; however, in this book we will use only the **Tukey method** which is also called **honestly significant difference** (HSD). The HSD value tells us what the difference between a pair of means should be in order to describe the means as significantly different from each other. Any difference that exceeds the HSD value is considered statistically significant. To simplify the computations, we will use Tukey's HSD method for equal group size. The formula for this HSD is:

$$HSD = Q_{(dfW, K)} \sqrt{\frac{MS_W}{n}}$$

Where $Q =$ a value obtained from the Studentized Range Statistic table (Appendix Table E)

$df_W =$ the within groups degrees of freedom

$K -$ the number of groups (or means)

$MS_W =$ the within groups mean square

$n =$ the number of people in a group

The first step is to consult a table called the Studentized Range Statistic (Appendix Table E). The table contains Q values for the .05 and .01 level of significance. The rows list the degrees of freedom within (df_W) and the columns list the number of groups (K). In our example, df_W are 16, and K is 4. The corresponding

Q value for the .05 level is 4.05, and for the .01 level it is 5.19. According to Table 11.3, MS_W is 1.48 and n is 5.   The computations of the HSD value at the .05 and .01 level of significance are:

$$HSD_{(.05)} = 4.05_{(16,4)} \sqrt{\frac{1.48}{5}} = 4.05 \sqrt{0.295} =$$

$$= 4.05 (0.54) = 2.19$$

$$HSD_{(.01)} = 5.19_{(16,4)} \sqrt{\frac{1.48}{5}} = 5.19 \sqrt{0.295} =$$

$$= 5.19 (0.54) = 2.80$$

Once we find the HSD value, we set up a table in which we list all the means in ascending order, and subtract the lower mean from the higher mean at each intersection (Table 11.4). For example:

$$MEAN_2 - MEAN_3 = 13.2 - 11.2 = 2.00$$

Table 11.4   Means of Four Groups: Post Hoc Comparison

	$\bar{X}_3=11.2$	$\bar{X}_2=13.2$	$\bar{X}_1=13.8$	$\bar{X}_4=14.6$
$\bar{X}_3 = 11.2$	--	2.00	2.60*	3.40**
$\bar{X}_2 = 13.2$		--	0.60	1.40
$\bar{X}_1 = 13.8$			--	0.80
$\bar{X}_4 = 14.6$				--

* $p < .05$ ** $p < .01$

According to this table, the difference between the means of sections 1 and 3 is significant at the .05 level, and the difference between the means of sections 3 and 4 is significant at the .01 level. No other means are significantly different from each other. Figure 11.6 depicts the four groups:

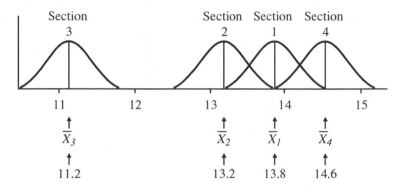

Figure 11.6 A graph illustrating the data in Table 11.4

The group using the cooperative learning method (section 4) scored the highest, followed closely by the CAI group (section 1), then the lecture group (section 2). The independent study group (section 1) scored the lowest. It scored 2.00 points below section 2, 2.60 points below section 1, and 3.40 points below section 4. These results may help Professor Learner decide which instructional methods should be used in the statistics course.

Two-Way ANOVA

Conceptualizing Two-Way ANOVA

One-way ANOVA is designed to study the relationship between *one* independent variable and a dependent variable. The two-way ANOVA studies the relationship between *two* independent variables and a dependent variable. The independent variables are also called **main effects**. When there are two or more independent variables, the design is called a **factorial analysis of variance**. One advantage of the factorial ANOVA is that it can reveal an *interaction* between independent variables, which is not apparent when a series of one-way ANOVA tests is conducted. To illustrate this point, let's look at the example which was used to demonstrate the computation of the one-way ANOVA.

Four different instructional methods were tested in four sections of a college statistics course. Students who registered to take the course were assigned at random to one of the four sections. The means on a quiz administered to students in all four sections were compared to each other, using one-way ANOVA. Suppose we want to further divide the students in each group by their major in college, by ability level, or by gender. It is possible to conduct another one-way ANOVA to compare, for example, the quiz scores of psychology students in all four instructional methods to the scores of their classmates who major in history. However, instead of doing two one-way ANOVA tests, one to compare the four methods and one to compare the two majors, we can do a two-way ANOVA. The two-way ANOVA allows us to compare simultaneously the method effect, the college major effect, and the effect of the interaction of the method and the major on the students' quiz scores. For example, psychology students may score higher using one method, whereas history students may do better using another method.

The total variation in a two-way ANOVA is partitioned into two main sources:

1. The **within**-group variation

2. The **between**-group variation, which is further partitioned into three components:

   a. the variation among the row means
   b. the variation among the column means
   c. the variation due to interaction

The sum of squares and the mean squares are computed for the within group, the two main effects (the independent variables), and the interaction.

Hypotheses for Two-Way ANOVA

Two-way analysis of variance tests three hypotheses about differences between the row variable, the column variable, and the interaction of these two independent variables (or factors). The three null hypotheses in our example are:

$H_{O(method)}$:   In the population, the means for all four methods are the same.

$H_{O(major)}$:   In the population, the means for the two majors are the same.

$H_{O(interaction)}$: In the population, there is no interaction between method and major.

Thus, a separate F-ratio is calculated for each of the hypotheses. These F-ratios are found by dividing each of the three mean squares (the mean square of the row variable, the mean square of the column variable, and the mean square of the interaction) by the within mean square.

Graphing the Interaction

It is often useful to graph interactions to study them further. Suppose, for example, we want to increase the attention span (the dependent variable) of third and sixth graders using two behavior modification methods. The grade level is one independent variable, and the behavior modification method is the second independent variable. Figure 11.7 shows two possible outcomes: the lines intersect if the interaction is significant (part a), and the lines are parallel if the interaction is not significant (part b).

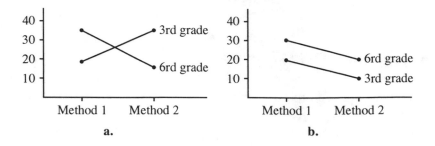

Figure 11.7 A graph showing a statistically significant interaction (part a) and a graph showing interaction that is not statistically significant (part b)

Part a of Figure 11.7 shows an interaction of grade level and method. Method 1 was more effective with the sixth graders, and method 2 was more effective with the third graders. Part b shows no interaction effect. Method 1 was more effective for both the third and the sixth graders, and method 2 was less effective for both grade levels. In addition, the sixth graders scored higher than the third graders using either method 1 or method 2.

The interaction may be significant even if the two lines do not intersect, as long as they are not parallel. The four means listed in Table 11.5 and the interaction which is graphed in Figure 11.8 show a significant interaction, although the two lines do not intersect. In this hypothetical example, the two independent variables are, as before, grade level and behavior modification method, and the dependent variable is the students' attention span. The figure shows that group A performed better using method 1, compared with method 2; while group B scored higher using method 2, compared with method 1.

Table 11.5   Means of Two Groups Using Two Different Behavior Modification Methods

	Method 1	Method 2
Group A	20	15
Group B	25	35

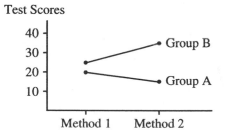

Figure 11.8 A graph of the data in Table 11.5 showing a significant interaction where the lines do not intersect

There are two types of interaction: (a) ordinal, where the lines do not intersect (see Figure 11.8); and (b) disordinal, where the lines intersect (see Figure 11.7, part a).

When, in addition to having a significant interaction, the two main effects (the row variable and the column variable) are also significant, it may be difficult to interpret the results. Figure 11.9 illustrates another hypothetical example of interaction, showing the means of two groups, A and B, and two methods, 1 and 2. As you can see, the interaction is significant (the lines cross), and overall, group A scored higher than group B. However, this was true only when method 2 was used, as group B scored higher than group A when method 1 was used. We can speculate that in addition to a significant F-ratio for the interaction, the two F-tests for main effects of methods and groups are also significant.

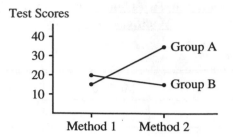

Figure 11.9 A graph showing a significant
interaction and significant main effects.

The Two-Way ANOVA Summary Table

The results of the computations of two-way ANOVA are
presented in a summary table, similar to that used for presenting
the results of one-way ANOVA (see Table 11.2). The two factors
(e.g., the groups and the methods) are called the **main effects** and
each is associated with an F-ratio. Similarly, the interaction is
analyzed using its own F-ratio. The computations of the degrees
of freedom associated with each of the three F tests are presented
in Table 11.6.

Table 11.6   Two-Way ANOVA Summary Table

Source	SS	*df*	MS	F	P
Main Effects					
Factor 1 (row)	SS_R	no. of levels - 1	MS_R	F_R	
Factor 2 (column)	SS_C	no. of levels - 1	MS_C	F_C	
Interaction	SS_{RxC}	$df_{row} \times df_{col.}$	MS_{RxC}	F_{RxC}	
Within Groups	SS_W	$N - K$	MS_W		
Total	SS_T	$N - 1$			

An Example of a Two-Way ANOVA

Two fourth-grade teachers in Lincoln School want to know if the gender of the main character in a story makes a difference in their students' interest in the story. The two fourth-grade classes are similar to each other in their student make-up and each includes 14 girls and 14 boys.[5] After reading their assigned stories, each class completes an interest inventory designed to measure interest in the stories read. Table 11.7 presents the scores of all the students, as well as the groups' means.

If we inspect the row means, we may conclude that there are no gender differences, because the boys and the girls have almost identical mean scores (16.46 and 16.39, respectively). It appears that the gender of the story's main character does not affect the fourth graders' level of interest in the story, as the two column means are the same (both are 16.43). However, boys and girls *did* react differently toward the two stories, as can be seen by inspecting the means in Table 11.7 and by graphing the interaction (Figure 11.10).

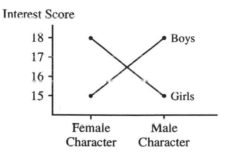

Figure 11.10 A graph showing the data in Table 11.7

---

[5] **A HINT:** Although ANOVA assumes that the groups are random samples from their respective populations, in studies conducted in a typical school this assumption may not be fully met. As mentioned before, empirical studies have shown that ANOVA can be conducted under such conditions without seriously affecting the results, especially when the group sizes are similar.

Table 11.7   Scores and Means of Boys and Girls Reading Stories
With Male Versus Female Main Characters

Type of Story			
	Female as Main Character	Male as Main Character	Total
Boys	14 13 17 10 18 16 15 15 15 16 14 17 16 15 $\bar{X}=15.07$	19 17 18 20 18 17 16 18 20 19 18 17 16 17 $\bar{X}=17.86$	$\bar{X}=16.46$
Girls	17 20 19 19 20 18 16 15 17 19 18 16 17 18 $\bar{X}=17.79$	18 14 16 15 14 13 17 15 14 14 13 16 15 16 $\bar{X}=15.00$	$\bar{X}=16.39$
Total	$\bar{X}=16.43$	$\bar{X}=16.43$	

The detailed computations of the three F-ratios are not included in this book.[6] The data presented in Table 11.8 were analyzed by a computer, and a discussion of the results follows.[7]

Table 11.8   Two-Way ANOVA Summary Table

Source	SS	df	MS	F
Main Effects				
Gender	0.07	1	0.07	0.03
Type of Character	0.00	1	0.00	0.00
Interaction	108.64	1	108.64	43.13*
Within	131.00	52	2.52	
Total	239.71	55	4.36	

*$p<.0001$

If we had conducted two one-way ANOVA tests instead of the two-way ANOVA, we might have concluded the following: (a) the gender of the main character in the story does *not* make a difference (nonsignificant F-ratio for the columns); and (b) there is no difference in the level of interest in the stories exhibited by boys and girls (nonsignificant F-ratio for rows). However, upon inspecting the means in Table 11.7, the interaction diagram in Figure 11.10, and the level of statistical significance in Table 11.8, it becomes clear that there *is* a difference between boys and girls in their level of interest toward the two stories. The boys are more interested in a story with a male character, and the girls are more

---

[6] **A HINT:** It is very easy to do a two-way ANOVA on the computer (as opposed to doing the computations by hand, which is tedious and time-consuming). Because computers are readily available today, we decided not to include the formulas and the computations for two-way ANOVA.

[7] **A HINT:** The "Within" (i.e., within groups) listed under the "Source" column is also called **Residual** or **Error**.

interested in a story with a female main character. If this were a real study, instead of a fictitious one, the implications for educators would have been that the selection of stories should be made carefully, taking into consideration the gender of the main character in the story.

Summary

1. **The one-way analysis of variance** (ANOVA) can be thought of as an extension of t-test for independent samples, used when there are two or more independent groups.

2. The **independent variable** is the categorical variable which defines the groups whose means are being compared. The **dependent variable** is the variable being measured whose means are being compared.

3. There are several assumptions for applying ANOVA, discussed at the beginning of this chapter.

4. When one independent variable is used, the design is called a **one-way ANOVA**; when two independent variables are used, the design is called a **two-way ANOVA**. The general name for designs with two or more independent variables is **factorial ANOVA**.

5. The **null hypothesis** (H_o) in a one-way ANOVA states that there is no significant difference between the means; the **alternative hypothesis** (H_A) states that at least two means differ significantly from each other.

6. The **variability** in a one-way ANOVA is divided into three sums of squares (SS): the **within** groups sum of squares (SS_W), the **between** groups sum of squares (SS_B), and the **total** sum of square (SS_T).

7. SS_B and SS_W are divided by their corresponding *df* to obtain the **mean square between** (MS_B) and **mean square within** (MS_W).

8. The computations of ANOVA involve several steps:
    a. computing the sums of squares (SS_W, SS_B, and SS_T)
    b. computing the mean squares (MS) for between groups (MS_B) and within groups (MS_W) by dividing the sum of squares by the corresponding *df*
    c. dividing MS_B by MS_W to find the *F*-ratio
    d. checking the table of critical values to decide whether to retain or reject the null hypothesis
    e. conducting a **post hoc comparison** if the null hypothesis was rejected to ascertain which means differ significantly from each other.

9. The results of the ANOVA analysis are usually presented in a **summary table**.

10. When two independent variables (or factors) are being compared simultaneously, the **two-way ANOVA** is used. These independent variables are also called **main effects**. Two-way ANOVA is done to enable us to study the **interaction** of the two factors, and the effect of each of the two factors on the dependent variable.

11. In order to better understand an interaction, it is often useful to graph it. A nonsignificant interaction is represented by **parallel** lines and a significant interaction is represented by **nonparallel** lines.

Chapter 12
CHI SQUARE

The **chi square** test, represented by χ^2 (the Greek letter chi, squared), is applied to discrete data (i.e., nominal, categorical data). The units of measurement are frequency counts rather than scores. The chi square was developed by Karl Pearson (who also developed the Pearson product moment correlation) in 1900, in order to measure how well observed data fit a theoretical distribution of data. The chi square belongs to a group of statistical methods called **nonparametric**, or distribution-free. These statistical tests can be applied to data that do not meet certain assumptions (e.g., being measured on an interval or ratio scale, or being normally distributed) which are required when using other tests, such as the t-test. The independent variables in chi square have at least two levels (or categories). For example, the variable *gender* has two levels, male and female. The variable *political party* may have four levels: Republican, Democrat, Independent, and Other. The categories may be created by using ordinal scale data (e.g., high, middle, and low socioeconomic status); or they may be created by using a nominal scale, which has no particular order (e.g., rural, urban, and suburban school districts).

The chi square is used extensively in analyzing questionnaire data, where groups or responses are assigned a numerical code. For example, the gender of the respondents might be coded as "1" if they are male and "2" if they are female; or "no" may be coded as "1" and "yes" may be coded as "2." When numbers are used to code categorical data, they comprise a nominal scale. (See Chapter 1 for a discussion of measurement scales.)

There are two types of frequencies in chi square: observed and expected. The **observed frequencies** are based on real (empirical) observation and on head count. An example of observed frequencies is the number of people who responded "yes" or "no" to a particular question. These observed frequencies are compared with **expected frequencies** which are theoretical or based on prior knowledge.[1] The chi square is used to test whether there is a significant difference between the observed frequencies and the frequencies which are expected when the null hypothesis is true. The total number of expected frequencies has to equal the total number of observed frequencies.

Significant difference between observed frequencies + frequencies expected when null H is true

Assumptions Required for Chi Square

1. The observations should be *independent* of each other. A person's response cannot be counted in more than one category, and the total number of observed frequencies should not exceed the number of subjects/participants. For example, a person may not be asked on two different occasions to respond to the same question, as if two people each responded once.

2. The data must be in the form of *frequencies*. The total number of the observed frequencies must equal the total number of the expected frequencies.

3. The categories, especially those that comprise an ordinal or an interval scale, should be created in some *logical*, defensible way. For example, suppose one of the variables is level of income, and we want to divide it into three categories: High (H), Middle (M),

---

[1] **A HINT:** The process for deriving the expected frequencies is included in the explanation of each type of chi square which follows.

and Low (L). The criteria used to establish the categories should be chosen carefully. Income is a continuous variable, so we need to establish logical cutoff points to separate the three categories.

Using Chi Square

The chi square statistic can be used in two main research situations:

1. In studies where there is *one* variable (one-way classification), and the expected frequencies are of *equal* or *unequal* probability. This chi square test is also called a **Test of Goodness of Fit**, because it tests how well the distribution of the observed frequencies fits the distribution of the expected frequencies.

2. In studies where there are *two* variables (two-way classification).   This chi square is also called a **Test of Independence**.

One Variable Chi Square: Goodness of Fit Test

Equal Expected Frequencies

The observed frequencies, as always, are based on empirical data; that is, on observation. We collect data by recording the number of occurrences in each category. For example, we can use chi square to test whether a coin is fair by tossing the coin 100 times and recording as observed frequencies the number of heads and tails. The expected frequencies are based on the assumption that the coin is fair; thus, half of the time it should land heads, and half of the time, tails. The null hypothesis states that the coin is fair and, consequently, would land as many times heads as tails.

Suppose we toss a coin 100 times, and record 55 heads and 45 tails. If the coin is fair (the null hypothesis is true), we would expect 50 heads and 50 tails. Is the coin biased or fair? As with the *t*-test and other statistics, we cannot eyeball these numbers and determine whether the difference between 55 and 45 is large enough to indicate a biased coin, or whether this difference is small enough to have occurred purely by chance. The χ^2 statistic can be used to determine whether the coin is biased. The formula for χ^2 is:

$$\chi^2 = \sum [\frac{(O - E)^2}{E}]$$

Where $\chi^2 =$ the chi square statistic

$O =$ the observed frequencies for each cell

$E =$ the expected frequencies for each cell

Each pair of observed frequencies and expected frequencies is called a cell. To compute χ^2, for each cell we first compute $(O-E)^2$, divided by E. We then add the results of these computations to obtain the χ^2 value. In this coin tossing example, we repeat the first step twice, once for heads and once for tails (Table 12.1). The computations result in a χ^2 value of 1.00.

Once the chi square value is computed, we follow the same steps as with the *t*-test. The next step, then, is to test for statistical significance using the table of critical values for chi square (Appendix Table F). The degrees of freedom (*df*) are the number of categories, or levels, minus 1. In our example, the variable has two levels, heads and tails, resulting in a *df* of 1 (2-1=1). As before, unless told otherwise, start by checking the critical value under *p*=.05 level of significance. The critical value across from a *df* of 1 and under a *p* of .05 is 3.841. The obtained χ^2 value of 1.00 does not exceed this critical value; therefore, we retain the null hypothesis. Our conclusion is that the coin is fair, even though when we tossed it 100 times it landed heads more times than tails. The difference between heads and tails is small enough to have happened by chance alone, and is probably due to a random error rather than a systematic error (i.e., a biased coin).

Table 12.1   Observed and Equal Expected Frequencies for Heads and Tails

	O (observed)	E (expected)	$\dfrac{(O-E)^2}{E}$
Heads	55	50	$\dfrac{(55-50)^2}{50} = \dfrac{25}{50} = 0.50$
Tails	45	50	$\dfrac{(45-50)^2}{50} = \dfrac{25}{50} = 0.50$
TOTAL	**100**	**100**	$\chi^2 = 1.00$

Next is another example of a one-variable chi square with equal expected frequencies. The students in Mr. Smart's fifth-grade class noticed that many of them had birthdays in the spring. They wanted to find out if indeed more babies are born in any particular season, or if there is an equal number of births in each of the four seasons (i.e., the number of babies born is independent of the season). The fifth graders surveyed 100 students, chosen at random from all the students in their school, and classified them into those born in the Fall (September, October, November); Winter (December, January, February); Spring (March, April, May); and Summer (June, July, August). The expected frequencies in each season are 25 (i.e., one-fourth of 100), representing the null hypothesis which states that there is no difference between the seasons. The null hypothesis (H_0) is:

$$H_O : O_{FALL} = O_{WINTER} = O_{SPRING} = O_{SUMMER}$$

Table 12.2   Observed and Equal Expected Frequencies for the Number of Students Born in Each of the Four Seasons

	O	E	$\dfrac{(O - E)^2}{E}$	
Fall	30	25	$\dfrac{(30-25)^2}{25}$	= 1.00
Winter	10	25	$\dfrac{(10-25)^2}{25}$	= 9.00
Spring	35	25	$\dfrac{(35-25)^2}{25}$	= 4.00
Summer	25	25	$\dfrac{(25-25)^2}{25}$	= 0.00
TOTAL	**100**	**100**	χ^2	**= 14.00**

The computation of chi square is carried out as before. For each cell (i.e., a pair of O and E) we compute:

$$\frac{(O-E)^2}{E}$$

With four levels, we repeat the computation four times, then add up the result of the computations for each level to get the χ^2 value.

The next step is to compare the obtained χ^2 value of 14.00 to the appropriate critical value. This is an example of a one-variable chi square, which has four levels, the seasons. Thus, df=3 (4-1=3). Our obtained χ^2 value of 14.00 exceeds the critical value with df=3 and p=.05 which is 7.815 (written as $\chi^2_{crit(.05,3)}$=7.815). (See Appendix Table F.) We also exceed the value under p=.02 (9.837) and p=.01 (11.341). However, our obtained value of 14.00 does not exceed the critical value under p=.001 which is 16.268. Therefore, we report the last p value we did exceed. Since we exceeded p=.01, rather than just equal it, we report the p value as $p < .01$.[2]   Because we exceeded the critical value, the null hypothesis is rejected. That is, the hypothesis stating that the same number of children are born in each of the four seasons is rejected. We conclude that there is a relationship between the season and the number of children born in a particular season. Specifically, after inspecting the data in Table 12.2, we can conclude that more children than expected were born in the spring, and less than expected in the winter.

A comparison of the computations of chi square in Tables 12.1 and 12.2 helps to explain why the first chi square was not statistically significant, while the second one was significant. The size of the χ^2 value can be traced to the formula:

$$\chi^2 = \sum \frac{(O - E)^2}{E}$$

The numerator is the difference between the *observed* and *expected* frequencies.   In Table 12.1, there are very small differences between the observed and expected frequencies in each cell, resulting in small numerators and a low chi square value. On the other hand, when there is a large discrepancy between the

---

[2] **A HINT:** Remember that in the table of critical values the p values get smaller as you move to the right. In this example, we passed p=.01, but did not quite make it to p=.001. Thus, we report $p < .01$ (somewhere between .01 and .001).

observed and expected frequencies, the numerator is large, and, in turn, so is the chi square value. This is what has happened in Table 12.2, especially for Winter and Spring.

Unequal Expected Frequencies

This type of chi square is used primarily to compare similarities and differences between a group's observed frequencies and some other criteria.   The criteria may be based on the population distribution, and they serve as the expected frequencies.   The researcher has to know the expected frequencies *a priori* (ahead of time) in order to conduct this type of chi square analysis.   An example may help to illustrate this chi square.

The School of Education in Teachers College was accused by the local media of grade inflation. Reporters contended that too many grades of A and B were given to undeserving students. The Dean of the school argued that the distribution of grades given to students in the School of Education was similar to the distribution in other similar institutions. The chi square statistic is selected to analyze the data and compare the distribution of grades in the School of Education (observed frequencies) with the grades in other colleges (expected frequencies) (Table 12.3). The null hypothesis states that there is no difference in the distribution of grades between the School Of Education and other similar institutions. If the two distributions of observed and expected frequencies are similar, the resulting chi square would be small, thus leading the researchers to retain the null hypothesis. (As was discussed before, in order to be able to conduct this type of chi square, the researcher has to have a priori knowledge about the distribution of the expected frequencies.)

The critical value of χ^2 at $p=.05$ and *df* of 4 is 9.488 ($\chi^2_{crit(.05,4)}$ = 9.488). (See Appendix Table F.) Our obtained value of 5.25 does not exceed the critical value, leading us to retain the null hypothesis.   Further inspection of the data shows that in comparison with other similar institutions, more grades of A and B and fewer grades of D and F were given in the School of Education.   However, these differences are not statistically significant and do not indicate a great departure from the "norm." The Dean may still want to review the grading process in the school, as they seem to differ somewhat from the standards in other colleges.

Table 12.3   **Observed and Unequal Expected Frequencies for Five Letter Grades**

Grade	O	E	$\frac{(O - E)^2}{E}$	
A	16	10	$\frac{(16-10)^2}{10}$	= 3.60
B	22	20	$\frac{(22-20)^2}{20}$	= 0.20
C	38	40	$\frac{(38-40)^2}{40}$	= 0.10
D	17	20	$\frac{(17-20)^2}{20}$	= 0.45
F	7	10	$\frac{(7-10)^2}{10}$	= 0.90
TOTAL	100	100	$\chi^2 = 5.25$	

Chi Square for Two Variables: Test of Independence

The second type of chi square is used to test whether *two* independent variables are related to, or are independent of, each other.

For example, a researcher may want to investigate whether there is a difference in the political party affiliation between teachers and parents in the school district. The researcher may survey 100 teachers and 100 parents, asking them to indicate whether they are Democrat, Republican, or Independent.[3] The responses of all participants are then tallied and arranged in a 2x3 ("two by three") table, as follows (Table 12.4):

Table 12.4   Observed Frequencies: Teacher and Parent Survey About Political Parties Affiliation

	Democrats	Republicans	Independents	TOTAL
Teachers	60	35	5	100
Parents	50	45	5	100
TOTAL	110	80	10	200

The null hypothesis states that political party affiliation is independent of group membership; i.e., there is no difference in the political affiliation distribution between the teachers and the parents. The degrees of freedom for a two-variable chi square are calculated as the number of rows minus 1, multiplied by the number of columns minus 1: (Row - 1)(Column - 1). In our example, there are 2 rows and 3 columns, so df are 2 (df=[2-1][3-1]=2).

The most common tables in chi square are those that have two levels in each of the two variables (e.g., boys/girls and yes/no). These are called 2x2 ("two by two") tables, or contingency tables. Next, we use an

---

[3] **A HINT:** When one variable is group membership (e.g., boys and girls), and the other variable is the responses of the group members (e.g., "yes" or "no"), the groups are usually recorded as rows and the responses are presented in the columns.

example to take you through several of the steps in the computations of chi square using data presented in a 2x2 table. For this example, suppose a group of 80 regular students and 90 special education students were asked to respond to the following statement: "I believe my classmates like me" by circling "yes" or "no."   Table 12.5 shows how they responded (the observed frequencies):

Table 12.5   Observed Frequencies: Regular and Special Education Students and Their Responses to the Statement: "I Believe My Classmates Like Me"

	Yes	No	TOTAL
Regular Students	62	18	80
Special Ed. Students	57	33	90
TOTAL	119	51	170

Grand Total

Even without conducting any statistical test, it is clear that the majority of students in both groups perceive their classmates to like them. But is that perception significantly stronger in one group compared with the other one? As before, we cannot simply eyeball the data and come up with a conclusion.

The expected frequencies are based on the null hypothesis which states that there is no relationship between the group membership ("Regular" vs. "Special Education") and the students' perceptions. In other words, the null hypothesis states that the two variables (group membership and perception) are independent of each other. Table 12.6 lists the observed and expected frequencies, and the totals. (The detailed computations of the *expected* frequencies are presented at the end of this chapter.)

Table 12.6 Observed and Expected Frequencies of Regular and Special Education Students and Their Responses to the Statement: I Believe My Classmates Like Me"

| | Yes | | No | | |
Group	Observed	Expected	Observed	Expected	Total
Regular Students	62	56	18	24	**80**
Spec. Ed Students	57	63	33	27	**90**

As before, for each cell we compute: $\dfrac{(O - E)^2}{E}$

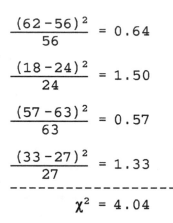

$$\frac{(62-56)^2}{56} = 0.64$$

$$\frac{(18-24)^2}{24} = 1.50$$

$$\frac{(57-63)^2}{63} = 0.57$$

$$\frac{(33-27)^2}{27} = 1.33$$

$$----------------$$

$$\chi^2 = 4.04$$

After obtaining the χ^2, we consult the table of critical values (see Appendix Table F).   Degrees of freedom are calculated as: $(2-1)(2-1)=1$.   Our obtained χ^2 value of 4.04 exceeds the critical value under p of .05 and 1 *df* ($\chi^2{}_{\text{crit}(.05,1)}=3.81$), but not the value under $p=.02$ and 1 *df* ($\chi^2{}_{\text{crit}(.02,1)}=5.41$).   Therefore, we report the results of this chi square test to be significant at $p <.05$ and reject the null hypothesis. The differences in the responses of the two groups of students are too large to have occurred purely by chance. We conclude that although in both groups the majority of students feel their classmates like them, the percent of regular education students responding positively to the question posed is higher than that of the special education students. The results of our study suggest that students' responses may depend on their group membership.

Using Percentages in Chi Square

In computing chi square, the frequencies, both observed and expected, may be presented as percentages instead of actual head counts. However, a chi square value which is obtained by using percentages in the calculations needs to be corrected in order to reflect the actual sample size. The chi square value that should be reported is the corrected chi square value. When the sample size is smaller than 100, the corrected chi square will be lower than the one obtained from calculations with percentages; and when the sample size is bigger than 100, the corrected chi square will be higher than that obtained from calculations using percentages. The correction for sample size is done by multiplying the chi square value which was obtained based on percentages by sample size (n), and dividing by 100. The formula is:

$$\chi^2_{corrected} = \frac{(\chi^2_{obtained})\,(n)}{100}$$

Where $\chi^2_{corrected}$ = the corrected χ^2

   $\chi^2_{obtained}$ = the obtained χ^2

   n = the sample size

For example, assume we have a sample size of 70 converted to 100% to do our computations, and we come up with χ^2 value of 10.00. The corrected χ^2 is calculated as follows:

$$\chi^2_{corrected} = \frac{(\chi^2_{obtained})\ (70)}{100} =$$

$$= \frac{(10.00)\ (70)}{100} = \frac{700}{100} = 7.00$$

Or, for example, if a χ^2 of 10.00 was obtained from a sample of 400 using percentages, the corrected χ^2 should be:

$$\chi^2_{corrected} = \frac{(10.00)\ (400)}{100} = \frac{4000}{100} = 40.00$$

The correction applies to all types of chi square (one-way classification as well as two-way classification). Since you are most likely to use computers in order to find the chi square value, it is probably a good idea to use the actual head count. This way, no correction will be needed.

Sample Size

When the expected frequencies are small and approach zero, the χ^2 value tends to be inflated, leading to a rejection of the null hypothesis when it should, in fact, be retained. Thus, we run the risk of making a Type I error (see Chapter 1). For 2x2 tables, when at least one expected frequency is less than 5, most textbooks suggest using **Yates' correction**, which yields smaller chi square values.[4] However, recent research has demonstrated that this correction may cause an overcorrection, and some textbooks

---

[4] **A HINT:** Some textbooks take a more conservative approach and recommend using Yates' correction when the number of expected frequency is *not higher than* 10.

question whether Yates' correction should be used.   To avoid having too few observations in a cell, similar categories may be combined.   For example, suppose we are coding data from a questionnaire with a response scale of Strongly Agree (SA), Agree (A), Disagree (D), and Strongly Disagree (SD), and the sample size is small.   To create cells with a sufficient number of observations, the responses of SA may be combined with A, and SD responses may be combined with D.

An excessively large sample size should also be avoided because it tends to detect small, unimportant differences and identify them as statistically significant.

Computation of Expected Frequencies for Chi Square with Two Variables

The detailed computation of the expected frequencies for chi square with two variables is presented next.   However, with computers readily available, it is unlikely that you will need to compute these by hand!   The data used to demonstrate the computations (Table 12.7) are the same as those presented in Table 12.5.

Table 12.7   Observed Frequencies of Regular and Special Education Students and Their Responses to a Question (Same Data as in Table 12.5)

	Yes	No	TOTAL
Regular Students	62	18	80
Special Ed. Students	57	33	90
TOTAL	119	51	170

⇑
Grand Total

We label the cells as A, B, C, and D, as follows:

A	B
C	D

To find the expected frequencies, we first compute the observed totals for rows (R) and for columns (C). Next, we calculate the grand total which is the combined number of observed frequencies. In this example, the grand total is 170 which would be obtained either by adding up the row totals or by adding up the column totals. Next, to find the expected frequency (E) for each cell, we multiply the total for that cell's row by the column's total for that cell, and divide the product by the grand total. The formula for the expected frequency for each cell is:

$$E_{cell} = \frac{(Total\ Row)(Total\ Column)}{Grand\ Total}$$

Next, we demonstrate the computation of the expected frequencies for cells A, B, C, and D, using the data in Table 12.7

$$E_{(cell\ A)} = \frac{(80)(119)}{170} = 56 \qquad E_{(cell\ B)} = \frac{(80)(51)}{170} = 24$$

$$E_{(cell\ C)} = \frac{(90)(119)}{170} = 63 \qquad E_{(cell\ D)} = \frac{(90)(51)}{170} = 27$$

Once the expected frequencies are calculated, we proceed as before (see the computations which follow Table 12.6).

Summary

1. The **chi square** (χ^2) procedure is applied to discrete, categorical data, where the units of measurement are frequency counts.

2. The chi square is considered a **nonparametric**, or **assumption-free**, statistic. It is used extensively in analyzing questionnaire data.

3. There are two types of frequencies in chi square: observed and expected. The **observed** frequencies, which are based on empirical data, are compared with the **expected** frequencies, which are theoretical or based on *a priori* knowledge. The observed and expected frequencies can be expressed as actual head counts or as percentages.

4. The chi square assumptions are: (a) the observations are **independent** of each other; (b) the data are in a **frequency** form; and (c) the categories are created in some **logical** way.

5. The chi square is used in two types of situations: (a) when there is one variable (the **goodness of fit test**); and (b) when there are two variables (the **test of independence**).

6. The chi square with one variable may have either equal expected frequencies; or unequal expected frequencies, which are known *a priori* (ahead of time) and are provided by the researcher.

7. The chi square for two variables is used to test whether two variables are related to, or are independent of, each other. Each of the two variables has to have at least two levels (e.g., male/female, true/false, above/below).

8.   The expected frequencies in chi square for two variables are
     based on the null hypothesis which states that there is no
     relationship between the two variables (e.g., no relationship
     between group membership, male vs. female; and their
     responses, true vs. false).

9.   Chi square is computed using the formula:

$$\chi^2 = \sum \frac{(O - E)^2}{E}$$

10. Once the chi square value is computed, it is compared with
     the appropriate critical value. If the obtained value *exceeds*
     that critical value, the null hypothesis is rejected. If the
     obtained value *does not exceed* the critical value, the null
     hypothesis is retained.

11. When percentages are used in place of an actual head count
     (i.e., observations), the obtained chi square should be
     corrected to reflect the fact that percentages were used. The
     corrected chi square value is the one reported.

12. When the expected frequencies are very small, we run the
     risk of rejecting the null hypothesis when, in fact, it should
     be retained (Type I error).

Part Six

RELIABILITY
AND VALIDITY

Chapter 13
RELIABILITY

The term *reliable*, when used to describe a person, usually means that this person is dependable, consistent, and trustworthy. Similarly, a reliable measure is expected to provide consistent and accurate results. If we use a reliable measure over and over again to measure physical traits, the same or very similar results should be obtained each time. For example, when we repeatedly use a precise scale to measure weight, we are likely to obtain the same weight time after time. However, when dealing with the affective domain (e.g., test anxiety or motivation) or even with the cognitive domain (e.g., academic achievement), the performance of individuals tends to change and be much less consistent. Factors such as moods, pressure, fatigue, and anxiety tend to affect performance. Therefore, even with a reliable measure, it is hard to achieve a high level of consistency between measures.

Since this book is intended for educators, our discussion of reliability will focus on procedures used in education. **Reliability** refers to the consistency of the measurement obtained for the same persons upon repeated testing. This consistency may be determined by using the same measure twice, administering two equivalent forms of the measure, or using a series of items designed to measure similar concepts.

The symbol used to indicate the reliability level is r, the same as that used for Pearson product-moment correlation coefficient (see Chapter 8). As will be explained later in this chapter, several procedures to assess reliability use correlation, so it is not surprising that the two share the same symbol. In theory, reliability can range from 0 to 1.00, but the reliability of measures of human traits and behaviors never quite reaches 1.00. Some very good achievement tests may reach .98, but probably not higher than that.

The reliability of an instrument is usually evaluated by the measure developer, rather than by the user. If the user applies the measure to groups and conditions similar to those used by the instrument developer, then the user can assume that the measure has the same reliability as that reported by the measure constructor.

Understanding the Theory of Reliability

The classical theory of reliability states that an observed score, X (e.g., a score obtained on an achievement test), contains two components: a **true score** (T) and an **error score** (E). The observed score can be described as:

$$X = T + E$$

The true score reflects the *real* level of performance of a person. However, this true score cannot be observed or measured directly. Based on the assumption that the error scores (E) are random and do not correlate with the true scores (T), the observed scores (X) are used to estimate the true scores. For some people, X is an *overestimate* of their T; and for other people, X is an *underestimate* of their T.

Theoretically, the true score of a person can be determined by administering the same measure over and over, recording the scores each time, and then averaging all the scores. In practice, though, people are tested with the same measure only once or twice at the most.

Reliability can be represented by this formula:

$$Rel = 1 - \frac{S_e^2}{S_x^2}$$

Where   Rel =   the reliability

S_e^2 =   the error variance

S_x^2 =   the variance of the observed scores (which was defined simply as the *variance* in Chapter 5)

From this formula, we can conclude that in order to make the reliability as close to 1.00 as possible (i.e., maximize the reliability), the ratio

$$\frac{S_e^2}{S_x^2}$$

should be as small as possible. This ratio can be decreased either by *decreasing* the numerator, S_e^2, or by *increasing* the denominator, S_x^2. The error scores' variance (S_e^2) can be decreased by writing good test items, including clear instructions, and providing optimum environment for the examinees taking the test. The observed scores' variance (S_x^2) can be increased by using heterogeneous groups of examinees (in terms of ability and performance), or by writing longer tests.

Methods of Assessing Reliability

Test-Retest
Test-retest reliability is assessed by administering the same test *twice* to the same group of people. The scores of the examinees

from the two testings are correlated and the correlation coefficient becomes the reliability index. The time interval between the two testings is important and should be reported when the reliability coefficient is reported. When the interval between testings is short, the reliability is likely to be higher than in cases when the interval between testings is long.

The test-retest method of assessing reliability seems the most obvious one, because reliability is related to consistency over time. However, there are several problems involved in this method of assessing reliability. First, people need to be tested twice, which may be time-consuming and expensive. Second, some memory or experience from the first test is likely to affect individuals' performance on the retest. Increasing the time interval between the two testing sessions may reduce this effect, but with a longer interval, new experiences or learning may occur and affect performance. Generally, it is recommended that the interval between retests should not exceed 6 months.

Due to the problems associated with the test-retest method, this method is not considered a conclusive measure of reliability in education and psychology. It may be used, though, in combination with other methods designed to assess test reliability.

Alternate Forms

The alternate form method of assessing reliability is based on the assumption that if students are being tested twice, with two alternate forms of the same test, their scores on the two forms will be the same. Alternate forms reliability is obtained when a group of students is administered the two forms and their two scores are correlated with each other. As with test-retest, the correlation coefficient serves as the index of reliability. The two forms of the test should be equivalent in terms of their statistical properties (e.g., equal means, variances, and item intercorrelation), as well as the content coverage and the types of items used.

There are two major problems involved in using this reliability assessment method. The first is that the students have to be tested twice, as was the problem with the test-retest method. The second problem is that it is very difficult, and often impractical, to develop an alternate form. If the purpose of the test developer is merely to assess the reliability of a test, then the alternate form method is unlikely to be used, because it requires having a second form of the test. However, many commercial testing companies, especially those which develop achievement tests, construct alternate forms for other purposes. Thus, these forms can also be used to assess reliability. Alternate forms are useful for security reasons (e.g., every other student gets the same form to reduce copying and cheating). They are also useful in some research studies, when one form is administered as a pretest and the other form as a posttest, in order to eliminate the possible effect that previous exposure to the test may have on subsequent testing scores.

Measures of Internal Consistency

One major disadvantage of the two aforementioned reliability assessment methods is that the examinees have to be tested twice. The **internal consistency** approach allows the use of scores from a single testing session to estimate the reliability. In essence, each item on a test can be viewed as a single measurement, and the test can be viewed as a series of repeated measures. The internal consistency methods are based on the assumption that when a test measures a single basic concept, items correlate with each other and people who answer one item correctly are likely to correctly answer similar items. The reliability estimates obtained by internal consistency methods are usually similar to those obtained by correlating two equivalent forms. There are several methods which can be used to estimate the test's internal consistency.

The split-half method.

In this procedure, the test is split into two halves and the scores of the examinees on one half are correlated with their scores on the other half. We consider each half to be an alternate form of the test. The most common way to split a test is to divide it into odd and even items, although any way which creates two similar halves is acceptable. However, dividing the test into the first half and the second half may create two halves that are not comparable. These two halves may differ in terms of content coverage, item difficulty, and students' level of fatigue and practice.

The first step in the computation of the split-half reliability procedure is to obtain the scores from the two halves for each person. The scores from one half are then correlated with the scores from the other half. Unlike the first two methods discussed (test-retest and alternate forms), this correlation is not an accurate assessment of the test reliability. In fact, it underestimates the reliability because it is computed for a test half as long as the actual test for which we wish to obtain the reliability. Research has demonstrated that all things being equal, a longer test is more reliable. That is, if we have two tests with similar items, but one is shorter than the other, we can predict that the longer test is more reliable than the shorter test.

In order to calculate the reliability for a full length test, the **Spearman-Brown prophecy formula** is used. This formula uses the reliability obtained for the half test to estimate the reliability of a full-length test. The Spearman-Brown prophecy formula is:

$$r_{full} = \frac{(2)(r_{half})}{1 + r_{half}}$$

Where r_{full} =   the reliability for the whole test

r_{half} =   the reliability for the half test (i.e., the correlation of the two halves)

Suppose we want to estimate the reliability of a 30-item test and the correlation of the odd-item half with the even-item half is .50. This correlation estimates the reliability for a 15-item test, whereas our test has 30 items. In order to estimate the reliability for the full-length test, the Spearman-Brown formula is applied:

$$r_{full} = \frac{(2)(.50)}{1 + .50} = \frac{1.00}{1.50} = .67$$

In this example, the test constructor should report the test split-half reliability as .67.

Kuder-Richardson methods.   G. F. Kuder and M. W. Richardson developed a series of formulas in an article published in 1937. Two of these, KR-20 and KR-21, are used today to measure an agreement, or intercorrelation, among test items. As with the split-half method, these procedures can only be used for items that are scored dichotomously (right or wrong). KR-20 can be thought of as the average of all possible split-half coefficients obtained for a group of examinees. KR-21 is easier to compute, but it is appropriate only when the level of difficulty of all items is similar, a requirement which is not easily satisfied.

Coefficient alpha.   This procedure was developed by Lee Cronbach in 1951. It yields results similar to KR-20 when used with dichotomous items. However, coefficient alpha can be used for tests with various item formats. For example, it can be applied to instruments with the Likert scale, where each item may be scored on a scale of 1-5. Coefficient alpha is considered by researchers to provide good reliability estimates in most situations.

A well-known computer program, SPSS (Statistical Package for the Social Sciences), provides coefficient alpha as a part of its reliability analysis. Since SPSS is widely used by researchers, readers of educational and psychological research are likely to see coefficient alpha being reported as an index of reliability.

Inter-Scorer Reliability

Occasionally, the measure used is not an objective instrument, such as a multiple-choice test; rather, it involves a degree of subjectivity and judgment. For example, the process of scoring essay tests or observing and rating behavior calls for subjective decisions on the part of those who have to grade the tests or rate behaviors. For example, when applying for entrance into a doctoral program in education, applicants may be required to submit a writing sample. The essays are then read by two or more readers who assign a score on each criterion using a rating scale. The essays may be scored using criteria such as content, organization, syntax and grammar, completeness, and originality.

The scores from two or more essay readers can be used in two ways: (a) to compute a correlation coefficient, or (b) to compute the percentage of agreement. The correlation coefficient and the percentage of agreement indicate the reliability and the consistency of the measure as used by the judges. A high correlation coefficient shows consistency between the readers. By providing clear guidelines for scoring, as well as providing good training, it is possible to increase the inter-scorer reliability and agreement.

The Standard Error of Measurement

The reliability and accuracy of a test can be expressed in terms of the standard error of measurement (SEM). The SEM provides information about the variability of a person's scores obtained upon repeated administrations of a test. The SEM is especially suitable for the interpretation of individual scores. Since, as mentioned before, measures of human traits and behaviors contain an error component, any score obtained by such a measure is not a completely accurate representation of the person's true performance. The more reliable the test (i.e., r closer to 1.00), the smaller the error component. The SEM allows us to estimate the range of scores wherein the true score lies, and it is computed as follows:

$$SEM = SD \sqrt{1 - Rel}$$

Where   SEM =   the standard error of measurement

           SD =   the standard deviation of the measure

           Rel =   the reliability of the measure

A numerical example will help illustrate how the SEM is computed. Suppose an achievement test has a standard deviation (*SD*) of 10, and a reliability of .91. The test's SEM is computed as:

$$SEM = 10 \sqrt{1 - .91} = 10 \sqrt{0.09} = (10)(0.3) = 3$$

Relating SEM to the normal curve model (see Chapter 6), we can state that 68% of the time the examinees' *true* scores would lie within ±1 SEM of their *observed* scores and 95% of the time the students' true scores would lie within ±2 SEM of their observed scores. For example, if a student obtained a score of 80 on this achievement test, 68% of the time the student's true score would lie 3 points above or below the observed score of 80. That is, between 77 and 83 and 95% of the time between 74 and 86. Clearly, it is desirable to have a small SEM, because then the band of estimate (the range within which the true score lies) is narrower and the true score is closer to the observed score.

If you inspect the formula for the computation of SEM, you would realize that the reliability of a test affects its SEM. A lower reliability results in a higher SEM and a wider, less precise band of estimate. Assume that the reliability of the test had been .64 instead of .91. SEM would then be computed as:

$$SEM = 10 \sqrt{1 - .64} = 10 \sqrt{0.36} = (10)(0.6) = 6$$

An SEM of 6 means that 68% of the time the student's true score would have been 6 points above or below the student's observed score of 80 (i.e., between 74 and 86), and 95% percent of the time, the true score would have been between 68 and 92. It is as if we are saying that although the student obtained a score of 80, we are 68% sure that the true score is somewhere between 6 points above to 6 points below that score.

Factors Affecting Reliability

Heterogeneity

When the group used to derive the reliability estimate is heterogeneous with regard to the property being measured (e.g., reading comprehension, mathematics computation, or attitudes toward corporal punishment), the variability of the test scores is higher and, consequently, the reliability estimate is higher. (The effect of the variance of observed scores on the reliability was explained at the beginning of this chapter under Understanding the Theory of Reliability.) The test manual which reports the test's reliability is likely to include information on the group used to assess the reliability. If, for example, the group included students from grades 3 through 5, but the test is to be used with third graders only, the reliability of the test for these students is probably lower than that reported in the manual.

Test Length

As was mentioned before, all things being equal, a longer test is more reliable. In a short test the probability of guessing right is high. Therefore, a longer test gives a more stable estimate of the student's performance, because the effect of guessing is reduced. The split-half reliability, which uses Spearman-Brown formula, demonstrates the effect of test length on reliability. It shows that a full-length test is more reliable than a test half as long. If you check the test manual of a commercial test, you can see that the reliability levels of the subsections of the test are usually lower than the reliability levels of the whole test. In determining the desired length of any given test, though, it may be necessary to consider other variables, such as time constraints, or the ages of the prospective students who will be taking the test.

Difficulty of Items

Tests which are too easy or too difficult produce little variability among the scores obtained by the examinees, and therefore tend to have a lower reliability.

Quality of Items

Improving the quality of items increases an instrument's reliability. The process starts by writing clear, unambiguous items, providing good instructions for the test-takers and the test-administrators, and standardizing the administration and scoring procedures. Ideally, the instrument can then be field-tested with a group similar to the one intended to take the test in the future. An item analysis can be performed to reveal weaknesses in the items, and help improve the test by reducing the error variance.

How High Should the Reliability Be?

Usually, teacher-made tests tend to have lower reliability levels than tests prepared by commercial companies or by professional test writers. Teachers may not have the time or the expertise to construct the tests, and they may not perform item analysis or revise the items where needed.

Another point to keep in mind is that tests which measure the *affective* domain tend to have a lower reliability than tests that measure the *cognitive* domain. The main reason for this phenomenon is that affective domain behavior is less consistent than cognitive domain behavior.

As a rule, important decisions, such as admitting students into a program, should not be based on a single test score because every test has a certain level of error. Batteries of achievement tests should report the reliability levels for the subtests, as well as for the total test. Additionally, the standard error of measurement (SEM) should be reported, whenever possible, to indicate the test's margin of error.

Deciding on a desired level of reliability depends to a great extent on the intended use of the test results.   In exploratory research, even a modest reliability of .50 to .60 is acceptable, although a higher reliability is always preferable.   For group decisions, reliability levels in the .60s may be acceptable.   For example, if a study involves a comparison of experimental and control groups, individual scores are not usually being compared; rather, group values (e.g., mean scores) are likely to be compared. On the other hand, when important decisions are made based on the results of the test, the reliability coefficients should be very high.   Most commercial tests used for decisions regarding individuals have reliability levels of at least .90.   Even though many classroom teachers do not have the time or the expertise to assess the reliability of the tests they construct, they should be aware of the issue of reliability in educational and psychological testing.

Summary

1. **Reliability** refers to the consistency of a measurement obtained for the same person upon repeated testing.   A reliable measure yields the same or similar results every time it is used.

2. The affective and cognitive domains are more difficult to measure reliably than are physical traits.

3. The *real* level of performance for any individual, or the **true score** (T), cannot be observed directly.   The **observed score** (X) is likely to overestimate or underestimate the true score for any given individual. The observed score equals the sum of the true score and the **error score.**

4. **Reliability** can be represented by the formula:

$$Reliability \ (Rel) = 1 - \frac{S_e^2}{S_x^2}$$

Where: S^2_e =   the error variance

S^2_x =   the variance of the observed scores

5. Methods of decreasing the error component (S^2_e) include writing good items, giving clear instructions, and providing an optimal environment for the examinees.   Methods of increasing the variance of the observed scores include using heterogeneous groups of examinees and writing longer tests.

6. The reliability of a particular measure may be assessed using these three methods: the **test-retest,** the **alternate forms,** and the **internal consistency.**

7. The **test-retest** reliability is assessed by administering the same test twice to the same persons. With the **alternate forms** method of assessing reliability, the same group of students is tested twice with two alternate forms of the same test. For both of these methods, the index of reliability is the correlation coefficient of the two scores.

8. Measures of **internal consistency** use the scores from a single testing session to measure reliability.   In this method, each individual item becomes a single measurement, while the test as a whole is a series of repeated measures.   Internal consistency methods include the **split-half, Kuder-Richardson** (KR-20 and KR-21), and **coefficient alpha.**

9. The **standard error of measurement** (SEM) measures the reliability and accuracy of the test in relation to its ability to accurately estimate the range of scores within which the true

score lies. SEM is calculated using this formula:

$$SEM = SD \sqrt{1 - Rel}$$

Where: SD = the standard deviation of the measure

Rel = the reliability of the measure (r)

10. A smaller SEM allows for a more accurate estimate of the true score and, therefore, indicates a more reliable measure.

11. Factors such as the heterogeneity of the group, the test length, and the difficulty and quality of the items affect the reliability of the measure. Individual items should be unambiguous and neither too easy nor too difficult.

12. Teacher-made tests tend to have lower reliability levels than commercial tests.

13. Tests used to measure the affective domain tend to have a lower reliability than tests used to measure the cognitive domain.

Chapter 14
VALIDITY

The **validity** of a test refers to the appropriateness of specific inferences and interpretations made using the test scores. It is not sufficient to say that a test is "valid;" rather, the *intended use* of the test should be indicated. Keep in mind that validity is not inherent in the instrument itself and that an instrument is considered valid for a particular purpose only. For example, a test that is valid as a measure of reading comprehension in third grade is not valid as a measure of science in fifth grade. Validation of a test involves conducting empirical studies where data are collected to establish the instrument validity. A valid test is assumed to be reliable and consistent; however, a reliable test may be valid only for a specific purpose.

There are three basic types of validity, according to *Standards for Educational and Psychological Testing* (AERA APA-NCME, 1985, pp. 9-18): content validity, criterion-related validity and construct validity.[1] Although not listed in the *Standards* as a type of validity, face validity is also important for a more comprehensive discussion of validity, and is included in this chapter.

---

[1] **A HINT:** We recommend that as test users you familiarize yourself with this publication which discusses various issues related to educational and psychological testing. *Standards for Educational and Psychological Testing* (1985) was developed by a joint committee of The American Educational Research Association (AERA), The American Psychological Association (APA), and The National Council on Measurement in Education (NCME). It is published by the American Psychological Association, 1200 Seventeenth Street, NW, Washington, DC, 20036.

Content Validity

Content validity refers to the adequacy with which an instrument measures a representative sample of behaviors and content domain about which inferences are to be made. Of the three types of validity described in *Standards*, content validity is the most important for achievement tests. In order to establish the content validity of the test, its items are examined and compared to the content of the unit to be tested, or to the behaviors and skills to be measured. In the case of achievement tests, the test constructor should ensure that the items are an adequate sample of the content to be tested. If instructional objectives are available, the teacher may choose to examine the match between the test items and the objectives. Well-defined content domain and behaviors help increase the test's content validity.

Teachers who write their own achievement tests should make sure that items on the test correspond to what was covered in class in terms of content, behaviors, and skills. For example, a teacher who teaches a unit on the Civil War and emphasizes understanding reasons and processes, should not write test items that ask students to *recall* dates, events and names, because such items lower the validity of the test.

Another example might take you back to your college years. Many of us can recall taking examinations which were very different from what we expected. We expected certain material to be covered on the examination but this was not the case. Part of the problem, no doubt, was the low content validity of these examinations and the mismatch between what was covered in class and what was included on the test.

Educators who are assigned the responsibility of choosing a series of standardized, commercial achievement tests for their school need to compare the test items to their curriculum and make sure they match. A standardized test may have a high content validity for some schools, but a low content validity for other schools, because curricula are likely to differ from school to school.

Criterion-Related Validity

Criterion-related validity refers to the extent to which the performance on a measuring instrument is related to the performance on some other external measure, labeled as the **criterion**. There are two types of criterion-related validity: concurrent and predictive.

Concurrent validity

Concurrent validity refers to how well the test we wish to validate correlates with another well-established instrument which measures the same thing. This well-established instrument is designated the **criterion**. For example, a newly-created short version of a well-established test may be correlated with the full-length test. A high correlation between the two tests indicates that they measure similar characteristics and traits. In order to establish concurrent validity, the two measures are administered to the same group of people, and the scores on the two measures are correlated. The correlation coefficient serves as an index of concurrent validity.

To illustrate, suppose a researcher develops a new IQ test which takes 35 minutes to administer and 35 minutes to score. This is much faster than the commonly-used IQ tests, the WISC-R and the Stanford-Binet (S-B). In order to establish the concurrent validity of the new IQ test, the researcher may correlate it with the WISC-R and the S-B by administering all three tests to the same group of people. A high positive correlation of the new test with the WISC-R and with the S-B would lend support to the validity of the new test.

Predictive validity

Predictive validity refers to how well a test predicts some future performance. This type of validity is especially useful for aptitude and readiness tests which are designed to predict some future performance. The test to be validated is the **predictor** (e.g., SAT and ACT) and the future performance is the **criterion** (e.g., GPA of college freshmen). Data are collected for the same group of people on both the predictor and the criterion, and the scores on the two measures are correlated. The correlation, called the **validity coefficient**, indicates the extent of the instrument's predictive validity. Unlike concurrent validity where both instruments are administered at about the same time, predictive validity involves administering the predictor at the present time, while the criterion is administered later in the future.

Suppose a researcher wants to establish the predictive validity of Gordon's Intermediate Measure of Audiation (IMA), a music aptitude test for elementary school children. Forty third-graders are administered the AMA music aptitude test and are then given musical instruments in their schools. At the end of the year, the music teacher is asked to rate each student's musical achievement using a scale of 10 (excellent) to 1 (poor). Next, the aptitude scores are correlated with the teacher ratings. A positive high correlation indicates that the aptitude test has a high predictive validity, because it predicted accurately the students' end-of-year achievement in music.

You should keep in mind that tests that are intended to predict future performance may provide incomplete information about the criterion. For example, the IMA music aptitude test may not always predict how well a student plays a musical instrument a year later. The reason is that this test may measure natural aptitude, but probably not other factors such as motivation, perseverance, quality of music instruction, and parental support.

Construct Validity

The term *construct* is used to describe characteristics that cannot be measured directly, such as intelligence, sociability, and aggression. **Construct validity** refers to the extent to which a test measures and provides accurate information about a theoretical trait or characteristic.   Construct validity is of interest mostly to psychologists and educators. The process of establishing the test's construct validity can be quite complicated.   The researcher administers the test to be validated to a group of people, and then collects other pieces of data on these people.   Suppose, for example, that a new scale has been developed in order to measure test anxiety. To demonstrate that the scale indeed measures test anxiety, the researcher first administers the scale to a group of respondents, and then collects additional information about these people. Those who score low on the scale are considered to have a low level of test anxiety and are expected to behave in various situations in a way consistent with low anxiety. Conversely, those who score high on the test are expected to behave in ways which are compatible with a high level of test anxiety. Thus, establishing the construct validity consists of accumulating supporting evidence. Evidence for construct validity is not gathered just once for one sample; rather, it is collected with the use of many samples and multiple sources of data.

An example may help to illustrate one way the test developer can assess the construct validity of test anxiety.   First, the researcher administers the test to two randomly assigned groups. A t-test may be used to establish that the means of the two groups are not significantly different from each other. Then, one of the groups receives some intervention to reduce test anxiety. Finally, both groups again take the test-anxiety instrument, and their mean scores are compared. If the group members who participated in the workshop score lower on the anxiety text, compared with the control group of members, some evidence is provided to support the validity of the test as a measure of text anxiety.

Face Validity

Face validity refers to the extent to which an instrument *appears* to measure what it is intended to measure. When the measures employed are clearly related to a task, the instrument face validity is fairly obvious. For example, assessing the applicant's qualification for a job which entails typing by having the person type seems to be a valid request, and the measure (i.e., typing) has face validity. On the other hand, when the relationship of the test to the construct being assessed is unclear, the measure quite often does not have face validity. For example, in psychological testing, when using an instrument such as the Rorschach, one may question how ink blots are related to personality disorders.

The extent to which a test appears valid to the examinees and to other people involved in the testing process (e.g., administrators and decision makers) may determine how well the test is accepted and used. Additionally, face validity helps to keep test takers motivated and interested, because they can see the relevancy of the test to the perceived task. A test with a high face validity which is used to screen a pool of applicants for certain positions is quite defensible as an appropriate instrument, because applicants can see the test as relevant and perceive it as an appropriate measure.

Face validity is likely to be assessed based on a superficial inspection of a test. However, this inspection is not sufficient. The mere *appearance* of face validity is not a guarantee that a test is valid and that it truly measures what it is supposed to measure. You should be aware of the fact that face validity is not always found in discussions of validity, and it may not be considered by all to be as important as the other types of validity.

Assessing Validity

Although we have identified several different types of validity, they are not necessarily separate or independent of each other. Establishing the measure's validity usually involves a series of steps of gathering data. Information provided by the test developer on the test validity should include a description of the sample used in the validation process. Ideally, the characteristics of this sample are similar to those of the test users.

Assessing the content validity of a test does not involve numerical calculation. Rather, it is a process of examining the test in relation to the content it is supposed to measure. In measuring criterion-related validity, the validity coefficient is used to describe the correlation between a test and a criterion. To be useful, the criterion has to be reliable and appropriate. The process of establishing the construct validity of an instrument includes the use of statistical methods (e.g., correlation), as well as procedures for gathering and comparing various measures.

Test Bias

Standardized tests, especially those used for admission, placement, and grading, are viewed at times as being **biased** against one group or another. A test is considered biased if it consistently and unfairly discriminates against a group of people that takes the test.[2] For example, certain tests are said to be gender biased, usually discriminating against female examinees. Other tests may be considered biased against racial or cultural minorities.

---

[2] **A HINT:** Norm-referenced tests are constructed to discriminate *among* examinees of different ability levels. This type of discrimination is not to be confused with the notion of test bias, where a test systematically discriminates against a particular group of examinees.

Summary

1.   **Validity** refers to the inferences and interpretations made using the test scores. The intended use of the test should be indicated, because an instrument is considered valid for a particular purpose only.

2.   The three basic types of validity are: **content validity**, **criterion-related validity**, and **construct validity**.

3.   **Content validity** is measured by comparing the test items with the unit, behaviors, or skills which that test is attempting to measure.

4.   Tests have **criterion-related validity** with respect to the relationship of performance on two separate measures. One measure is the newly developed test, and the other measure serves as a criterion. There are two types of criterion-related validity: **concurrent** and **predictive**.

5.   A test has **concurrent validity** if its results correlate with another well-established instrument which measures the same thing.

6.   A test has **predictive validity** if it can successfully predict future performance in a given area. In such a case the test is the predictor and future performance is the criterion used to establish validity.

7.   **Construct validity** refers to the ability of the test to measure and provide information about traits which cannot be measured directly, such as intelligence, sociability, and aggression.

8.   To establish the construct validity, it is necessary to collect additional data over a period of time and to correlate these data with the test results. By doing so, we can accumulate evidence to support the assertion that the instrument measures certain theoretical traits or characteristics.

9.   **Face validity**, which is not a formal type of validity, refers to the extent to which an instrument appears to measure what it is intended to measure.

10.   Validity may be assessed using multiple sources and multiple methods.

11.   A test is considered **biased** if it systematically discriminates against a particular group of examinees.

Part Seven

PUTTING IT
ALL TOGETHER

Chapter 15
SIMULATIONS AND EXAMPLES

Introduction

Following are 22 examples of different research situations. After reading each passage, decide which statistical test should be used to answer the research question and to analyze the data.

Also included is a decision flowchart of the statistical tests covered in this book. You may use the flowchart to help you proceed step-by-step through the decision process, as you try to determine the statistical test which should be used to answer the research question. To use the chart, first determine the scale of measurement. This first level of the flowchart is divided into nominal, ordinal, and interval/ratio scales. The second level shows the decision boxes about the type of hypothesis being tested and are divided into two types of hypotheses: hypotheses of difference and hypotheses of association. After reading each passage you should decide whether you are testing a hypothesis of difference or association. (See the following explanation of these two types of hypotheses.) Next, look at the groups or measures being studied: are they paired or independent of each other? Another question you may want to ask yourself pertains to the number of groups in the study: do we have one group, two groups, or more than two groups?

Choosing a Statistical Test: A Decision Flowchart

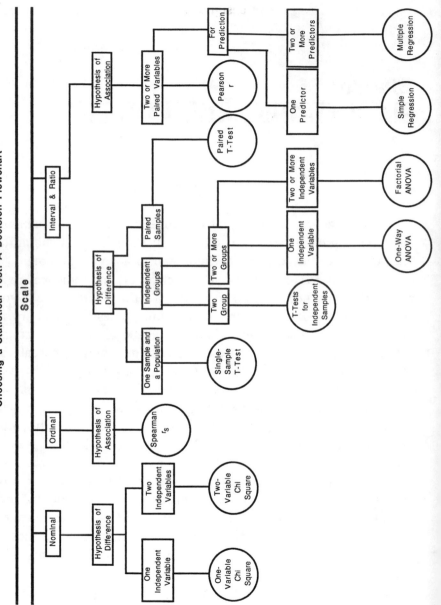

Certain statistical tests designed for hypotheses of **differences** may also be thought of as tests used for hypotheses of **association**. For example, chi square may be used to test whether there is a *difference* in the responses of two groups to a particular question. However, chi square may also be thought of as a test designed to study the *association* between two variables: group membership, and the responses of the group members to some question. In other words, we ask ourselves whether membership in a particular group is associated with a particular response (i.e., are people more likely to respond in a certain way because they belong to a particular group).

Another example may be the use of *t*-test for independent samples. A study may be conducted to test whether there is a *difference* in the mean reading scores obtained by two groups using different reading methods. Or, conversely, we may ask if higher reading scores are *associated* with a particular teaching method.

In a way, *association* can be thought of as the flip side of *difference* and sometimes it is simply a matter of two parts of the same question. For example, we can design a study to test whether two variables are *associated* with, or *different* from, each other. In general, statistical tests may be classified into those designed to test hypotheses of *association* and those designed to test hypotheses of *difference*. It may be easier for you to distinguish between these two types of tests if you remember the following: tests that are designed to measure *association* between variables can indicate the presence or absence of such association, while in addition they can also indicate the **degree** (or extent) of such association. For example, Pearson *r* which is used to test hypotheses of association, can also provide information about the degree of association between two paired variables. This is done through the use of the correlation coefficient *r*. On the other hand, while tests that are designed to measure *differences* can also indicate the presence of *relationship* between the independent and the dependent variables, these tests cannot indicate the degree of the relationship. For example, one-way ANOVA may be used to measure the relationships between teaching methods and test scores, but it cannot describe the magnitude of these relationships.

In deciding which statistical test may be used to answer the research question and to analyze data in the research passages which follow, choose from these statistical tests which were discussed in the book:

1. T-test: (a) independent samples; (b) paired samples; (c) a single sample

2. Chi square: (a) one variable, equal probabilities; (b) one variable, unequal probabilities; (c) two variables

3. One-way ANOVA

4. Two-way ANOVA

5. Pearson r

6. Spearman r_s

7. Simple regression

8. Multiple regression.

To help you get the "hang of it," we will now walk you through two examples. These simulations will help show you how to proceed with the rest of the examples as you try to determine which statistical test should be used to analyze the data. Our experience has taught us that it is often useful to ask ourselves a series of questions. The answers to these questions help in determining the statistical test to be used. It is also useful at times to imagine some data points and to illustrate what the data might look like. As you work through the 22 passages, we suggest that you ask yourself the same six questions as those presented at the end of each of the two practice passages which follow. You can compare your responses with those provided in the second part of this chapter, titled "Answers."

SAMPLE PASSAGES AND A STEP-BY-STEP

EXPLANATION OF THE ANSWERS

Sample Passage 1

Many studies comparing cooperative learning to traditional teaching have found that the social self-concept of many students is improved when cooperative learning is used. One elementary school decides to investigate whether the students' social self-concept is improved when cooperative learning methods are implemented. Two of the fourth-grade classes are using cooperative learning and the other two continue with traditional approaches. At the end of the school year, a measure of self-concept is administered to all fourth-grade students.

Answer

1. **What is being measured and how?**
   Social self-concept, using a measure of self-concept.

2. **What is the scale of measurement?**
   Assume an interval scale, since almost all educational tests use data measured on an interval scale.

3. **What hypothesis is being tested?**
   Hypothesis of difference: the study explores differences in self-concept between students in classes using cooperative learning and those using traditional teaching.

4. **How many sets of test scores?**
Two - one for the cooperative learning group and one for the traditional approach.

5. **Are the measures paired or independent of each other?**
The measures are independent of each other.

6. **What might the data look like?**

Cooperative Learning	Traditional
45	34
50	29
38	41
Mean 1	Mean 2

Solution: Since the means of two independent groups are being compared, use *t*-test for independent samples.

Sample Passage 2

School board members all over the United States have noticed that district residents who have school-age children attending the district's schools are more likely than other residents to support a tax increase to improve education. In a suburban school district, a non-binding referendum about raising taxes to pay for education in the district is put on the ballot. The voters are asked to indicate their support or opposition to the proposal by marking the ballot with a Yes or No vote. The voters are also asked to indicate whether they have school-age children in the district's schools. The responses of the voters are compared to determine whether those with children in the district's schools are more likely to support the tax increase, compared with voters who do not have children in the district's schools.

<u>Answer:</u>

1. **What is being measured and how?**
   The number of voters with and without children in the district's schools who support or oppose a tax increase, using a question on a survey.

2. **What is the scale of measurement?**
   Nominal (group membership and type of response).

3. **What hypothesis is being tested?**
   A hypothesis of difference: the study explores differences in opinion regarding a tax increase between residents with and without school-age children in the district.

4. **How many sets of scores?**
   Two - one set of responses for voters with children in the district's schools and one set for voters without children in the district's schools.

5. **Are the measures paired or independent of each other?**
   The measures are independent of each other.

6. What might the data look like?

Group		Increase Taxes	
		Yes	No
Children in the district	Yes	87	13
	No	21	79

Solution: Data are presented in a form of frequencies; therefore, use chi square. Since there are two variables (groups and response options), use two-variable chi square.

SIMULATION PASSAGES

1. A director of a large child-care center decides to train all her teachers in the use of CPR. The Red Cross is invited to provide the training to the teachers. To assess the teachers' increase in knowledge of CPR, the Red Cross suggests to the center's director that all the teachers complete a competency test before and after the training program. After completing the pretest, the teachers participate in a two-day CPR training program. After the training, they again complete the CPR competency test. The center's director, the teachers, and the Red Cross examine the posttest scores to determine whether they are significantly higher than the pretest scores obtained before the training.

2. A sixth-grade teacher notices that when the students in his class talk about the television programs they watched the evening before, the boys tend to discuss different programs than the girls do. To test whether there is a gender difference in the *type* of program watched by the children, the teacher decides to collect data from the sixth graders. He explains to his students the research question and asks them to keep a record of all the television programs they watch for one whole week. To increase the sample size, the students in the other two sixth-grade classes are also asked to keep track of the weekly television programs they watch. Together with his students, the teacher compiles the data gathered by 110 sixth-grade students. The television programs watched by the students are then classified into five categories: action, drama, comedy, nature, and news. To determine whether there is a difference in the type of programs watched by boys and girls, the teacher and the students record the number of students who watch each *category*, broken down by *gender*.

3. In the last election, a referendum was passed to raise school taxes in the district by 5%. After much discussion, three areas of critical need emerged: (a) expand courses, (b) update equipment, and (c) increase teachers' salaries. However, the school board cannot agree about the proper use of the additional money. In an attempt to determine whether there are significant differences between the various groups in the district, the School Board surveys the district's parents, teachers, and administrators, presenting to them the three areas of critical need and asking them to indicate which of the three they deem most urgent. The school board is interested in finding out whether there are differences among the three groups of respondents (parents, teachers, and administrators) regarding the three options for the use of the additional tax revenue.

4.   Is there such a thing as a student who is a high achiever in all subjects? Or a student who is a low achiever in all subjects? In an effort to contribute to the answer to these questions, a junior high school principal selects a random sample of 200 students from her school, and compares their standardized achievement test scores in mathematics, reading, language arts, study skills, and science. She wants to ascertain whether there is a relationship between students' scores on these five subjects.

5.   A statistics instructor at a liberal arts college has noticed that psychology students seem to have more positive attitudes toward statistics than other students. Sociology students also seem to have a positive attitude, whereas English students seem to like statistics the least. To test whether there is some relationship between college major and students' attitudes toward statistics, the Attitude Toward Statistics (ATS) scale is given to all the students on the first day of the fall semester. The responses of psychology, sociology, English, and history students are then compared to each other to determine if there is a difference in the attitudes toward statistics exhibited by these students.

6.   A school district is under court order to maintain a racial balance in all its schools.   Each school in the district is required to reflect the racial/ethnic make-up of all the students in the district. The district has 41% white students, 29% black students, 24% Hispanic students, and 6% Asian students. In order to ascertain whether his school represents the district's demographic distribution, a principal decides to examine the racial/ethnic distribution of the 350 students in his school in comparison to the district's distribution.

7.   There are educators who claim that parents of younger children tend to be more satisfied with their children's schools, compared to parents of older children. A Likert-type scale,

developed by the staff in a local school, is administered annually at the end of the school year to measure the level of parents' satisfaction regarding the services, curricula, and programs provided by the school. The scale includes 20 questions with responses to each question ranging from 1 (very dissatisfied) to 5 (very satisfied). Thus, an overall score of 100 indicates a very high level of satisfaction, and an overall score of 20 indicates a very low level of satisfaction. The scale is administered to the parents of kindergarten, third, fifth, and seventh graders, and a score of overall satisfaction is obtained for each of the respondents. The researchers want to find out whether there is a difference in the level of satisfaction among the parents of the different grade levels.

8. Many studies about birth order and its relationship to a host of variables have been conducted in the last 50 years. The results are inconclusive at best. Many researchers, however, insist that first-born children tend to be overachievers and more successful than their younger siblings. Just as many researchers oppose this position, which they believe is overly simplistic. They cite various research statistics to support their view. They contend that other variables, such as socioeconomic status (SES) and gender, are just as important as birth order in determining a person's achievement and success. A researcher decides to explore a possible relationship between *birth order, SES*, and the children's *academic achievement*. The researcher uses students' school records to gather information about standardized achievement test scores for a randomly-selected group of 100 *first-born* high-school children from low, middle, upper-middle, and upper SES. Similar information is gathered for a group of 100 randomly selected *second-born* high-school children from low, middle, upper-middle, and upper SES who are *not related* to the group of first-born children.

9. The faculty in a large liberal arts college feel that the psychology professors get paid more than faculty in other departments. The professors want to test whether the mean annual income of psychology professors is significantly higher than that of faculty in all the other departments combined.

10. Many English teachers cite research showing that students who use computers for word processing write longer essays compared to students using pencil and paper. Based on this research, a junior high school decides to introduce computers to seventh-grade students in their English classes. Before introducing computers into all the seventh-grade English classes, a study is conducted in which the students in two seventh-grade classes spend four weeks learning the computer keyboard and mastering a word processing program. The students in one class are then asked to write an essay using a word-processing program, while the students in the other class are asked to write essays on the same topic using pencil and paper. The measured variable is the length of the essays, measured as the number of words.

11. The students in a first-grade class are practicing classification and counting using colored candy. The teacher contacts the manufacturer of the candy to find out if a controlled ratio of the colors of the candy is maintained by the manufacturer. The manufacturer informs the teacher that they follow a strict five-color ratio. To test whether the "typical" bag of candies represents the color ratio advertised by the manufacturer, the first graders enlist the help of the seventh graders who are learning statistics. The first-graders take 10 large bags of the candy and select at random 100 candies from these bags. Next, the students classify the 100 candies into five piles by color and count the number of candies in each pile. The first-graders and their older peers then determine whether their randomly-selected candies represent the distribution of five colors according to the manufacture specifications.

12. Two second-grade teachers who teach similar classes decide to test a new method for teaching spelling. To determine if the new method enables students to spell better, a study is conducted by the two teachers. Each week, the students in both classes learn how to spell the same 10 new words. For two weeks, one teacher uses the new approach while the other teacher uses the traditional approach. At the end of each week, the same 10-word test is given to the students in both classes. The score for each student is the combined number of words spelled correctly on the two 10-words spelling tests. The mean of the scores obtained by the class using the traditional approach is compared to the mean of the scores obtained by the class using the new approach.

13. After working with middle-school students for a number of years, the school's social worker has noticed that certain students who seem to do quite well in one subject may not do as well in other subjects. To further investigate this phenomenon, the social worker selects at random 10 sixth-grade students and asks the students' English teacher to rank-order them on their academic performance from the highest achiever (1) to the lowest achiever (10). The same task is given to the students' mathematics teacher. The social worker wants to find out if there is an agreement between the two rank-orders assigned by the two teachers to each of the 10 students.

14. In preparation for the standardized achievement test administered each year in the spring, a fifth-grade English teacher wants to practice with her students reading a passage and extracting meaning from the passage. First, the teacher uses Form A of a sample test to assess the students. Then, for two weeks, the teacher practices with the students how to read and interpret passages. At the end of the two weeks, all the fifth graders take Form B of the sample test. The scores obtained by the students on the prepractice test (Form A) are

compared to the scores obtained by them on the postpractice test (Form B).

15. The students in a high school mathematics class are learning about probability. They conduct an experiment with a four-sided spinner. The students hypothesize that the spinner would land an equal number of times on each of the four sides. To test their hypothesis, the students conduct an experiment in which they spin the spinner 200 times. They record the outcomes, and then the number of times the spinner lands on each side is compared to the expected frequencies. Since there are four sides, out of 200 spins, the students expect the spinner to land 50 times on each side.

16. The directors of admissions in a large graduate school want to re-examine three variables currently used to select students for admission into the graduate programs. They want to examine whether these variables are good predictors of students' success in the program, as measured by the students' graduate school GPA. The three variables being used for selecting students are the students' Verbal and Quantitative scores on the Graduate Record Examination (GRE) and their college GPA. The admissions directors decide to conduct a study to determine how well these three variables predict graduate school GPA. Five hundred students who have completed their graduate studies are randomly selected and their school records are used to obtain information about their GRE scores, undergraduate GPA, and graduate school GPA.

17. A school wants to change the color of its logo. A survey is conducted to choose the color, and the top three colors are selected. Then, all students are asked to indicate which of these three colors they like the most. The school administration decides that for a color to be chosen as the new logo color, it has to be preferred over the other two colors by a statistically significant number of students ($p<.05$), not just

by a simple majority. The color preferences of 100 randomly-selected students are compared to determine if one of the three colors has been chosen by a significantly higher number of students, compared with the other two colors.

18. Many school districts administer readiness tests to their entering kindergarten students. In order to convince potential users of a readiness test that it can accurately predict students' academic performance in first grade, the test publisher conducts the following study. The publisher offers to administer the readiness test, free of charge, to kindergarten students in several school districts in various demographic areas. After the test is administered, the readiness test score for each student is recorded. At the end of the first grade, all students are administered a standardized achievement test. The readiness test scores obtained a year earlier and the achievement test scores are studied to determine whether the readiness test can serve as a good predictor of first grade achievement.

19. The local media has noted the public's complaints about the academic performance of athletes in state universities. Many believe athletes are not held to the same high academic standards as other students in the university. To refute these complaints, the administration at one state university conducts a study to compare the GPA of the athletes to that of the other students. The GPA of 50 athletes, selected at random out of the university's 300 athletes, is compared to the GPA of the students at large to determine whether the athletes' GPA is significantly lower than that of the non-athletes, as is claimed by the media.

20. Television is viewed by many as a major contributor to a variety of social problems, including increased violence and lower literacy rates. A group of parents and teachers decides to investigate whether there is a relationship between the

number of hours children watch television and their GPA. After being assured of complete confidentiality, all students in a middle school are asked to keep a diary for two weeks and record the number of hours they watch television each day. For each of the children, information is available about their GPA (measured on a scale of 0.00-4.00) and the number of hours per week they have spent watching television. Those conducting the study want to find out if there is a relationship between these two variables. The researchers emphasize, however, that no causal relationship can be inferred from such a study, only a possible association between the number of hours of television viewing and students' GPA.

21. Research to date has documented that high school boys enjoy using computers more than high school girls. Some say that this phenomenon may be the result of the fact that most computer games are oriented toward boys' interests and are action-oriented. A study is conducted with a randomly selected group of 500 fifth-grade boys and girls. Each child is given one computer game to use, and the children's attitudes toward computers are measured at the end of a two-week period, using a Likert scale. Two types of games are used: action-oriented and social-oriented games. Half of the boys and half of the girls are given the action-oriented game, and the other half are given the social-oriented game. The researchers want to find out which computer game seems to appeal more to fifth graders; whether there are gender differences; and whether these differences depend, at least to some extent, on the type of computer games used by the children.

22. Are you likely to make more money and have a better paying job if you have a college degree? Would you make even more money if you go to graduate school? Many of us would like to have an answer to these questions. A nationally-known public opinion poll company surveys a stratified sample of

3000 people to determine the number of years they attended school and their annual income. The researchers want to determine whether the number of years of schooling is a good predictor of income.

Answers

Passage 1

1. What is being measured and how?
Knowledge of CPR, measured by a competency test.

2. What is the scale of measurement?
Interval.

3. What hypothesis is being tested?
A hypothesis of difference: the study investigates differences in teachers' knowledge of CPR before and after participating in a training course.

4. How many sets of scores?
Two - pretest and posttest scores for a group of teachers.

5. Are the measures paired or independent of each other?
Paired - the two scores are obtained for the same group of teachers.

6. What might the data look like?

Pretest	Posttest
8	20
10	27
7	26
Mean Pretest	Mean Posttest

Solution: Since two means obtained for the same group of teachers are being compared, use a *t*-test for paired samples.

Passage 2

1. **What is being measured and how?**
   The number of boys and girls who watch each of the five types of television programs; students own records are being used.

2. **What is the scale of measurement?**
   Nominal.

3. **What hypothesis is being tested?**
   A hypothesis of difference: differences between sixth-grade boys and girls in the type of program they watch are being studied.

4. **How many sets of scores?**
   Two - one set of frequencies for five television program types for boys, and one set for girls.

5. **Are the measures paired or independent of each other?**
   The measures are independent of each other.

6. **What might the data look like?**

TV Program

Group	Action	Drama	Comedy	Nature	News
Boys	45	9	23	10	13
Girls	26	20	25	14	15

Solution: The data are presented in a form of frequencies; therefore, use chi square. Since there are two variables (gender and type of television program), use two-variable chi square.

Passage 3

1. **What is being measured and how?**
   The number of parents, teachers, and administrators who support each of the three critical need areas; a survey is being used.

2. **What is the scale of measurement?**
   Nominal.

3. **What hypothesis is being tested?**
   A hypothesis of difference: the study explores differences between parents, teachers, and administrators regarding three areas of critical need.

4. **How many sets of scores?**
   Three - one set of three critical-need frequencies for parents, one set for teachers, and one set for administrators.

5. **Are the measures paired or independent of each other?**
   The measures are independent of each other.

6. **What might the data look like?**

Group	Expand Courses	Update Equipment	Increase Teachers' Salaries
Parents	40	23	37
Teachers	3	8	89
Administrators	9	31	60

Solution: The data are presented in a form of frequencies; therefore, use chi square. Since there are two variables (groups of respondents and response options), use two-variable chi square.

Passage 4

1. **What is being measured and how?**
   The achievement scores of 200 students on five subjects.

2. **What is the scale of measurement?**
   Interval.

3. **What hypothesis is being tested?**
   A hypothesis of association: the study investigates relationships among the scores obtained by 200 junior high students on five standardized achievement tests.

4. **How many sets of scores?**
   Five scores are available for each student.

5. **Are the measures paired or independent of each other?**
   Paired - all five scores are obtained for the same group of students.

6. **What might the data look like?**

Student	Math	Reading	Language Arts	Study Skills	Science
A	64	58	49	51	53
B	78	85	81	77	80
C	91	89	93	90	95

> **Solution:** Since the association between five measures obtained for the same group of people is assessed, use correlation; because the scales of the measures are interval, use Pearson r.

Passage 5

1. **What is being measured and how?**
   Students' attitudes toward statistics, using the ATS scale.

2. **What is the scale of measurement?**
   Interval.

3. **What hypothesis is being tested?**
   A hypothesis of difference: the study explores differences
   in attitudes toward statistics between psychology, sociology,
   English, and history college students.

4. **How many sets of scores?**
   Four - for the four college majors.

5. **Are the measures paired or independent of each other?**
   The scores of the four groups are independent of each other.

6. **What might the data look like?**

Psychology Students	Sociology Students	English Students	History Students
45	49	21	28
48	35	38	31
40	40	29	39
Mean 1	Mean 2	Mean 3	Mean 4

Solution: Since means of four independent groups are being compared, use one-way ANOVA.

Passage 6

1. What is being measured and how?
The number of white, black, Hispanic, and Asian students in the school and in the district; students' records are being used.

2. What is the scale of measurement?
Nominal.

3. What hypothesis is being tested?
A hypothesis of difference: differences in the racial/ethnic distribution of a school in comparison to the district where the school is located are being studied.

4. How many sets of scores?
Two - one set of racial/ethnic groups for the school and one set for the district.

5. Are the measures paired or independent of each other?
The measures are independent of each other.

6. What might the data look like?

Racial/Ethnic Group	School (Observed)	District (Expected)*
White	154	143.5
Black	73	101.5
Hispanic	102	84
Asian	21	21
TOTAL	**350**	**350.0**

* Note: The observed frequencies for the school represent actual "head count" for that school. The expected frequencies for the district represent percentages, rather than actual "head

count." However, the ratio of the percentages for the district are the same as those listed for the district in passage number 6. As you may remember, the number of observed frequencies should always equal the number of expected frequencies. Therefore, both columns (observed and expected) equal 350. (See Chapter 12 which discusses chi square for further explanation of the use of percentages.)

Solution: Data are presented in a form of frequencies; therefore, use chi square. Since only one variable is used (racial/ethnic groups) and the expected frequencies are unequal, use one-variable chi square with unequal expected frequencies.

Passage 7

1. **What is being measured and how?**
   The level of parents' satisfaction, measured by a Likert scale.

2. **What is the scale of measurement?**
   Interval.

3. **What hypothesis is being tested?**
   A hypothesis of difference: the study is designed to determine whether there are differences in the level of satisfaction with their children's schools displayed by parents of kindergarten, third, fifth, and seventh graders.

4. How many sets of scores?
Four - one set each for the parents of kindergartners, third graders, fifth graders, and seventh graders.

5. Are the measures paired or independent of each other?
The measures obtained for the four groups are independent of each other.

6. What might the data look like?

Kindergartners' Parents	3rd Graders' Parents	5th Graders' Parents	7th Graders' Parents
89	73	54	35
93	87	89	61
90	89	56	42
Mean 1	Mean 2	Mean 3	Mean 4

Solution: Since means of four independent groups are being compared, use one-way ANOVA.

Passage 8

1. What is being measured and how?
The academic achievement of first-born and second-born children from low, middle, upper-middle, and upper SES are being measured, using school's records.

2. What is the scale of measurement?
Interval.

3. **What hypothesis is being tested?**
A hypothesis of difference: the study investigates whether there are differences in academic achievement between first and second born high-school children who are not related to each other. These children come from low, middle, upper-middle, and high SES.

4. **How many sets of scores?**
For each of the four SES, achievement scores for first-born and second-born children are being gathered.

5. **Are the measures paired or independent of each other?**
The measures are independent of each other.

6. **What might the data look like?**

	First Born	Second Born	TOTAL
Low SES	Mean	Mean	MEAN
Middle SES	Mean	Mean	MEAN
Upper-Middle SES	Mean	Mean	MEAN
Upper SES	Mean	Mean	MEAN
TOTAL	MEAN	MEAN	

Solution: Because means are being compared and there are two independent variables (birth order and SES), use two-way ANOVA.

Passage 9

1. What is being measured and how?

The mean annual income of professors in the psychology department and that of professors in other departments.

2. What is the scale of measurement?

Ratio.

3. What hypothesis is being tested?

A hypothesis of difference: the study focuses on possible differences in the mean annual income between psychology professors and other faculty in a liberal arts college.

4. How many sets of scores?

Two - the mean annual income of psychology professors is compared to the mean annual income of faculty in other departments.

5. Are the measures paired or independent of each other?

The measures are independent of each other.

6. What might the data look like?

Psy. Dept. Annual Income
45,670	Overall faculty
53,460	mean income; μ
51,200	

Mean of psychology faculty

Solution: Since a mean of one group is being compared to the mean of a population, use a t-test for a single sample.

Passage 10

1. What is being measured and how?
Length of essays written by seventh graders, expressed as the number of words.

2. What is the scale of measurement?
Ratio.

3. What hypothesis is being tested?
A hypothesis of difference: the study explores whether there is a difference in the length of essays written by junior high school students using computers for word processing and essays written by similar students using pencil and paper.

4. How many sets of scores?
Two - one set of scores for one group and one set of scores for the second group.

5. Are the scores paired or independent of each other?
The two measures are independent of each other.

6. What might the data look like?

Group 1	Group 2
201	198
180	173
195	170
Mean 1	Mean 2

Solution: Since the means of two independent groups are being compared, use a *t*-test for independent samples.

Passage 11

1. What is being measured and how?
Candy, which is counted and divided according to color.

2. What is the scale of measurement?
Nominal.

3. What hypothesis is being tested?
A hypothesis of difference: in the study, the five-color ratio of candy specified by the candy manufacturer, is compared to the color ratio of 100 candies bought at a store.

4. How many sets of scores?
Two--the five-color distribution of 100 randomly-selected candy, and the five-color ratio the manufacturer provided.

5. Are the measures paired or independent of each other?
The measures are independent of each other.

6. What might the data look like?

Color	Observed Frequencies	Expected Frequencies. (Manufacture Specification)
Brown	35	31
Green	21	19
Yellow	13	11
Red	12	21
White	19	18

Solution: Data are presented in a form of frequencies; therefore, use chi square. Because there is only one variable (the color of the candy) and the expected frequencies are unequal, use one-variable chi square with unequal expected frequencies.

Passage 12

1. What is being measured and how?
The students' spelling ability, using a weekly 10-word spelling test.

2. What is the scale of measurement?
Interval.

3. What hypothesis is being tested?
A hypothesis of difference: the mean scores on two weekly 10-word spelling tests given to two classes using different spelling instructional approaches are compared to each other in this study.

4. How many sets of scores?
Two - one for one class and one for the second class.

5. Are the measures paired or independent of each other?
The two groups are independent of each other.

6. What might the data look like?

Group 1	Group 2
18	16
20	17
15	12
Mean 1	Mean 2

Solution: Since the means of two independent groups are being compared, use a *t*-test for independent samples.

Passage 13

1. What is being measured and how?
The ranks assigned to 10 randomly-selected students by the English teacher and by the mathematics teacher.

2. What is the scale of measurement?
Ordinal.

3. What hypothesis is being tested?
A hypothesis of association: the study compares two separate ranks assigned to a group of 10 students by two teachers.

4. How many sets of scores?
Two ranks are assigned to each student by the teachers.

5. Are the measures paired or independent of each other?
Paired - the two sets of ranks are assigned to the same group of students.

6. What might the data look like?

Student No.	Ranks Assigned by English Teacher	Ranks Assigned by Mathematics Teacher
A	8	5
B	3	7
C	2	6

Solution: Since the association between two measures obtained for the same group of students is assessed, use correlation; since the scale of the measures is ordinal, use Spearman r_s.

Passage 14

1. What is being measured and how?
Reading ability, measured by a reading test.

2. What is the scale of measurement used?
Interval.

3. What hypothesis is being tested?
A hypothesis of association: the purpose of the study is to compare reading scores obtained by fifth graders on two tests administered by their English teacher before and after the students practiced reading skills for two weeks.

4. How many sets of test scores?
Two - pretest and posttest scores.

5. Are the scores paired or independent of each other?
Paired - the pretest and posttest scores are obtained for the same group of students.

6. What might the data look like?

Student No.	Pretest	Posttest
A	34	47
B	45	58
C	41	50
	Mean Pretest	Mean Posttest

Solution: Since the two means being compared were obtained for the same group of students, use a paired *t*-test.

Passage 15

1. What is being measured and how?
The number of times the spinner lands on each of the four sides is being recorded.

2. What is the scale of measurement?
Nominal.

3. What hypothesis is being tested?
A hypothesis of difference: the passage describes a study in which the number of times a spinner lands on each of its four sides is compared to the expected number of times the spinner should have landed on the four sides. This expected number is based on the hypothesis that the spinner would land an equal number of times on each side.

4. How many sets of scores?
Two - one set of four observed frequencies is compared to a set of four expected frequencies.

5. Are the measures paired or independent of each other?
The measures are independent of each other.

6. What might the data look like?

Spinner Outcomes	Observed Frequencies	Expected Frequencies
Side 1	29	25
Side 2	25	25
Side 3	22	25
Side 4	24	25

> **Solution: Data are presented in a form of frequencies;
> therefore, use chi square.** Since only one variable is being
> used (the sides of a spinner) and the expected frequencies are
> of equal probabilities, use one-variable chi square with equal
> expected frequencies.

Passage 16

1. What is being measured and how?
The scores of 500 graduate students on the GRE, their
undergraduate GPA, and their graduate school GPA are
obtained from the students' school records.

2. What is the scale of measurement?
Interval.

3. What hypothesis is being tested?
A hypothesis of association: students' scores on the Verbal
and Quantitative sections of the GRE, the students'
undergraduate GPA, and the relation of these three scores
to the students' graduate school GPA are being investigated
in this study.

4. How many sets of scores?
For each student four scores are available: GRE - Verbal,
GRE - Quantitative, undergraduate school GPA, and
graduate school GPA.

5. Are the measures paired or independent of each other?
Paired - they are all obtained for the same group of
students.

6. What might the data look like?

Student No.	GRE Verbal	GRE Quantitative	College GPA	Graduate GPA
A	630	589	3.05	3.47
B	721	682	3.69	3.75
C	589	605	3.45	3.43

Solution: Since all four measures are obtained for the same group of students and three of these measures (GRE - Verbal, GRE - Quantitative, and undergraduate GPA) are used to predict the fourth one (graduate school GPA), use multiple regression.

Passage 17

1. What is being measured?
The color preference of 200 randomly-selected students, as measured by a survey.

2. What is the scale of measurement?
Nominal.

3. What hypothesis is being tested?
A hypothesis of difference: the study explores differences in the number of students who have selected one of three colors as the new color for their school logo. The equal expected frequencies are based on the assumption that there is no difference in color preference among the three colors.

4. How many sets of test scores?
Two - one set for the three observed frequencies and one set for the three expected frequencies.

5. Are the measures paired or independent?
The preferences of the students are independent of each other.

6. What might the data look like?

| | Number of Students | |
Color Preferred	Observed	Expected
Green	25	33.33
Purple	57	33.33
Royal Blue	38	33.33

Solution: Data are presented in a form of frequencies; therefore, use chi square. Since only one variable is used (the color of the logo) and the expected frequencies are of equal probabilities, use one variable chi square with equal expected frequencies.

Passage 18

1. What is being measured and how?

Readiness scores and first grade achievement test scores are obtained for a group of first graders, using a readiness test and an achievement test.

2. What is the scale of measurement?

Interval.

3. What hypothesis is being tested?

A hypothesis of association: relationship between students' kindergarten scores on a readiness test and their first grade scores on an academic performance test are being studied.

4. How many sets of scores?

Two - a readiness score and an achievement score are obtained for each student.

5. Are the measures paired or independent of each other?

Paired - both are obtained for the same group of students.

6. What might the data look like?

Student No.	Readiness Test Scores	Achievement Test Scores
A	35	68
B	29	75
C	33	82

Solution: Since both measures are obtained for the same group of students and one variable is used to predict the other variable, use simple regression.

Passage 19

1. What is being measured and how?
The GPA scores of athletes and the GPA scores of the students-at-large, using school's records.

2. What is the scale of measurement?
Interval.

3. What hypothesis is being tested?
A hypothesis of difference: the study investigates differences in the GPA of 50 college students athletes and the GPA of non-athlete students.

4. How many sets of scores?
Two - a mean GPA for the athletes and a mean GPA for the rest of the students.

5. Are the measures paired or independent of each other?
The scores are independent of each other.

6. What might the data look like?

GPA of Athletes	
3.1	Mean GPA of
2.8	non-athlete students: μ
3.2	
Mean GPA	

Solution: Since the mean of one group is being compared to the mean of a population, use *t*-test for a single sample.

Passage 20

1. What is being measured and how?
The number of hours the children watch television and their GPA.

2. What is the scale of measurement?
The number of hours is measured on a ratio scale and GPA is measured on an interval scale.

3. What hypothesis is being tested?
A hypothesis of association: the study explores relationships between the number of hours middle-school students watch television and their GPA .

4. How many sets of scores?
Two - the number of hours each student watches television and the student's GPA.

5. Are the measures paired or independent of each other?
Paired - both scores are obtained for the same group of students.

6. What might the data look like?

Student	No. of Hours/Week	GPA
David	32	2.97
Jean	28	3.78
Harry	33	3.22

Solution: Since the association between two measures obtained for the same group of children is assessed, use correlation; since the scales of the measures are ratio (number of hours/week) and interval (GPA), use Pearson r.

Passage 21

1. What is being measured and how?
The attitudes of fifth-grade boys and girls toward two types of computer games are being measured, using a Likert scale.

2. What is the scale of measurement?
Interval.

3. What hypothesis is being tested?
A hypothesis of difference: differences in attitudes toward computers of high-school boys and high-school girls using social-oriented and action-oriented computer games are being studied.

4. How many sets of scores?
Four - two scores (one for each type of game) for the boys and two scores for the girls.

5. Are the measures paired or independent of each other?
The measures are independent of each other.

6. What might the data look like?

	Action-Oriented Games	Social-Oriented Games	TOTAL
Boys	Mean	Mean	MEAN
Girls	Mean	Mean	MEAN
TOTAL	MEAN	MEAN	

Solution: Because means are being compared and there are two independent variables (gender and type of game), use two-way ANOVA.

Passage 22

1. What is being measured and how?
Years of schooling and annual income of 3000 people are being studied using information gathered by a survey.

2. What is the scale of measurement?
Ratio.

3. What hypothesis is being tested?
A hypothesis of association: the study investigates the relationships between the number of years of schooling and annual income of a stratified group of 3000 people.

4. How many sets of scores?
Two - for each person information is available about years of schooling and annual income.

5. Are the measures paired or independent of each other?
Paired - both measures are obtained for the same group of people.

6. What might the data look like?

Person No.	Years of Schooling	Annual Income
A	12	$ 33,000
B	19	$110,000
C	16	$ 57,000

Solution: Since both measures are obtained for the same group of people, and one variable is used to predict the second variable, use simple regression.

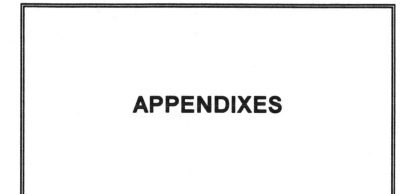

APPENDIXES

Page 110 For Use

Appendix A   Z Scores and Percentage of Area under the Normal Curve Between any Given Z- Score and the Mean[1]

(1) Standard Score z	(2) Area from Mean to z	(1) Standard Score z	(2) Area from Mean to z
0.00	.0000	0.25	.0987 *10%*
0.01	.0040	0.26	.1026
0.02	.0080	0.27	.1064 *11%*
0.03	.0120	0.28	.1103 *11%*
0.04	.0160	0.29	.1141 *11%*
0.05	.0199 *.02%*	0.30	.1179 *12%*
0.06	.0239	0.31	.1217
0.07	.0279	0.32	.1255 *13%*
0.08	.0319	0.33	.1293
0.09	.0359 *.04%*	0.34	.1331
0.10	.0398 *.04%*	0.35	.1368
0.11	.0438 *.04%*	0.36	.1406
0.12	.0478 *.05%*	0.37	.1443
0.13	.0517 *.05%*	0.38	.1480
0.14	.0557	0.39	.1517
0.15	.0596 *.06%*	0.40	.1554
0.16	.0636 *.06%*	0.41	.1591
0.17	.0675 *.07%*	0.42	.1628
0.18	.0714 *.07%*	0.43	.1664
0.19	.0753 *.08%*	0.44	.1700
0.20	.0793 *.08%*	0.45	.1736
0.21	.0832	0.46	.1772
0.22	.0871 *.09%*	0.47	.1808
0.23	.0910 *.09%*	0.48	.1844
0.24	.0948 *.09%*	0.49	.1879 — *19%*

(handwritten) Add % to 50 =

(handwritten) 19 + 50 = 69% Percentile Rank

[1]Adapted from A.L. Edwards, *Statistical Methods for the Behavioral Sciences*, Holt, Rinehart and Winston, Inc., 1954, pp. 490-99, with permission of the author.

(1) Standard Score	(2) Area from Mean to	(1) Standard Score	(2) Area from Mean to
z	z	z	z
0.50	.1915	0.80	.2281
0.51	.1950	0.81	.2910
0.52	.1985	0.82	.2939
0.53	.2019	0.83	.2967
0.54	.2054	0.84	.2995
0.55	.2088	0.85	.3023
0.56	.2123	0.86	.3051
0.57	.2157	0.87	.3078
0.58	.2190	0.88	.3106
0.59	.2224	0.89	.3133
0.60	.2257	0.90	.3159
0.61	.2291	0.91	.3186
0.62	.2324	0.92	.3212
0.63	.2357	0.93	.3238
0.64	.2389	0.94	.3264
0.65	.2422	0.95	.3289
0.66	.2454	0.96	.3315
0.67	.2486	0.97	.3340
0.68	.2517	0.98	.3365
0.69	.2549	0.99	.3389
0.70	.2580	1.00	.3413
0.71	.2611	1.01	.3438
0.72	.2642	1.02	.3461
0.73	.2673	1.03	.3485
0.74	.2704	1.04	.3508
0.75	.2734	1.05	.3531
0.76	.2764	1.06	.3554
0.77	.2794	1.07	.3577
0.78	.2823	1.08	.3599
0.79	.2852	1.09	.3621

(1) Standard Score z	(2) Area from Mean to z	(1) Standard Score z	(2) Area from Mean to z
1.10	.3643	1.40	.4192
1.11	.3665	1.41	.4207
1.12	.3686	1.42	.4222
1.13	.3708	1.43	.4236
1.14	.3729	1.44	.4251
1.15	.3749	1.45	.4265
1.16	.3770	1.46	.4279
1.17	.3790	1.47	.4292
1.18	.3810	1.48	.4306
1.19	.3830	1.49	.4319
1.20	.3849	1.50	.4332
1.21	.3869	1.51	.4345
1.22	.3888	1.52	.4357
1.23	.3907	1.53	.4370
1.24	.3925	1.54	.4382
1.25	.3944	1.55	.4394
1.26	.3962	1.56	.4406
1.27	.3980	1.57	.4418
1.28	.3997	1.58	.4429
1.29	.4015	1.59	.4441
1.30	.4032	1.60	.4452
1.31	.4049	1.61	.4463
1.32	.4066	1.62	.4474
1.33	.4082	1.63	.4484
1.34	.4099	1.64	.4495
1.35	.4115	1.65	.4505
1.36	.4131	1.66	.4515
1.37	.4147	1.67	.4525
1.38	.4162	1.68	.4535
1.39	.4177	1.69	.4545

(1) Standard Score z	(2) Area from Mean to z	(1) Standard Score z	(2) Area from Mean to z
1.70	.4554	2.00	.4772
1.71	.4564	2.01	.4778
1.72	.4573	2.02	.4783
1.73	.4582	2.03	.4788
1.74	.4591	2.04	.4793
1.75	.4599	2.05	.4798
1.76	.4608	2.06	.4803
1.77	.4616	2.07	.4808
1.78	.4625	2.08	.4812
1.79	.4633	2.09	.4817
1.80	.4641	2.10	.4821
1.81	.4649	2.11	.4826
1.82	.4656	2.12	.4830
1.83	.4664	2.13	.4834
1.84	.4671	2.14	.4838
1.85	.4678	2.15	.4842
1.86	.4686	2.16	.4846
1.87	.4693	2.17	.4850
1.88	.4699	2.18	.4854
1.89	.4706	2.19	.4857
1.90	.4713	2.20	.4861
1.91	.4719	2.21	.4864
1.92	.4726	2.22	.4868
1.93	.4732	2.23	.4871
1.94	.4738	2.24	.4875
1.95	.4744	2.25	.4878
1.96	.4750	2.26	.4881
1.97	.4756	2.27	.4884
1.98	.4761	2.28	.4887
1.99	.4767	2.29	.4890

(1) Standard Score z	(2) Area from Mean to z	(1) Standard Score z	(2) Area from Mean to z
2.30	.4893	2.60	.4953
2.31	.4896	2.61	.4955
2.32	.4898	2.62	.4956
2.33	.4901	2.63	.4957
2.34	.4904	2.64	.4959
2.35	.4906	2.65	.4960
2.36	.4909	2.66	.4961
2.37	.4911	2.67	.4962
2.38	.4913	2.68	.4963
2.39	.4916	2.69	.4964
2.40	.4918	2.70	.4965
2.41	.4920	2.71	.4966
2.42	.4922	2.72	.4967
2.43	.4925	2.73	.4968
2.44	.4927	2.74	.4969
2.45	.4929	2.75	.4970
2.46	.4931	2.76	.4971
2.47	.4932	2.77	.4972
2.48	.4934	2.78	.4973
2.49	.4936	2.79	.4974
2.50	.4938	2.80	.4974
2.51	.4940	2.81	.4975
2.52	.4941	2.82	.4976
2.53	.4943	2.83	.4977
2.54	.4945	2.84	.4977
2.55	.4946	2.85	.4978
2.56	.4948	2.86	.4979
2.57	.4949	2.87	.4979
2.58	.4951	2.88	.4980
2.59	.4952	2.89	.4981

(1) Standard Score z	(2) Area from Mean to z	(1) Standard Score z	(2) Area from Mean to z
2.90	.4981	3.20	.4993
2.91	.4982	3.21	.4993
2.92	.4982	3.22	.4994
2.93	.4983	3.23	.4994
2.94	.4984	3.24	.4994
2.95	.4984	3.30	.4995
2.96	.4985	3.40	.4997
2.97	.4985	3.50	.4998
2.98	.4986	3.60	.4998
2.99	.4986	3.70	.4999
3.00	.4987		
3.01	.4987		
3.02	.4987		
3.03	.4988		
3.04	.4988		
3.05	.4989		
3.06	.4989		
3.07	.4989		
3.08	.4990		
3.09	.4990		
3.10	.4990		
3.11	.4991		
3.12	.4991		
3.13	.4991		
3.14	.4992		
3.15	.4992		
3.16	.4992		
3.17	.4992		
3.18	.4993		
3.19	.4993		

Appendix B Values of the Correlation Coefficient (Pearson's *r*) for Different Levels of Significance

df	p level			
	.10	.05	.02	.01
1	.988	.997	.9995	.9999
2	.900	.950	.980	.990
3	.805	.878	.934	.959
4	.729	.811	.882	.917
5	.669	.754	.833	.874
6	.622	.707	.789	.834
7	.582	.666	.750	.798
8	.549	.632	.716	.765
9	.521	.602	.685	.735
10	.497	.576	.658	.708
11	.476	.553	.634	.684
12	.458	.532	.612	.661
13	.441	.514	.592	.641
14	.426	.497	.574	.623
15	.412	.482	.558	.606
16	.400	.468	.542	.590
17	.389	.456	.528	.575
18	.378	.444	.516	.561
19	.369	.433	.503	.549
20	.360	.423	.492	.537
21	.352	.413	.482	.526
22	.344	.404	.472	.515
23	.337	.396	.462	.505
24	.330	.388	.453	.496
25	.323	.381	.445	.487
26	.317	.374	.437	.479
27	.311	.367	.430	.471
28	.306	.361	.423	.463
29	.301	.355	.416	.456
30	.296	.349	.409	.449
35	.275	.325	.381	.418
40	.257	.304	.358	.393
45	.243	.288	.338	.372
50	.231	.273	.322	.354
60	.211	.250	.295	.325
70	.195	.232	.274	.302
80	.183	.217	.256	.283
90	.173	.205	.242	.267
100	.164	.195	.230	.254

Source: Reprinted from Table VA in Fisher & Yates, *Statistical Methods for Research Workers*, published by Oliver and Boyd Ltd., Edinburgh, and by permission of the University of Adelaide.

Note: Degrees of freedom (*df*) are the number of pairs of scores minus 2.

If 1 tailed 2 tailed double scap

critical values

the more confidence the higher you go the right you can predict Confidence in your research

Appendix C — Distribution of *t*

df	Level of significance for one-tailed test					
	.10	.05	.025	.01	.005	.0005
	Level of significance for two-tailed test					
	.20	.10	.05	.02	.01	.001
1	3.078	6.314	12.706	31.821	63.657	636.619
2	1.886	2.920	4.303	6.965	9.925	31.598
3	1.638	2.353	3.182	4.541	5.841	12.941
4	1.533	2.132	2.776	3.747	4.604	8.610
5	1.476	2.015	2.571	3.365	4.032	6.859
6	1.440	1.943	2.447	3.143	3.707	5.959
7	1.415	1.895	2.365	2.998	3.499	5.405
8	1.397	1.860	2.306	2.896	3.355	5.041
9	1.383	1.833	2.262	2.821	3.250	4.781
10	1.372	1.812	2.228	2.764	3.169	4.587
11	1.363	1.796	2.201	2.718	3.106	4.437
12	1.356	1.782	2.179	2.681	3.055	4.318
13	1.350	1.771	2.160	2.650	3.012	4.221
14	1.345	1.761	2.145	2.624	2.977	4.140
15	1.341	1.753	2.131	2.602	2.947	4.073
16	1.337	1.746	2.120	2.583	2.921	4.015
17	1.333	1.740	2.110	2.567	2.898	3.965
18	1.330	1.734	2.101	2.552	2.878	3.922
19	1.328	1.729	2.093	2.539	2.861	3.883
20	1.325	1.725	2.086	2.528	2.845	3.850
21	1.323	1.721	2.080	2.518	2.831	3.819
22	1.321	1.717	2.074	2.508	2.819	3.792
23	1.319	1.714	2.069	2.500	2.807	3.767
24	1.318	1.711	2.064	2.492	2.797	3.745
25	1.316	1.708	2.060	2.485	2.787	3.725
26	1.315	1.706	2.056	2.479	2.779	3.707
27	1.314	1.703	2.052	2.473	2.771	3.690
28	1.313	1.701	2.048	2.467	2.763	3.674
29	1.311	1.699	2.045	2.462	2.756	3.659
30	1.310	1.697	2.042	2.457	2.750	3.646
40	1.303	1.684	2.021	2.423	2.704	3.551
60	1.296	1.671	2.000	2.390	2.660	3.460
120	1.289	1.658	1.980	2.358	2.617	3.373
∞	1.282	1.645	1.960	2.326	2.576	3.291

Source: Taken from Table IV of Fisher & Yates: *Statistical Tables for Biological, Agricultural and Medicinal Research* published by Longman Group UK Ltd., London, by permission of the publishers.

Appendix Table D

The 5 percent (Lightface Type) and 1 percent (Boldface Type) Points for the Distribution of F

Degrees of freedom for numerator

n_1	1	2	3	4	5	6	7	8	9	10	11	12
1	161	200	216	225	230	234	237	239	241	242	243	244
	4,052	**4,999**	**5,403**	**5,625**	**5,764**	**5,859**	**5,928**	**5,981**	**6,022**	**6,056**	**6,082**	**6,106**
2	18.51	19.00	19.16	19.25	19.30	19.33	19.36	19.37	19.38	19.39	19.40	19.41
	98.49	**99.00**	**99.17**	**99.25**	**99.30**	**99.33**	**99.34**	**99.36**	**99.38**	**99.40**	**99.41**	**99.42**
3	10.13	9.55	9.28	9.12	9.01	8.94	8.88	8.84	8.81	8.78	8.76	8.74
	34.12	**30.82**	**29.46**	**28.71**	**28.24**	**27.91**	**27.67**	**27.49**	**27.34**	**27.23**	**27.13**	**27.05**
4	7.71	6.94	6.59	6.39	6.26	6.16	6.09	6.04	6.00	5.96	5.93	5.91
	21.20	**18.00**	**16.69**	**15.98**	**15.52**	**15.21**	**14.98**	**14.80**	**14.66**	**14.54**	**14.45**	**14.37**
5	6.61	5.79	5.41	5.19	5.05	4.95	4.88	4.82	4.78	4.74	4.70	4.68
	16.26	**13.27**	**12.06**	**11.39**	**10.97**	**10.67**	**10.45**	**10.27**	**10.15**	**10.05**	**9.96**	**9.89**
6	5.99	5.14	4.76	4.53	4.39	4.28	4.21	4.15	4.10	4.06	4.03	4.00
	13.74	**10.92**	**9.78**	**9.15**	**8.75**	**8.47**	**8.26**	**8.10**	**7.98**	**7.87**	**7.79**	**7.72**

Source: Reproduced from G. W. Snedecor, *Statistical Methods*, 5th ed., Iowa State University, Iowa, by permission of the author and publisher.

Appendix Table D, cont.

					Degrees of freedom for numerator							
n_1	1	2	3	4	5	6	7	8	9	10	11	12
7	5.59	4.74	4.35	4.12	3.97	3.87	3.79	3.73	3.68	3.63	3.60	3.57
	12.25	**9.55**	**8.45**	**7.85**	**7.46**	**7.19**	**7.00**	**6.84**	**6.71**	**6.62**	**6.54**	**6.47**
8	5.32	4.46	4.07	3.84	3.69	3.58	3.50	3.44	3.39	3.34	3.31	3.28
	11.26	**8.65**	**7.59**	**7.01**	**6.63**	**6.37**	**6.19**	**6.03**	**5.91**	**5.82**	**5.74**	**5.67**
9	5.12	4.26	3.86	3.63	3.48	3.37	3.29	3.23	3.18	3.13	3.10	3.07
	10.56	**8.02**	**6.99**	**6.42**	**6.06**	**5.80**	**5.62**	**5.47**	**5.35**	**5.26**	**5.18**	**5.11**
10	4.96	4.10	3.71	3.48	3.33	3.22	3.14	3.07	3.02	2.97	2.94	2.91
	10.04	**7.56**	**6.55**	**5.99**	**5.64**	**5.39**	**5.21**	**5.06**	**4.95**	**4.85**	**4.78**	**4.71**
11	4.84	3.98	3.59	3.36	3.20	3.09	3.01	2.95	2.90	2.86	2.82	2.79
	9.65	**7.20**	**6.22**	**5.67**	**5.32**	**5.07**	**4.88**	**4.74**	**4.63**	**4.54**	**4.46**	**4.40**
12	4.75	3.88	3.49	3.26	3.11	3.00	2.92	2.85	2.80	2.76	2.72	2.69
	9.33	**6.93**	**5.95**	**5.41**	**5.06**	**4.82**	**4.65**	**4.50**	**4.39**	**4.30**	**4.22**	**4.16**
13	4.67	3.80	3.41	3.18	3.02	2.92	2.84	2.77	2.72	2.67	2.63	2.60
	9.07	**6.70**	**5.74**	**5.20**	**4.86**	**4.62**	**4.44**	**4.30**	**4.19**	**4.10**	**4.02**	**3.96**

Appendix Table D, cont.

n_1		Degrees of freedom for numerator										
	1	2	3	4	5	6	7	8	9	10	11	12
14	4.60 **8.86**	3.74 **6.51**	3.34 **5.56**	3.11 **5.03**	2.96 **4.69**	2.85 **4.46**	2.77 **4.28**	2.70 **4.14**	2.65 **4.03**	2.60 **3.94**	2.56 **3.86**	2.53 **3.80**
15	4.54 **8.68**	3.68 **6.36**	3.29 **5.42**	3.06 **4.89**	2.90 **4.56**	2.79 **4.32**	2.70 **4.14**	2.64 **4.00**	2.59 **3.89**	2.55 **3.80**	2.51 **3.73**	2.48 **3.67**
16	4.49 **8.53**	3.63 **6.23**	3.24 **5.29**	3.01 **4.77**	2.85 **4.44**	2.74 **4.20**	2.66 **4.03**	2.59 **3.89**	2.54 **3.78**	2.49 **3.69**	2.45 **3.61**	2.42 **3.55**
17	4.45 **8.40**	3.59 **6.11**	3.20 **5.18**	2.96 **4.67**	2.81 **4.34**	2.70 **4.10**	2.62 **3.93**	2.55 **3.79**	2.50 **3.68**	2.45 **3.59**	2.41 **3.52**	2.38 **3.45**
18	4.41 **8.28**	3.55 **6.01**	3.16 **5.09**	2.93 **4.58**	2.77 **4.25**	2.66 **4.01**	2.58 **3.85**	2.51 **3.71**	2.46 **3.60**	2.41 **3.51**	2.37 **3.44**	2.34 **3.37**
19	4.38 **8.18**	3.52 **5.93**	3.13 **5.01**	2.90 **4.50**	2.74 **4.17**	2.63 **3.94**	2.55 **3.77**	2.48 **3.63**	2.43 **3.52**	2.38 **3.43**	2.34 **3.36**	2.31 **3.30**
20	4.35 **8.10**	3.49 **5.85**	3.10 **4.94**	2.87 **4.43**	2.71 **4.10**	2.60 **3.87**	2.52 **3.71**	2.45 **3.56**	2.40 **3.45**	2.35 **3.37**	2.31 **3.30**	2.28 **3.23**

Appendix Table D, cont.

	Degrees of freedom for numerator											
n_1	1	2	3	4	5	6	7	8	9	10	11	12
21	4.32 / **8.02**	3.47 / **5.78**	3.07 / **4.87**	2.84 / **4.37**	2.68 / **4.04**	2.57 / **3.81**	2.49 / **3.65**	2.42 / **3.51**	2.37 / **3.40**	2.32 / **3.31**	2.28 / **3.24**	2.25 / **3.17**
22	4.30 / **7.94**	3.44 / **5.72**	3.05 / **4.82**	2.82 / **4.31**	2.66 / **3.99**	2.55 / **3.76**	2.47 / **3.59**	2.40 / **3.45**	2.35 / **3.35**	2.30 / **3.26**	2.26 / **3.18**	2.23 / **3.12**
23	4.28 / **7.88**	3.42 / **5.66**	3.03 / **4.76**	2.80 / **4.26**	2.64 / **3.94**	2.53 / **3.71**	2.45 / **3.54**	2.38 / **3.41**	2.32 / **3.30**	2.28 / **3.21**	2.24 / **3.14**	2.20 / **3.07**
24	4.26 / **7.82**	3.40 / **5.61**	3.01 / **4.72**	2.78 / **4.22**	2.62 / **3.90**	2.51 / **3.67**	2.43 / **3.50**	2.36 / **3.36**	2.30 / **3.25**	2.26 / **3.17**	2.22 / **3.09**	2.18 / **3.03**
25	4.24 / **7.77**	3.38 / **5.57**	2.99 / **4.68**	2.76 / **4.18**	2.60 / **3.86**	2.49 / **3.63**	2.41 / **3.46**	2.34 / **3.32**	2.28 / **3.21**	2.24 / **3.13**	2.20 / **3.05**	2.16 / **2.99**
26	4.22 / **7.72**	3.37 / **5.53**	2.98 / **4.64**	2.74 / **4.14**	2.59 / **3.82**	2.47 / **3.59**	2.39 / **3.42**	2.32 / **3.29**	2.27 / **3.17**	2.22 / **3.09**	2.18 / **3.02**	2.15 / **2.96**
27	4.21 / **7.68**	3.35 / **5.49**	2.96 / **4.60**	2.73 / **4.11**	2.57 / **3.79**	2.46 / **3.56**	2.37 / **3.39**	2.30 / **3.26**	2.25 / **3.14**	2.20 / **3.06**	2.16 / **2.98**	2.13 / **2.93**

Appendix Table D, cont.

n_1	Degrees of freedom for numerator											
	1	2	3	4	5	6	7	8	9	10	11	12
28	4.20 **7.64**	3.34 **5.45**	2.95 **4.57**	2.71 **4.07**	2.56 **3.76**	2.44 **3.53**	2.36 **3.36**	2.29 **3.23**	2.24 **3.11**	2.19 **3.03**	2.15 **2.95**	2.12 **2.90**
29	4.18 **7.60**	3.33 **5.42**	2.93 **4.54**	2.70 **4.04**	2.54 **3.73**	2.43 **3.50**	2.35 **3.33**	2.28 **3.20**	2.22 **3.08**	2.18 **3.00**	2.14 **2.92**	2.10 **2.87**
30	4.17 **7.56**	3.32 **5.39**	2.92 **4.51**	2.69 **4.02**	2.53 **3.70**	2.42 **3.47**	2.34 **3.30**	2.27 **3.17**	2.21 **3.06**	2.16 **2.98**	2.12 **2.90**	2.09 **2.84**
32	4.15 **7.50**	3.30 **5.34**	2.90 **4.46**	2.67 **3.97**	2.51 **3.66**	2.40 **3.42**	2.32 **3.25**	2.25 **3.12**	2.19 **3.01**	2.14 **2.94**	2.10 **2.86**	2.07 **2.80**
34	4.13 **7.44**	3.28 **5.29**	2.88 **4.42**	2.65 **3.93**	2.49 **3.61**	2.38 **3.38**	2.30 **3.21**	2.23 **3.08**	2.17 **2.97**	2.12 **2.89**	2.08 **2.82**	2.05 **2.76**
36	4.11 **7.39**	3.26 **5.25**	2.86 **4.38**	2.63 **3.89**	2.48 **3.58**	2.36 **3.35**	2.28 **3.18**	2.21 **3.04**	2.15 **2.94**	2.10 **2.86**	2.06 **2.78**	2.03 **2.72**
38	4.10 **7.35**	3.25 **5.21**	2.85 **4.34**	2.62 **3.86**	2.46 **3.54**	2.35 **3.32**	2.26 **3.15**	2.19 **3.02**	2.14 **2.91**	2.09 **2.82**	2.05 **2.75**	2.02 **2.69**

Appendix Table D, cont.

Degrees of freedom for numerator

n_1	1	2	3	4	5	6	7	8	9	10	11	12
40	4.08 **7.31**	3.23 **5.18**	2.84 **4.31**	2.61 **3.83**	2.45 **3.51**	2.34 **3.29**	2.25 **3.12**	2.18 **2.99**	2.12 **2.88**	2.07 **2.80**	2.04 **2.73**	2.00 **2.66**
42	4.07 **7.27**	3.22 **5.15**	2.83 **4.29**	2.59 **3.80**	2.44 **3.49**	2.32 **3.26**	2.24 **3.10**	2.17 **2.96**	2.11 **2.86**	2.06 **2.77**	2.02 **2.70**	1.99 **2.64**
44	4.06 **7.24**	3.21 **5.12**	2.82 **4.26**	2.58 **3.78**	2.43 **3.46**	2.31 **3.24**	2.23 **3.07**	2.16 **2.94**	2.10 **2.84**	2.05 **2.75**	2.01 **2.68**	1.98 **2.62**
46	4.05 **7.21**	3.20 **5.10**	2.81 **4.24**	2.57 **3.76**	2.42 **3.44**	2.30 **3.22**	2.22 **3.05**	2.14 **2.92**	2.09 **2.82**	2.04 **2.73**	2.00 **2.66**	1.97 **2.60**
48	4.04 **7.19**	3.19 **5.08**	2.80 **4.22**	2.56 **3.74**	2.41 **3.42**	2.30 **3.20**	2.21 **3.04**	2.14 **2.90**	2.08 **2.80**	2.03 **2.71**	1.99 **2.64**	1.96 **2.58**
50	4.03 **7.17**	3.18 **5.06**	2.79 **4.20**	2.56 **3.72**	2.40 **3.41**	2.29 **3.18**	2.20 **3.02**	2.13 **2.88**	2.07 **2.78**	2.02 **2.70**	1.98 **2.62**	1.95 **2.56**
55	4.02 **7.12**	3.17 **5.01**	2.78 **4.16**	2.54 **3.68**	2.38 **3.37**	2.27 **3.15**	2.18 **2.98**	2.11 **2.85**	2.05 **2.75**	2.00 **2.66**	1.97 **2.59**	1.93 **2.53**

Appendix Table D, cont

Degrees of freedom for numerator

n_1	1	2	3	4	5	6	7	8	9	10	11	12
60	4.00 **7.08**	3.15 **4.98**	2.76 **4.13**	2.52 **3.65**	2.37 **3.34**	2.25 **3.12**	2.17 **2.95**	2.10 **2.82**	2.04 **2.72**	1.99 **2.63**	1.95 **2.56**	1.92 **2.50**
65	3.99 **7.04**	3.14 **4.95**	2.75 **4.10**	2.51 **3.62**	2.36 **3.31**	2.24 **3.09**	2.15 **2.93**	2.08 **2.79**	2.02 **2.70**	1.98 **2.61**	1.94 **2.54**	1.90 **2.47**
70	3.98 **7.01**	3.13 **4.92**	2.74 **4.08**	2.50 **3.60**	2.35 **3.29**	2.23 **3.07**	2.14 **2.91**	2.07 **2.77**	2.01 **2.67**	1.97 **2.59**	1.93 **2.51**	1.89 **2.45**
80	3.96 **6.96**	3.11 **4.88**	2.72 **4.04**	2.48 **3.56**	2.33 **3.25**	2.21 **3.04**	2.12 **2.87**	2.05 **2.74**	1.99 **2.64**	1.95 **2.55**	1.91 **2.48**	1.88 **2.41**
100	3.94 **6.90**	3.09 **4.82**	2.70 **3.98**	2.46 **3.51**	2.30 **3.20**	2.19 **2.99**	2.10 **2.82**	2.03 **2.69**	1.97 **2.59**	1.92 **2.51**	1.88 **2.43**	1.85 **2.36**
125	3.92 **6.84**	3.07 **4.78**	2.68 **3.94**	2.44 **3.47**	2.29 **3.17**	2.17 **2.95**	2.08 **2.79**	2.01 **2.65**	1.95 **2.56**	1.90 **2.47**	1.86 **2.40**	1.83 **2.33**
150	3.91 **6.81**	3.06 **4.75**	2.67 **3.91**	2.43 **3.44**	2.27 **3.14**	2.16 **2.92**	2.07 **2.76**	2.00 **2.62**	1.94 **2.53**	1.89 **2.44**	1.85 **2.37**	1.82 **2.30**

Appendix Table D, cont.

		Degrees of freedom for numerator										
n_1	1	2	3	4	5	6	7	8	9	10	11	12
200	3.89	3.04	2.65	2.41	2.26	2.14	2.05	1.98	1.92	1.87	1.83	1.80
	6.76	**4.71**	**3.88**	**3.41**	**3.11**	**2.90**	**2.73**	**2.60**	**2.50**	**2.41**	**2.34**	**2.28**
400	3.86	3.02	2.62	2.39	2.23	2.12	2.03	1.96	1.90	1.85	1.81	1.78
	6.70	**4.66**	**3.83**	**3.36**	**3.06**	**2.85**	**2.69**	**2.55**	**2.46**	**2.37**	**2.29**	**2.23**
1000	3.85	3.00	2.61	2.38	2.22	2.10	2.02	1.95	1.89	1.84	1.80	1.76
	6.66	**4.62**	**3.80**	**3.34**	**3.04**	**2.82**	**2.66**	**2.53**	**2.43**	**2.34**	**2.26**	**2.20**
∞	3.84	2.99	2.60	2.37	2.21	2.09	2.01	1.94	1.88	1.83	1.79	1.75
	6.64	**4.60**	**3.78**	**3.32**	**3.02**	**2.80**	**2.64**	**2.51**	**2.41**	**2.32**	**2.24**	**2.18**

Appendix Table E   Distribution of Studentized Range Statistic

df for within mean square	α	k = number of groups													
		2	3	4	5	6	7	8	9	10	11	12	13	14	15
1	.05	18.0	27.0	32.8	37.1	40.4	43.1	45.4	47.4	49.1	50.6	52.0	53.2	54.3	55.4
	.01	90.0	135	164	186	202	216	227	237	246	253	260	266	272	277
2	.05	6.09	8.3	9.8	10.9	11.7	12.4	13.0	13.5	14.0	14.4	14.7	15.1	15.4	15.7
	.01	14.0	19.0	22.3	24.7	26.6	28.2	29.5	30.7	31.7	32.6	33.4	34.1	34.8	35.4
3	.05	4.50	5.91	6.82	7.50	8.04	8.48	8.85	9.18	9.46	9.72	9.95	10.2	10.4	10.5
	.01	8.26	10.6	12.2	13.3	14.2	15.0	15.6	16.2	16.7	17.1	17.5	17.9	18.2	18.5
4	.05	3.93	5.04	5.76	6.29	6.71	7.05	7.35	7.60	7.83	8.03	8.21	8.37	8.52	8.66
	.01	6.51	8.12	9.17	9.96	10.6	11.1	11.5	11.9	12.3	12.6	12.8	13.1	13.3	13.5
5	.05	3.64	4.60	5.22	5.67	6.03	6.33	6.58	6.80	6.99	7.17	7.32	7.47	7.60	7.72
	.01	5.70	6.97	7.80	8.42	8.91	9.32	9.67	9.97	10.2	10.5	10.7	10.9	11.1	11.2
6	.05	3.46	4.34	4.90	5.31	5.63	5.89	6.12	6.32	6.49	6.65	6.79	6.92	7.03	7.14
	.01	5.24	6.33	7.03	7.55	7.97	8.32	8.61	8.87	9.10	9.30	9.49	9.65	9.81	9.95
7	.05	3.34	4.16	4.69	5.06	5.36	5.61	5.82	6.00	6.16	6.30	6.43	6.55	6.66	6.76
	.01	4.95	5.92	6.54	7.01	7.37	7.68	7.94	8.17	8.37	8.55	8.71	8.86	9.00	9.12

Source: Reprinted from September 1, 1971 issue of Business Week by special permission, © 1971 by McGraw-Hill, Inc. Table adapted fr. Table 11.2 in The Probability Integrals of the Range and of the Studentized Range, prepared by H. Leon Harter, Donald S. Clemm, and Eugene H. Guthrie, published in WADEC Tech. Rep. 58-484, vol. 2, 1959, Wright Air Development Ctr.

Appendix Table E, cont.

df for within mean square	α	k = number of groups													
		2	3	4	5	6	7	8	9	10	11	12	13	14	15
8	.05	3.26	4.04	4.53	4.89	5.17	5.40	5.60	5.77	5.92	6.05	6.18	6.29	6.39	6.48
	.01	4.74	5.63	6.20	6.63	6.96	7.24	7.47	7.68	7.87	8.03	8.18	8.31	8.44	8.55
9	.05	3.20	3.95	4.42	4.76	5.02	5.24	5.43	5.60	5.74	5.87	5.98	6.09	6.19	6.28
	.01	4.60	5.43	5.96	6.35	6.66	6.91	7.13	7.32	7.49	7.65	7.78	7.91	8.03	8.13
10	.05	3.15	3.88	4.33	4.65	4.91	5.12	5.30	5.46	5.60	5.72	5.83	5.93	6.03	6.11
	.01	4.48	5.27	5.77	6.14	6.43	6.67	6.87	7.05	7.21	7.36	7.48	7.60	7.71	7.81
11	.05	3.11	3.82	4.26	4.57	4.82	5.03	5.20	5.35	5.49	5.61	5.71	5.81	5.90	5.99
	.01	4.39	5.14	5.62	5.97	6.25	6.48	6.67	6.84	6.99	7.13	7.26	7.36	7.46	7.56
12	.05	3.08	3.77	4.20	4.51	4.75	4.95	5.12	5.27	5.40	5.51	5.62	5.71	5.80	5.88
	.01	4.32	5.04	5.50	5.84	6.10	6.32	6.51	6.67	6.81	6.94	7.06	7.17	7.26	7.36
13	.05	3.06	3.73	4.15	4.45	4.69	4.88	5.05	5.19	5.32	5.43	5.53	5.63	5.71	5.79
	.01	4.26	4.96	5.40	5.73	5.98	6.19	6.37	6.53	6.67	6.79	6.90	7.01	7.10	7.19
14	.05	3.03	3.70	4.11	4.41	4.64	4.83	4.99	5.13	5.25	5.36	5.46	5.55	5.64	5.72
	.01	4.21	4.89	5.32	5.63	5.88	6.08	6.26	6.41	6.54	6.66	6.77	6.87	6.96	7.05

Appendix Table E, cont.

df for within mean square	α	k = number of groups 2	3	4	5	6	7	8	9	10	11	12	13	14	15
16	.05	3.00	3.65	4.05	4.33	4.56	4.74	4.90	5.03	5.15	5.26	5.35	5.44	5.52	5.59
	.01	4.13	4.78	5.19	5.49	5.72	5.92	6.08	6.22	6.35	6.46	6.56	6.66	6.74	6.82
18	.05	2.97	3.61	4.00	4.28	4.49	4.67	4.82	4.96	5.07	5.17	5.27	5.35	5.43	5.50
	.01	4.07	4.70	5.09	5.38	5.60	5.79	5.94	6.08	6.20	6.31	6.41	6.50	6.58	6.65
20	.05	2.95	3.58	3.96	4.23	4.45	4.62	4.77	4.90	5.01	5.11	5.20	5.28	5.36	5.43
	.01	4.02	4.64	5.02	5.29	5.51	5.69	5.84	5.97	6.09	6.19	6.29	6.37	6.45	6.52
24	.05	2.92	3.53	3.90	4.17	4.37	4.54	4.68	4.81	4.92	5.01	5.10	5.18	5.25	5.32
	.01	3.96	4.54	4.91	5.17	5.37	5.54	5.69	5.81	5.92	6.02	6.11	6.19	6.26	6.33
30	.05	2.89	3.49	3.84	4.10	4.30	4.46	4.60	4.72	4.83	4.92	5.00	5.08	5.15	5.21
	.01	3.89	4.45	4.80	5.05	5.24	5.40	5.54	5.56	5.76	5.85	5.93	6.01	6.08	6.14
40	.05	2.86	3.44	3.79	4.04	4.23	4.39	4.52	4.63	4.74	4.82	4.91	4.98	5.05	5.11
	.01	3.82	4.37	4.70	4.93	5.11	5.27	5.39	5.50	5.60	5.69	5.77	5.84	5.90	5.96
60	.05	2.83	3.40	3.74	3.98	4.16	4.31	4.44	4.55	4.65	4.73	4.81	4.88	4.94	5.00
	.01	3.76	4.28	4.60	4.82	4.99	5.13	5.25	5.36	5.45	5.53	5.60	5.67	5.73	5.79

Appendix Table E, cont.

df for within mean square	α	k = number of groups													
		2	3	4	5	6	7	8	9	10	11	12	13	14	15
120	.05	2.80	3.36	3.69	3.92	4.10	4.24	4.36	4.48	4.56	4.64	4.72	4.78	4.84	4.90
	.01	3.70	4.20	4.50	4.71	4.87	5.01	5.12	5.21	5.30	5.38	5.44	5.51	5.56	5.61
∞	.05	2.77	3.31	3.63	3.86	4.03	4.17	4.29	4.39	4.47	4.55	4.62	4.68	4.74	4.80
	.01	3.64	4.12	4.40	4.60	4.76	4.88	4.99	5.08	5.16	5.23	5.29	5.35	5.40	5.45

Critical Value (handwritten)

Appendix F   Distribution of Chi Square (χ^2)

P value is greater ← _one_ → _P < P is less if you have · 05 or more_ (handwritten annotations)

df	.10	.05	.02	.01	.001
1	2.706	3.841	5.412	6.635	10.827
2	4.605	5.991	7.824	9.210	13.815
3	6.251	7.815	9.837	11.341	16.268
4	7.779	9.488	11.668	13.277	18.465
5	9.236	11.070	13.388	15.086	20.517
6	10.645	12.592	15.033	16.812	22.457
7	12.017	14.067	16.622	18.475	24.322
8	13.362	15.507	18.168	20.090	26.125
9	14.684	16.919	19.679	21.666	27.877
10	15.987	18.307	21.161	23.209	29.588
11	17.275	19.675	22.618	24.725	31.264
12	18.549	21.026	24.054	26.217	32.909
13	19.812	22.362	25.472	27.688	34.528
14	21.064	23.685	26.873	29.141	36.123
15	22.307	24.996	28.259	30.578	37.697
16	23.542	26.296	29.633	32.000	39.252
17	24.769	27.587	30.995	33.409	40.790
18	25.989	28.869	32.346	34.805	42.312
19	27.204	30.144	33.687	36.191	43.820
20	28.412	31.410	35.020	37.566	45.315
21	29.615	32.671	36.343	38.932	46.797
22	30.813	33.924	37.659	40.289	48.268
23	32.007	35.172	38.968	41.638	49.728
24	33.196	36.415	40.270	42.980	51.179
25	34.382	37.652	41.566	44.314	52.620
26	35.563	38.885	42.856	45.642	54.052
27	36.741	40.113	44.140	46.963	55.476
28	37.916	41.337	45.419	48.278	56.893
29	39.087	42.557	46.693	49.588	58.302
30	40.256	43.773	47.962	50.892	59.703

Source: Taken from Table IV of Fisher & Yates: _Statistical Tables for Biological, Agricultural and Medical Research_ published by Longman Group UK Ltd., London, by permission of the publishers.

GLOSSARY OF STATISTICAL SYMBOLS

p	probability; level of significance
X	raw score
$X-\bar{X}$	deviation score (score minus mean)
N	number of people in a group (or population)
n	number of people in a group (or sample)
Σ	sum of (sigma, upper case)
$\bar{X}$	mean of sample
μ	mean of population (mu)
S	standard deviation (SD) of sample
S^2	variance of sample
σ	standard deviation (SD) of population (sigma, lower case)
σ^2	variance of population
z	z score
r	Pearson's correlation coefficient (also reliability)
df	degrees of freedom
r_s	Spearman rank-order correlation coefficient
$\hat{Y}$	predicted Y score (in regression)

b	slope (or coefficient; in regression)
a	intercept (or constant; in regression)
S_E	standard error of estimate (in regression)
χ^2	chi square
t	t value
F	F-ratio
SEM	standard error of measurement

GLOSSARY OF FORMULAS

Chapter 4

Mean

$$\overline{X} = \frac{\Sigma X}{n} \qquad or \qquad \mu = \frac{\Sigma X}{N}$$

Chapter 5

Variance: Deviation score method

$$\sigma^2 = \frac{\Sigma (X-\overline{X})^2}{N} \quad (for \; population)$$

$$S^2 = \frac{\Sigma (X-\overline{X})^2}{n-1} \quad (for \; sample)$$

Variance: Raw Score method

$$\sigma^2 = \frac{N\Sigma X^2 - (\Sigma X)^2}{N^2} \quad (for \; population)$$

$$S^2 = \frac{\Sigma X^2 - \frac{(\Sigma X)^2}{n}}{n-1} \quad (for \; sample)$$

Chapter 5 (cont.)

Standard deviation

$$\sigma = \sqrt{\sigma^2} \quad (for\ population)$$
$$S = \sqrt{S^2} \quad (for\ sample)$$

Chapter 6

Z score

$$z = \frac{X - \overline{X}}{SD}$$

T score

$$T = (z)\ 10 + 50$$

Chapter 8

Pearson correlation

$$r = \frac{\sum z_x z_y}{N}$$

$$r = \frac{N\sum XY - (\sum X)(\sum Y)}{\sqrt{N\sum X^2 - (\sum X)^2}\ \sqrt{N\sum Y^2 - (\sum Y)^2}}$$

Chapter 8 (cont.)

Spearman rank-order correlation

$$r_s = 1 - \frac{6\sum D^2}{N(N^2 - 1)}$$

Chapter 9

Prediction equation

$$\hat{Y} = bX + a$$

The slope (*b*)

$$b = r\frac{S_y}{S_x}$$

The intercept (*a*)

$$a = \bar{Y} - b\bar{X}$$

Standard error of estimate

$$S_E = S_Y \sqrt{1 - r^2}$$

Chapter 9 (cont.)

Multiple regression

$$\hat{Y} = b_1 X_1 + b_2 X_2 + a$$

Chapter 10

T-test for independent samples

$$t = \frac{\overline{X}_1 - \overline{X}_2}{\sqrt{\dfrac{(n_1 - 1) S_1^2 + (n_2 - 1) S_2^2}{n_1 + n_2 - 2} \left(\dfrac{1}{n_1} + \dfrac{1}{n_2} \right)}}$$

T-test for dependent samples

$$t = \frac{\Sigma D}{\sqrt{\dfrac{N \Sigma D^2 - (\Sigma D)^2}{n - 1}}}$$

T-test for single sample

$$t = \frac{\overline{X} - \mu}{S_{\overline{x}}}$$

and

$$S_{\overline{x}} = \frac{S}{\sqrt{n}}$$

Chapter 11

ANOVA

Sum of Squares - Total (SS_T)

$$SS_T = \sum X_T^2 - \frac{(\sum X_T)^2}{N_T}$$

Sum of Squares - Between (SS_B) (for four groups)

$$SS_B = \sum \left[\frac{(\sum X)^2}{n} \right] - \frac{(\sum X_T)^2}{N_T} =$$

$$= \left[\frac{(\sum X_1)^2}{n_1} + \frac{(\sum X_2)^2}{n_2} + \frac{(\sum X_3)^2}{n_3} + \frac{(\sum X_4)^2}{n_4} \right]$$

$$- \frac{(\sum X_T)^2}{N_T}$$

Sum of Squares - Within (SS_W) (for four groups)

$$SS_W = \sum \left[\sum X^2 - \frac{(\sum X)^2}{n} \right] =$$

$$= \left[\sum X_1^2 - \frac{(\sum X_1)^2}{n_1} \right] + \left[\sum X_2^2 - \frac{(\sum X_2)^2}{n_2} \right] +$$

$$+ \left[\sum X_3^2 - \frac{(\sum X_3)^2}{n_3} \right] + \left[\sum x_4^2 - \frac{(\sum X_4)^2}{n_4} \right]$$

Chapter 11 (cont.)

Mean Squares - Between (MS_B)

$$MS_B = \frac{SS_B}{K-1}$$

Mean Squares - Within (MS_W)

$$MS_W = \frac{SS_W}{N-K}$$

F-ratio

$$F = \frac{MS_B}{MS_W}$$

Tukey's HSD

$$HSD = Q_{(dfW, K)} \sqrt{\frac{MS_W}{n}}$$

Chapter 12

Chi square

$$\chi^2 = \sum \left[\frac{(O-E)^2}{E}\right]$$

Chapter 13

Spearman-Brown Prophecy Formula (for split-half reliability)

$$r_{full} = \frac{(2)\ (r_{half})}{1 + r_{half}}$$

Standard error of measurement (SEM)

$$SEM = SD \sqrt{1 - r}$$

Index

A priori (or planned)
comparison, 200
Alternative hypothesis, 10,
176
Amodal distribution, 60
ANOVA
assumptions for, 192
capabilities of, 191
computation of, 196
F test, 192
F-ratio, 197, 199, 200
factorial or multiple
classification, 210
independent variable and
dependent variable,
192
mean square between,
196
mean square within, 196
one-way, 192-94, 196,
198-200, 202, 288,
291
summary table, 206

ANOVA (cont.)
post hoc comparison,
200, 207-9
Studentized Range
Statistic, 207
sum of squares (within,
between and total),
194
Tukey method (or
honestly significant
difference, HSD),
207
two-way, 192, 209, 210,
212, 214, 215, 217,
292, 306
graphing the
interaction, 211-13
summary table, 214
types of variability
studied, 194
variance estimates, 196
Arithmetic mean, 62
Average, 62

Bar graph, 46, 48
  drawing, 48
Bimodal distribution, 60
Box plot, 54, 55

Chi square
  assumptions required for,
    22
  cell, 224
  equal expected
    frequencies, 223,
    225-27, 300
  expected frequencies,
    222, 302
  formula for, 224
  formula for correction
    for sample size, 233
  frequencies presented as
    percentages, 233
  how used, 221, 223
  observed frequencies,
    222
  for one variable, 223,
    224, 226, 227, 299
  and sample size, 234
  symbol for, 221
  for two variables, 229-
    31, 233, 235, 274,
    285, 286
  unequal expected
    frequencies, 228,
    229, 290, 295

Chi square (cont.)
  Yates' correction, 234
Class intervals, 33-35
Cluster sampling, 22
Coefficient of determination,
  142, 166. (*See also*
  shared variance)
Constant, 4
Construct validity, 258, 259
Content validity, 256
Content-referenced tests, 121
Correlation, 131, 287, 305
  computing, 135, 136,
    138
  correlation coefficient,
    127
  definition of, 127
  factors affecting, 139
  graphing, 127
  hypotheses for, 134
  negative, 130
  positive, 129
Correlation coefficient, 127
  evaluating, 133
  evaluation and
    interpretation of, 142
Correlation tables, 146
Criterion variable, 154
Criterion-referenced tests,
  121
  mastery/nonmastery, 121
  percent correct, 121

Criterion-related validity,
257
   concurrent validity, 257
   predictive validity, 257
Cumulative frequency
   distribution, 36, 37
   graphing, 43
   ogive (or "s" curve), 37
Curvilinear relationship, 132

Degrees of freedom (*df*), 12,
224
Dependent variable, 154
   in ANOVA, 192
Descriptive statistics, 18
Deviation score method, 76-
78, 81, 83, 90
Directional hypothesis, 176
Distribution
   amodal, 60
   bimodal, 60
   multimodal, 60
Domain-referenced tests, 121

Error score, 158, 164, 242
Error term, 197
Errors
   Type I and Type II, 12

F test, 192
F-ratio, 197, 199, 200
Face validity, 259, 260
Frequency axis, 38
Frequency distribution, 31,
33
   cumulative frequency
      and cumulative
      percentage, 36
Frequency polygon, 37, 39,
41, 42
   drawing, 40

Goodness of Fit test, 223
Grade equivalents, 119
   misinterpretations of, 119
Graphs, 37-39, 41, 42, 44,
45, 48-51, 54, 55
   axes, 38
   bar diagram (bar graph),
      48
   box plot, 54, 55
   frequency polygon, 37-
      39, 41, 42
   guidelines to follow
      when drawing, 38
   histogram, 37-39, 41, 42
   line graph, 49
   pictogram, 50
   pie graph, 44
   stem-and-leaf diagram,
      51, 53

Grouped distributions, 33

Histogram, 37, 39, 41, 42
    and bar graph, dif-
        ferences between, 48
Honestly significant
    difference (HSD), 207
    formula for, 207
Hypotheses, 10
    alternative, 10
    directional, 176
    nondirectional, 176
    null, 10
    statistical, 10

Incidental (convenience)
    sample, 23
Independent variable, 153
    in ANOVA, 192
Inferential statistics, 18
Intercorrelation tables, 143
    reading, 145

Likert scale, 8
Line graph, 49
Linear relationship, 132

Mean, 62-66, 68
    of combined groups, 66,
        68
    and extreme scores, 66
    formula for, 63
    and scales, 65
    weighted, 67, 68
Measure of central tendency,
    59
    comparing the mode,
        median, and mean,
        64-66
    mean, 62-66, 69
    median, 61, 62, 65, 66,
        69
    mode, 59, 60, 65, 66, 69
Measurement, 4
Measures
    qualitative, 3
    quantitative, 3
Median, 61, 62, 65, 66, 68
    and scales, 65
    statistical use of, 65
Mode, 59, 60, 65, 66, 68
    and scales, 65
    statistical use of, 65
Multimodal distribution, 60
Multiple regression, 167,
    168, 301
    multiple R, 167, 168
    regression equation, 167

Nondirectional hypothesis,
    176
Nonparametric statistics, 9,
    221
Norm-referenced tests, 116
Normal curve, 99-103
    calculating percentile
        rank, 109
    calculating percentile
        ranks, 109, 111
    for describing, predicting
        and estimating
        variables, 103
Normal distributions
    common characteristics,
        100
Normalizing standardized
    test scores
    grade equivalents, 119
    percentile ranks, 117,
        118
    stanines, 119
Norming group
    characteristics of, 116
Norms
    local, 116
    national, 116
Null hypothesis, 10, 177
    rejecting, 11
    retaining, 11

Ogive (or "s" curve), 37, 43

Parameter, 19
Parametric statistics, 9
Pearson, Karl, 132, 154, 221
Pearson product-moment
    coefficient, 131
    formula for computation
        of, 135, 137
    requirements, 132
Percentage of shared
    variance, 166
Percentile bands, 118
Percentile ranks, 109, 111,
    117
Percentiles, 109
Pictogram, 50
Pie graph, 44
Population, 17
Post hoc comparison
    computations of the HSD
        value, 208
Probability Level, 11

Qualitative research, 3
Quantitative research, 3

Range, 74
    calculating, 75
Raw score method, 83, 87,
    88, 90

Regression
    graphing the regression
        equation, 165
    intercept, 156
    line of best fit, 155
    multiple, 154, 167, 168,
        301
    prediction, 153
    predictor variable, 153
    regression line, 155
    shared variance
        (coefficient of
        determination), 166
    simple, 154, 155, 157-
        59, 161, 163, 165,
        166, 303, 307
    slope, 156
Regression equation, 155
Reliability
    alternate forms method,
        244, 245
    coefficient alpha method,
        247
    definition of, 241
    factors affecting, 250,
        251
    formula for, 243
    inter-scorer approach,
        247
    internal consistency
        approach, 245
    Kuder-Richardson
        methods, 247

Reliability (cont.)
    levels required for
        different purposes,
        251, 252
    Spearman-Brown
        Prophecy formula,
        246
    split-half method, 245,
        247
    standard error of
        measurement (SEM),
        248, 249
    test-retest method, 243
    true score and error
        score, 242

S curve (or ogive), 43
Sample, 17
    bias, 23
    cluster, 22
    incidental (convenience),
        23
    simple random, 20
    size of, 24
    stratified, 22
    systematic, 21
Sampling statistics, 18
Scales
    interval, 7
    nominal, 5
    ordinal, 6
    ratio, 7

Scattergram, 127
  drawing, 129
Scores axis, 38
Shared variance, 142. (*See also* coefficient of determination)
Simple random sample, 20
Simple regression, 155, 157-59, 161, 163, 165, 166, 303, 307
  formula for computing the intercept (a), 157
  formula for computing the slope (b), 156
  formula for computing the standard error of estimate, 159
  regression equation, 155
Skewed distribution, 64
Spearman rank-order correlation, 147-149, 297
  formula for computing, 147
Standard deviation, 75, 81
  calculation of, 75
  deviation score method, 76-78, 81, 83, 90
  factors affecting, 85
  raw score method, 87, 88, 90
  of a sample; symbol for, 86

Standard deviation (cont.)
  sensitivity to extreme scores, 84
  using, 83, 84
  and variance, comparing for populations and samples, 86
  and variance, summary of steps in the computation of, 87, 92
Standard error of estimate, 159, 165
Standard error of measurement (SEM), 248
  computation of, 248
Standard normal curve, 101
Standard scores, 104, 106-8
  T score, 108
  z score, 104, 106, 107
Standardized test reports, 119
Standardized tests, 116, 118
Stanines, 119
Statistic, 19
Statistical hypothesis, 10
Statistical significance, 11
Stem-and-leaf diagram, 51, 53
Stratified sample, 22
Systematic sample, 21

T scores, 107, 108
  converting from z scores,
    107
T-test
  assumption of the
    homogeneity of
    variances, 179
  definition of, 175
  hypotheses for, 176
  for independent samples,
    179, 181, 184, 272,
    294, 296
  for paired (dependent)
    samples, 186, 187,
    189, 284, 298
  pairing scores, 184
  for a single sample, 186,
    187, 189, 293, 304
  using, 178
T-test value
  calculating, 177
  formula for computation
    of, 180, 182
  one-tailed test, 178
  two-tailed test, 178
Test bias, 261
Test of Independence, 229
Test scores
  ways to report, 115
True score, 242
Type I error, 12
Type II error, 12

Validity
  assessing, 260
  construct, 258, 259
  content, 256
  criterion-related
    (concurrent and
    predictive), 257, 258
  definition of, 255
  face, 259, 260
  test bias, 261
  validity coefficient, 258
Validity coefficient, 258
Variability, 73, 74
Variables, 4
  continuous, 5
  discrete, 5
  normally distributed, 99
Variance
  deviation score method,
    79, 81, 83, 90
  estimates, 196
  factors affecting, 85
  raw score method, 83,
    87, 88, 90
  and SD, comparing for
    populations and
    samples, 86
  and SD, summary of
    steps in computation
    of, 87, 92
  of a sample, calculation
    of, 87

Variance (cont.)
    of a sample, symbol for, 86
    sensitivity to extreme scores, 84
    and standard deviation, 75
    using, 83, 84

Weighted mean, 67, 68
    formula used for computation of, 67

Yates' correction, 234

Z score, 104, 106, 107
    calculating from raw scores, 105